Navajo Tradition, Mormon Life

Navajo Tradition, Mormon Life

The Autobiography and Teachings of Jim Dandy

Robert S. McPherson, Jim Dandy, and Sarah E. Burak

THE UNIVERSITY OF UTAH PRESS

Salt Lake City

The Defiance House Man colophon is a registered trademark
of the University of Utah Press. It is based upon a four-foot-tall,
Ancient Puebloan pictograph (late PIII) near Glen Canyon, Utah.

16 15 14 13 12   1 2 3 4 5

Library of Congress Cataloging-in-Publication Data

McPherson, Robert S., 1947-
  Navajo tradition, Mormon life : the autobiography and teachings
    of Jim Dandy / Robert S. McPherson, Jim Dandy, and Sarah E. Burak.
    p. cm.
  Includes bibliographical references and index.
  ISBN 978-1-60781-194-7 (pbk. : alk. paper)
1. Dandy, Jim. 2. Mormons—Biography. 3. Navajo Indians—Biography.
    I. Dandy, Jim. II. Burak, Sarah E. III. Title.
  BX8695.D36M37 2012
  289.3092—dc23
  [B]
                                    2012009783

Index by Andrew L. Christenson

Printed and bound by Sheridan Books, Inc., Ann Arbor, Michigan.

*Jim would like to dedicate this book to Dale Tingey
and the American Indian Services,*

———

Bob would like to dedicate it to Betsy and the family,

———

*Sarah would like to dedicate it to her loving husband,
Britt, for all of his support*

CONTENTS

INTRODUCTION

Origin of the Project: The Blossoming *and Beyond*

In 2002 Dale and Margene Shumway published *The Blossoming*, accounts of Native American men and women who had participated as youth in the Church of Jesus Christ of Latter-day Saints (Mormon) Indian Placement Program.[1] Among the biographies was one entitled "A Real Jim Dandy," which told the story of a young Navajo boy who had attended boarding school and failed, "knew about '40 words of English,'" and was almost denied entrance into placement because he was too old.[2] Program officials finally approved his participation then assigned him to live in Plymouth, Utah, with the Jess Lamb family. Following graduation from high school in 1964, Jim served an LDS mission to the Navajos, received his bachelor's degree from Weber State University, and later went to work as a coach, counselor, teacher, and liaison in the San Juan School District, Utah. According to this narrative, although Jim's life was at times difficult, he persisted with dogged determination, overcoming shortfalls to live a life of service and accomplishment. Like others who had come from similar circumstances, been on placement, and gone on to a successful career, Jim appears to be typical of those found in the book.

In some ways that is true. But Jim's life has another side that is also typical yet rarely examined: the side nurtured with traditional Navajo practices and the teachings that he never left behind. They are manifest in his daily life and in those of hundreds of other previous participants in the Placement Program. Today many of these people enjoy successful lives in the dominant culture, are assimilated in their language and lifeways, hold good jobs, raise their children, and serve in the LDS Church. Jim and his wife, Betty, another graduate of the Placement Program, typify this pattern. Still, the roots of Navajo tradition run deep. In contrast, some Navajo people forsake their church membership, eventually forsake the teachings of the LDS Church, and return to those of their original culture but continue to succeed in the economy and workforce of the Anglo world. Yet another group consists of people like Ella Bedonie, who shared her life story in *Beyond the Four Corners of the World* by Emily Benedek.[3] She has remained adrift, finding no mooring in either tradition. Neither culture offers a total solution; only the family and the here-and-now are of much significance.

While recognizing that choices in lifestyle offer as much diversity as the people living them, this book is about one man whose existence is embedded in traditional teachings but who fully embraces Mormonism. His life is not one of philosophical struggle against the past followed by an epiphany in the present that places his feet on gospel sod never to depart. He offers no sense of a conflicted individual who overcomes challenges to arrive at a safe spiritual harbor. Instead Jim's life is one of finding congruence from the beginning between Navajo and Mormon beliefs. His highly traditional background—born in a hogan near Red Lake, Arizona, raised by a grandfather and father who were both medicine men, and involvement in many Navajo practices—frames his worldview today. The last four chapters of this book illustrate just how strongly.

I first met Jim thirty-five years ago in 1976 when I moved to Blanding, Utah. As friends and not-too-distant neighbors, we worked on a few local projects together. When I was writing on Navajo topics, he provided clarification of things I did not understand. He was always fun to talk to; whenever I appeared at his door, his ready smile wreathed his face, radiating warmth throughout his five-foot-five-inch frame. A firm handshake and a boisterous "Well hello, Bob!" always made me feel welcomed and open to a friendly chat that could last for hours. I was constantly impressed by his depth of knowledge.

One time as we worked together, Jim asked if I would record his life story. I readily agreed. Other projects and differing schedules postponed the effort. Jim was busy with family responsibilities and I had writing and teaching commitments, so the two of us never seemed to get together. Finally a break in the impasse came when Sarah Burak, a VISTA (Volunteer in Service to America) worker, received an assignment to assist in the Blanding community with a Navajo project. She had earned a bachelor's degree in anthropology from Troy University in Alabama and was interested in immersing herself in the local culture. Together we set a date, approached Jim about interviews, and reviewed possible topics. Following a long-standing practice with Navajo people, I purchased a Navajo wedding basket, turquoise and coral jewelry, and other items that I thought Jim would appreciate. He was delighted, expressing gratitude as he compared this transaction with the way sharing information used to be done in the past. Jim had freely given his knowledge to other people but had never been paid or given credit. This way was good, something that he could "stand behind" just as in the old days.

Twelve interviews followed, with a number of clarifying discussions. Sarah participated in the formal information-gathering then had the laborious task of transcribing and organizing the material into general categories. Anyone who has done this knows how dialogue often jumps around; vagueness creeps in through unclear pronouns and inexact references; and cultural understanding is assumed and hence not explained but also may not be present. Sarah worked hard to get it right, but sorting it all was a real challenge. Her assistance in shaping the general form of the manuscript was essential; to me fell the responsibility of fine-tuning and providing contextual information.

As part of this initial process, the three of us traveled to Red Lake in May 2008 to interview family members. During the trip it became even more apparent that Jim moved easily between the two worlds, at one moment teaching about traditional beliefs and the next minute hooting about a college escapade while attending Brigham Young University. For instance, as we drove amid the landscape of Monument Valley, he talked freely about various rock formations until we reached Owl Rock across the highway from El Capitan Peak (Aghaałá). Owls are powerful harbingers of bad news associated with death, and this rock served as a type of transmitter for that kind of information. Jim wanted nothing to do with even discussing the monolith.

Shortly afterward, Jim told of the time that he and Betty drew $1,000 out of the bank to pay a bill. She later reached into her purse to take something else out and did not notice as the envelope with money fell to the ground then blew under a car. When Betty went to retrieve the money from her purse, it was gone. Devastated, Jim went to one of his sisters, a hand trembler, who used her power of divination to see "a hand with the envelope in it waving." She told Jim not to worry, that he and Betty would get their money back. A few days later the police called, saying that a man had found the money with a bank stub and had turned them in to the authorities. The couple was elated.

Next Jim regaled us with a story of how he had fed horse meat to a group of Anglo and Navajo friends visiting his apartment while he was attending school. Everyone loved the dinner until he told them what it was and they went to the refrigerator to confirm it. The big hoof sticking upright on the top shelf convinced them that perhaps their dinner was not so good after all. Stories like these and others gave us insight into Jim's complexity and the ties he had with traditional culture. The interviews held with his brothers and sisters that day confirmed again his depth of belief in and practice of traditional Navajo teachings, a major theme that runs throughout this book.

When Sarah completed her work on the manuscript, I took over. As with most histories, it became evident that Jim spent a long time teaching about some topics and skimmed over others. Maintaining his tone, adding information that he assumed readers would know, and keeping a flow between topics were primary concerns. Moving any type of recorded speech to a written form changes the dynamics of communication. The expectations of a written language are very different; soon the question became how much editing to do without totally removing the speaker's voice and personality. I solved this problem by using different voices.

Context is important when two different cultural traditions—Navajo and Mormon—intertwine. Both history and belief systems play a crucial role in understanding Jim's life. Chapters 3 through 7 are autobiographical: Jim tells of moving from a totally traditional life to one in a white Mormon community. They contain a mix of voices, as I provide some clarification or transition. The last four chapters are Jim's: he looks at Navajo teachings, many of which he garnered from his father and grandfather. For a person unfamiliar with this worldview, confusion can arise, especially when depending on a single source. To clarify, I have introduced additional information in the endnotes as other Navajos share their insights to elucidate Jim's. They provide a rich background, turning what had been a monologue into a dialogue. Much of this material comes from a monthly publication called *Leading the Way*, edited by Kathleen Manolescu and John E. Salabye Jr. It serves as a platform for Navajo elders to share their wisdom and general information, which I have incorporated with the editors' permission. There could not be a better fit. The reader is urged to scour these endnotes for a more complete understanding of information introduced in the text.

Moving then editing elements of an oral interview for the written page requires choices. I lightly edited Jim's voice so that he could tell his own story while I clarified passages and entered vocabulary appropriate for the topic, providing enough variety so that common aspects of repetition in speech did not interfere with the reading experience. This book will not sound like a straight oral interview. Especially in the third chapter concerning Jim's birth and surrounding circumstances, I took the things that he said and wove them into a picture of Navajo life that he agreed was accurate. I have also used the words that Jim used, such as "Anasazi" not "Ancestral Puebloans" and "medicine man" instead of terms such as "chanter," "singer," "medicine person," or "ceremonial practitioner," which sometimes appear in literature attempting to be more academically or politically correct. Indeed, most Navajo people use Jim's words, while academicians, writing for a different audience, choose the others. I hope that this explanation assists the reader in understanding how to keep the authorial and interviewee roles separate. To avoid the generic masculine, "he" and "she" are alternated throughout. They do not imply gender-specific activities except where noted.

By maintaining the Navajo voice, I have avoided the more formal tone often found in books written by anthropologists and other social scientists. Their expectation is a text for the scholarly community. Take, for example, Gladys A. Reichard's encyclopedic work *Navaho Religion: A Study of Symbolism*. In comparing it to the way Navajos speak of their beliefs, the reader encounters a gaping chasm between the two that goes far beyond language. The whole feeling of the Navajo view is lost. This is not to suggest that one type of writing is good, the other bad. They both have their place. But in order to maintain Jim's voice and assist in this narrative, I have invited other Navajo people to share their insight. This has created a rich introduction to the Navajo worldview with aspects that are not often discussed in the literature. The reader should also understand that Navajo accounts or practices may vary because they are passed on through an oral tradition. Some families have certain teachings that others do not have because of ceremonies that members may have performed or experienced. Although Jim has approved the manuscript, I take full responsibility for any errors—of omission or commission—that may have crept in.

Where does this Dandy life history fit in the field of Navajo autobiography? In 2001 anthropologist Charlotte J. Frisbie published *Tall Woman: The Life Story of Rose Mitchell, a Navajo Woman, c. 1874–1977*. In the introduction, she provides an exhaustive list of finished works along with others in progress. To this list can now be added books by Emily Benedek, Louise Lamphere, Joanne McCloskey, and Walking Thunder.[4] With a few exceptions, the main emphasis in these works has been on elders who have lived the traditional life found in the livestock economy of the 1920s and 1930s. Others look at generational change, often comparing life in the past with problems of today. Heavy emphasis is placed on the traditional ways, however, with an underlying discordant note of lost values and a lost way of life. Jim is different, although it is impossible to miss the influence of traditional ways. He is a transitional figure who has successfully adapted to the changed world. He operates easily in the twenty-first century, as witnessed by his effectiveness in school-building and community leadership, while confronting other issues of life through traditional practices.

Jim Dandy's life is a rich mixture that holds interest for everyone. For those who want a glimpse into the complexity of Navajo philosophy, his teachings show how even contemporary events find an explanation rooted in the past. Others may be interested in what a successful experience in the Placement Program meant to a youth coming from the reservation. Teachers working with young Navajo students may be looking for answers as to why certain practices should be avoided in the classroom. Still others may be seeking to understand how two very different religious traditions can find compatibility on a common ground. For whatever the reason, Jim's life speaks to the human experience of growing up in the culturally rich Four Corners area and how one man's life has successfully bridged two different worlds.

HISTORICAL AND RELIGIOUS CONTEXT

CHAPTER ONE

JIM'S LIFE AND TIMES IN PERSPECTIVE

An Overview of Navajo and Mormon History

No one lives in a vacuum, and Jim Dandy is no exception. As a "transitional" figure, his life has been subject to a wide variety of forces. It began in a deeply traditional environment reminiscent of the time when Navajo people depended primarily on livestock and agriculture and now continues in the age of computers and a globalized economy. Change, at an ever increasing pace, characterized the last half of the twentieth century. This chapter and chapter 2 examine what change has occurred by providing two types of context—historical and religious. Both are broad topics. As overviews, each chapter focuses on those elements most prevalent in Jim's development.

The Navajos and the Church of Jesus Christ of Latter-day Saints (Mormons) have shared a long history as groups in the Southwest that settled next to or amid each other. For over 160 years they have rubbed shoulders, with sometimes amiable and at other times hostile results. The general tenor, however, has been compatibility. Scholars studying these groups have produced an extensive literature on each, but few have looked at them in relationship to each other. Considering both the realized and potential impact, this is somewhat surprising. While this chapter cannot be a complete remedy for this lacuna, it provides a brief history of Navajo and Mormon interaction, emphasizing the last half of the twentieth century and events that had the greatest impact on the life and times of Jim Dandy. Chapter 2 addresses the religious and philosophical beliefs of the two groups during this same period and how they perhaps have more in common than originally believed.

Navajos and Mormons have each been historically expansive in their settlement patterns in the Southwest. For the Navajos this started with their
return from Fort Sumner in 1868 and has continued to this day, quadrupling
the size of the reservation. With over a dozen major additions of land to the
initial treaty reservation of 1868, Navajo holdings are now 25,000 square
miles, making it larger than the state of Rhode Island.[1] Much of this growth
occurred to the north and west because of sparser populations, yet a fair
share of growth took place to the east and south when already established
communities and railroad lines permitted. During the last quarter of the nineteenth and first quarter of the twentieth centuries Mormons also expanded
dramatically. As the tentacles of land occupation spread throughout the Great
Basin and into the Southwest, they placed the Mormons in direct and continuous contact with the Navajos and other Indian groups of the region. The
individual efforts of men like Jacob Hamblin, Ira Hatch, and Thales Haskell
who began working with the Navajos in the 1850s gave way to more con-
certed interaction in the 1870s and 1880s as Mormon settlements grew along
the Little Colorado and San Juan rivers and into New Mexico, creating a
more intense type of contact between the two cultures.[2] Missionary work
designed to maintain peace on the frontier and forge alliances now shifted to
an emphasis on economic development.

A short list of these Mormon settlements hints at the extent of town-
building near the borders of the expanding Navajo Reservation. To the west
along the Little Colorado River in Arizona arose Cameron, Sunset, Saint
Joseph, Woodruff, Taylor, and Saint Johns; to the south, Holbrook and Snow-
flake; to the north, Tuba City and Moenkopi.[3] Along the San Juan River on
the northern periphery of the reservation were Bluff and Monticello, Utah;
Fruitland, Farmington, Waterflow, and Kirtland, New Mexico; and Mancos,
Colorado; and to the east sat Ramah, New Mexico.[4] Water and soil drew these
first settlers, who based their economy on subsistence farming and animal
husbandry. Eventually other people joined the original pioneers and fur-
thered specialization in trades and services supporting the small but growing
communities. Still, the question persisted as to how these nascent settlements
removed from efficient transportation and faced with small-scale production
could enter into the economic mainstream of the late nineteenth century. Part
of the answer arose in the trade of wool and blankets sold by the Navajos in
trading posts.

Mormon traders, beginning in the late 1870s and early 1880s, brought important features and effective skills to their posts. Considered by outsiders to be clannish, church members enjoyed the advantage of both an official and unofficial grapevine that made possibilities and options available. The church called some of its members to settle an area as part of their responsibility. They remained until "released" from their service and were then free to go elsewhere. Others joined the established community, seeing it as an opportunity to obtain land and open a business. For whatever reason, Mormon interaction with Navajos became increasingly frequent, leading anthropologist Clyde Kluckhohn to summarize this relationship in the 1940s as follows:

During the past forty years, more and more trading stores on and near the Reservation have come into the hands of Mormons. This trend is partly a function of geography, of intra-Mormon solidarity, and of economic practices characteristic of Mormons. But other evidence could be adduced to show that in the early days Mormons got along better with Indians than did most pioneers who entered the region. . . . Mormons tended to show more respect for and interest in Indian customs; more than other whites, perhaps, they gave Indians a sense of being a part (and a worthy part) of the world as a whole.[5]

As an example to illustrate how this translated into concrete terms, take Joseph Lehi Foutz, a man intimately familiar with the places where Jim was raised. Foutz spent his younger years exploring and working with Jacob Hamblin among the Paiute, Hopi, and Navajo tribes. Beginning in the 1870s, he started a career in trading that did not end until his death on March 19, 1907. In 1878 Foutz moved to Lee's Ferry in Arizona to escape federal officials hunting polygamists. He began trading at Moenkopi shortly after that then moved to Moenave on the periphery of the Hopi Reservation. Joseph Lee, son of John D. Lee, opened two posts for the Navajos (Red Lake and Blue Canyon), where Foutz worked before moving to Tuba City to trade. In 1900 the federal government bought these lands from the settlers and made it part of the Navajo Reservation. Foutz arrived in Kirtland, New Mexico, where opportunity encouraged the expansion of his trading business, now joined by his six sons. Adding sons-in-law and their families, an army of thirty-seven relatives, all of whom were LDS, were involved in trading by 1940.[6]

While it is very difficult to determine how many traders serving the Navajos during this time were LDS and how many of these were actually practicing their faith, a rough estimate could put the figure at perhaps half in some areas. This is particularly true where neighboring settlements were founded by Mormons. People familiar with the reservation and environs will realize that the following list of posts served by this net of relations is not comprehensive and that the turnover of ownership was frequent. Still, it is impossible to miss the frequency of Mormon-Navajo relations. In New Mexico Mormon-owned posts included Gallegos, Beclabito, Tocito, Sanostee, Smith Lake, Burnham, Bitsi, Whitewater, Pinedale, Shiprock, Fruitland, Sheep Springs, Tó Łigaai, and Coyote Canyon. Arizona posts included Keams Canyon, White Cone, Redrock, Teec Nos Pos, Red Mesa, Dinnehotso, Piñon, Sawmill, Wide Ruins, Hunter's Point, Tuba City, Moenave, Moenkopi, Greasewood, Red Lake, Blue Canyon, and Cedar Ridge. Located in Utah were Aneth, Bluff, Montezuma Creek, Mexican Hat, and Blanding, while Colorado had the Mancos Creek Trading Post.

Mormon traders interacted with Navajo clients on a daily basis. The posts became central features in an otherwise dispersed economy and society organized around the livestock industry. Positive personal relations across the counter translated into economic benefit. Traders often went far beyond the mere purchase of wool and rugs to extend credit for daily commodities, while serving as doctors, lawyers, advisors, and anything else required by the community. Navajo customers referred to them using kinship terms and turned to them for guidance in dealing with the foreign world outside of the reservation.[7] Most of these traders spoke the Navajo language, provided goods for community events, became enmeshed in the daily life of their customers, and understood the religious and social aspects of the culture served. Trader Will Evans, who ran different posts in New Mexico for fifty years beginning in 1898, primarily in Shiprock, provides a good example of such a trader. He became so immersed in Navajo history and culture that he actively pursued preserving it in written and artistic form. His book *Along Navajo Trails: Recollections of a Trader* provides an interesting mix of personal beliefs and Navajo cultural heritage.

The florescence of the trading post began declining in the 1930s with the advent of the livestock reduction era. The federal government determined that the reservation had too many sheep, goats, horses, and cows and that overgrazing of the land had become a huge problem that must be solved. Struggling in the depths of the Great Depression and suddenly sensitized to national environmental concerns, the government undertook to reduce stressful impact upon the land brought about by poor farming and livestock practices. Navajo herds became one of many targets for reduction, with thousands of animals being slaughtered to meet the carrying capacity of the land. In some instances as much as one-half of the livestock was driven into corrals or canyons, slaughtered, and left to rot. Considered an attempt to frustrate the Navajos' prosperity and a direct assault on their way of life, stock reduction became one of the most bitter pills that the People ever swallowed during their history.[8] From the government's perspective, the results were effective and the size of the herds became ecologically manageable. Far less beneficially, the Navajos were now forced from economic independence into greater dependence on the government and the wage economy of the dominant society.[9] The change was abrupt.

By the early 1940s, when Jim Dandy entered the world, the Navajos had lost much of their self-sufficiency, had participated in the Civilian Conservation Corps program both on and off the reservation, and were becoming involved in the war industries of World War II. These work opportunities served as stop-gap measures, postponing the reality that Navajo employment would depend on the private sector and its wage economy once the government withdrew job opportunities. The 1950s proved particularly difficult: men left home, sometimes taking their families, at other times going with other men in crews to work in construction, lay track for railroads, harvest seasonal crops as itinerant labor, and perform other menial tasks for a pittance. The women often remained at home, awaiting their husbands' return with a much-needed paycheck. The general tenor of traditional Navajo life had taken a sharp turn.

Amid this change the Southwest Indian Mission, formally designed for Mormon proselyting to the Navajos and Zunis, began. Its goal was to teach LDS doctrine in Indian languages. Stirrings of this nature occurred as early as 1940, but not until March 7, 1943, did the LDS Church officially establish the Navajo-Zuni mission. Ralph W. Evans, a son of Will Evans and trader from the Shiprock area, presided over a half-dozen part-time missionaries, most of whom were also traders, and was assisted by as many Navajo converts. The mission, renamed the Southwest Indian Mission on January 1, 1949, because of its expanding role, grew under the efforts of these primarily part-time missionaries.[10] At the same time, Apostle Spencer W. Kimball became increasingly interested in furthering the work among Native Americans, not only because he had grown up with many Indians in Arizona but also because he viewed them as "Royal Blood" due to their perceived affiliation with the Lamanites in the Book of Mormon.

One area that received particular interest at this time was Ramah, New Mexico, a small community established by Mormon settlers in 1876. What initially had started as a missionary effort in the last quarter of the nineteenth century soon devolved into one more example of a white community swallowing up resources where the Indians used to live. After seventy-five years of malaise, missionary efforts now renewed. But a non-LDS group, Harvard University's Project of the Laboratory of Social Relations, was conducting its "Comparative Study of Values in Five Cultures" at the same time. Beginning in 1949 and continuing until 1953, this group studied the interactions among the Mormons, Navajos, Zunis, Hispanics, and Texans, resulting in a book called *People of Rimrock: A Study of Values in Five Cultures*.

Noted anthropologist Clyde Kluckhohn led a team of experts who studied then summarized various relationships in the community. Of primary interest are those of the Indians and Mormons. Navajos viewed Mormons as being different from other white people, calling them "Gáamalii" (a name of unclear derivation). Although the Indians had lost some excellent land in the past, relations were peaceful, centering around three primary areas: missionaries–potential converts, employers-employees, and traders-customers; the last of these was "the key intercultural role in the operation of both Mormon and Navajo economic systems."[11] Even with this dependence, the Mormons held feelings of superiority over the Indians, viewing them as "dirty and uncivilized. Indians are not regarded as social equals. . . . While the Zunis and Navajos perceive the conflicting attitudes and aims of the Mormons in their relationships with them, the Mormons do not perceive this conflict at all realistically and are often surprised by the negative responses they receive to their missionary efforts," which during this time had been "reawakened."[12]

Members of the LDS, however, filtered their views of their neighbors through the Book of Mormon. Unlike other Christian denominations in the area, the Saints did not insist that traditional beliefs be dropped before investigating the church. "The Mormons believe that it is wrong to destroy the faith of the Indians, which is viewed not as a false but as a degenerate form of the 'true' religion. Mormons allow Indians to practice their own ceremonials and even attempt to relate elements of Indian religion to elements in the Bible and the Book of Mormon."[13] While this was never church policy, it indicates an acceptance and tolerance based in religious conviction.

During this difficult time for Navajo families in the 1950s, a new program offered by the LDS Church took root. It had a huge impact on Jim's life. The LDS Placement Program for the Navajos is an often misrepresented and understudied event in which over 35,000 Native American children (or according to one source twice that number) enrolled over a thirty-year period beginning in the 1950s.[14] While the draw for placement students extended throughout the American West—from the Dakotas to the Northwest and into parts of Canada—and embraced sixty-three different tribes, the "vast majority of students were Navajos" from Arizona, New Mexico, and Utah.[15] One study in 1981 estimated that "approximately 20% of the Navajo population, perhaps 40,000 tribal members, had been baptized as Mormons."[16] LDS Placement was not the only reason Navajo people joined the church, but it certainly was a prominent one during those years. Understanding how this program worked and what it meant in the lives of individual Navajos provides a context for what Jim and his family members encountered.

The Indian Student Placement Program (ISPP) unofficially began in 1947 when a young Navajo girl, Helen John, sought educational opportunities off the reservation.[17] While she and her family were working in the sugar-beet fields of Richfield, Utah, she befriended an LDS woman named Amy Avery. Helen told Avery that she wanted to remain in Richfield and continue her education in the local school. In response Amy called Golden Buchanan, coordinator of Indian affairs in the Sevier Stake (an ecclesiastical unit), for assistance. He in turn wrote to Spencer W. Kimball, then chairman of the LDS Church's Committee on Indian Relationships, an apostle in the hierarchy, and future president of the church. Kimball, raised close to the Navajo Reservation in Arizona and a friend of many Navajo people, championed the idea of improving relations with Indian communities. His view: "The difference between them and us is opportunity."[18] Seeing an opportunity for Helen, Kimball asked Buchanan and his family to take her into their home so that she could attend school. The family agreed, becoming the first foster family in the program. A handful of other Indian children followed suit that year. Spurred by their success, more Navajo parents requested placement for their children; by the 1953–54 school year, the program had grown to sixty-eight students.[19]

In July 1954 LDS leaders agreed to make the ISPP an official church program. They established general guidelines to protect both the students and the foster families and slowly increased enrollment. The church placed the program under the Social Service Department of the women's Relief Society, a licensed child placement agency, and assigned a social worker to interview and monitor each child.[20] Foster family rules specified that a receiving family was not to be coerced into accepting a placement student and that the child should not be regarded as a servant or guest in the home but as a member of the family. The student received responsibilities equivalent to those of the other children in the household. Foster families accepted financial responsibility for the individual, including paying for food, clothing, and school costs; they received no reimbursement from either the church or government except for medical care and travel expenses. All of this was based on the premise that the participating student was a member of the LDS Church.[21] By the school year 1968–69 the program had 46 caseworkers and 3,132 students.[22]

Attending school was a federal requirement, but choosing where to attend was left to parental discretion. If they chose placement, the student and family had to submit an application and undergo an interview process in which a caseworker evaluated their commitment to the program. Even after being accepted, the child and parents could decline or withdraw at any time. The foster family also had an evaluation to ensure that their home was safe and healthy for the student. With both families approved, the church provided information to increase understanding. The *Foster Parent Guide* included instructions on how to welcome the new child, deal with differences in communication, and adjust to two sets of parents. The text encouraged the children to write to their reservation families often and offered suggestions for appropriate names for the foster parents, such as "Father and Mother Jones," while stressing that "students should, in all situations, retain their own name."[23] Clayton Long, an attendee, recalls his experience: "When I walked in the home for the first time, my foster parents had performed an extreme makeover. They had Navajo rugs and a sheepskin on the floor, with all kinds of pictures and books about Navajos and a Navajo dictionary. I felt this was good. I saw something that reminded me of home and was familiar. So even though it was strange there were some things that felt right."[24] Of course not all families were this culturally sensitive; a few were just the opposite, but all were given instruction on how to be warm and sensitive.

The overall goal was "to make possible educational, spiritual, social, and cultural opportunities for Latter-day Saint children, and to provide opportunity for them to participate in non-Indian community life so that they can use their experience now and later for their own benefit and that of their people."[25] The program peaked in 1970, with approximately 5,000 students living with foster families.[26] A steady decline in participation began after the 1970s due to improved educational opportunities on the reservation, but the program has never been officially discontinued. Indian families can still request placement arrangements for children in special circumstances.[27]

Navajo parents often viewed placement as a more promising and healthier arrangement than the Bureau of Indian Affairs (BIA) boarding schools or the Intermountain Indian School, where many different tribes sent students. The military-like discipline and lack of parental care was hard for children. Ella Sakizzie remembers her boarding school experience, which was comparable to that of many others:

We were punished for all sorts of reasons. For instance, if a matron caught us talking to someone at night, she made us stand in the hallway with our arms above our head or stand in the corner while everyone else slept. Once is usually enough; you learn your lesson to go right to sleep. If you were caught stealing food while working in the kitchen, they made you eat nothing until the next mealtime. You had to stand on a table in front of everyone and eat raisins or prunes if that was what you had stolen. Everyone else would be eating their regular meal.[28]

Many parents thought that if their children must be away from them then they should be with a caring family who provided more attention and care. Others chose placement "because they felt that the Mormons would be able to provide more services, material benefits, and emotional support than other missionaries."[29] Even with the improvements over the boarding school, Elouise Goatson, a former placement student with ten years of boarding school experience, states: "But the Placement Program was not all in the best situation either. That might be some of the reasons why other placement students have drifted from it. If I didn't get my third foster family on my first year on placement, I would have never gone back."[30]

Not surprisingly, the ISPP received mixed reviews from participants and outsiders. Most students recall the fear and sadness they felt as they left their families and homes to take up residence with an Anglo family hundreds of miles away. Their journey started at an LDS Church on or close to the reservation, where they boarded a bus for a long ride. Tears were plentiful. When the bus arrived at the drop-off point, the students received something to eat, were bathed and deloused and often given a haircut, then met their foster family. Betty Dandy describes her experience: "When I first went on placement I was thinking where am I going? Where are they taking me? Of course I cried because I didn't want to leave home. I remember the first time that we went to Provo. I had never seen such big mountains. That made me feel really lonely. I said, 'Oh, I've never seen such mountains.'"[31] Leaving the red rock desert of the Navajo Reservation, a seemingly barren landscape of sagebrush and scrub oak, for the mountains of Utah served as a visual reminder of how far away home really was. Betty, like many Navajo children, came from a one-room hogan with a dirt floor and no running water, electricity, or modern furniture. They recall how strange it was to sleep in a bed instead of on a sheepskin and to have their own room. Even sharing a room with foster siblings provided more space and privacy than was familiar to them. For many Navajo children this was their first extended experience with whites. It took time for both sides to adjust. The goal of the program was to keep the same family-child arrangement for the student's entire school years. This was not always possible. Occasionally children moved through several different families for various reasons, including adjustment issues or illness of a foster parent.

Various groups both on and off the reservation viewed the ISPP as a vehicle of cultural genocide, inflicting psychological harm on the participants and removing the best and brightest from the reservation. There is truth to this. The LDS Church required children with above-average grades who were well adjusted within their society and had a good relationship with their natural families. Those directing the program maintained that the ISPP fostered leadership. Top students could weather the storms of transition better "because the cultural, educational and general adjustment problems are difficult enough without the added difficulty of working with children with poor adjustment or discipline problems."[32] The ISPP hoped to "produce leadership for Indian people from among their own ranks."[33]

One study argues that returning home in the summer proved emotionally difficult for the majority of students. During the school year they lived the values and social norms of an upper middle class family and received rewards for learning and practicing them. The author Martin Topper claimed: "The cultural shock of reintegration with life on the reservation and the reemergence of the painful memories of the original separation from its Navajo family can combine to create psychological tension in the child that can be dramatically resolved in the form of behavioral 'acting out.' . . . Perhaps the most basic problem that faces the Navajo adolescent returning from placement is that he or she must grow up to be an adult Navajo."[34]

In other words, regardless of the amount of education and training received, a placement student either returned to the reservation to interact in a culturally acceptable way or was relocated. When asked how she felt about returning home to her natural family, Tonia Halona, a former placement student, answered: "To be honest, I didn't like it very much. It was kind of different because my mom noticed a change. My mom took it to heart for a while because she didn't like how much I had grown up as far as my language."[35] But she also found support for her educational pursuits with her relatives. Unlike Halona, Jerrald Hogue was always excited to return home. "It was good to leave from placement. It was a good feeling to be able to see your family again. Then again, you hate to leave your friends up there. But going back up [to placement] was the hardest."[36]

A study of former placement students conducted by Bruce Chadwick, Stan Albrecht, and Howard Bahr found "as a consequence of the ISPS [Indian Student Placement Services], participants viewed themselves as reasonably competent in both worlds but totally belonging to neither."[37] Conversely, two-thirds of the participants stated that the program "made them feel closer to their Indian heritage," whereas fourteen percent felt separated from it.[38] Anna Begay Birtcher said: "Actually the Church has helped me appreciate my roots, my rich heritage, my 'Indianism.' My foster parents always talked of the positive characteristics of my Native American background."[39] This study also compared placement participants to a control group of Native Americans not enrolled in the program. Although the findings showed that those who did participate obtained higher levels of education, the study found no "unequivocal support for the long range economic success of ISPS participants" as well as no significant difference in social adjustment.[40] Still, a third of those who participated long enough graduated from high school—a figure that surpassed many reservation and trade schools. Eighty-eight percent of the natural parents expressed willingness to enroll their children in the program again,[41] while eighty-five percent of the foster parents would again choose to accept children into their home.[42] In regard to meeting the goal of further training in the LDS Church, ISPP "played an important role in enhancing religious faith, though it contributed somewhat less to permanently changing religious behavior."[43] The study's conclusion revealed that the long-term consequences were "either generally favorable or, at worst, neutral. Indeed, the most negative consequences were experienced by white foster siblings, not Indian students or their families."[44]

While most of these studies are based on questionnaires with measurable outcomes, the experience also had a less tangible side: spirituality, which only each individual can realize. Not only did placement students straddle two cultural worlds, but they were also caught between two spiritual realms. How broad was this separation between the ends of spirituality in traditional Navajo beliefs and those of the LDS Church? Starting at one end of this spectrum, one study suggested: "Crowded membership rolls notwithstanding, very few [Navajo Placement returnees] met even the minimum qualifying standards (as active church members). Many of those who had been baptized openly admit that they have never once attended an LDS church function."[45] Some critics, looking at the haste of baptism before receiving eligibility, referred to the process as "dip and ship." One Navajo man asserts: "I don't really follow either [Navajo religion or the LDS Church]. I think many placement people are like that."[46] Another says: "There's no way a Navajo Mormon can be as devoted to the church as a white Mormon."[47]

Lacee A. Harris struggled to comprehend his situation. "The more I grew to understand my Indianness, the less I understood how I fit into the Church. . . . I felt the Church really had no place for us as 'Indians.' We only belonged if we were Lamanites."[48] For Harris, this meant accepting that he had descended from a wicked group of people, as portrayed in the Book of

Mormon.[49] He felt that this required giving up his culture and replacing it with Mormon culture, the culture of middle-class whites. "The teachings of the church allow us to be both Indian and Mormon, but to expect Indians to be Anglo Mormons puts an enormous strain on some of the Indian people."[50] Elouise Goatson adds that Native Americans stopped attending the LDS Church "because showing pride and preserving your language and traditions are more important than trying to live the gospel."[51] To many it is black and white: no bridge could span the chasm.

The most complete story of a person who attended placement then struggled in its aftermath is told by Ella Bedonie, who shared her life in *Beyond the Four Corners of the World: A Navajo Woman's Journey* by Emily Benedek. As a young girl she attended placement and had a generally positive experience. When she returned to the reservation she maintained contact with her foster family. She eventually changed to the Native American Church but did not seem to find the peace she sought. The difficulties of daily living included a bout with cancer, during which she wondered about the futility of life. Materialism preempted the spiritual possibilities found in all three faiths. Ella finally declared that she had achieved the American dream of a house with a white picket fence but struggled to fill a void in her beliefs that left her empty, without peace. Her foster family tried to assist her through the difficult times, never abandoning her, but she distanced herself.

Today young scholars still criticize placement by using the current buzzword of racism. Elise Boxer's dissertation, for example, tells how the "LDS Church actively created and maintained a distinct indigenous identity based on religious ideologies. . . . [That] created a unique racialized space that simultaneously subjugated and venerated indigenous peoples in the LDS church."[52] This gave "meaning to the LDS church's colonization of indigenous peoples beyond the nineteenth century." While this rhetoric can be inflammatory and echoes selected sentiments expressed during the 1970s, evidence does not indicate that this was a deliberate plan by promoters and participants in the program or the dominant experience of those who received the services. No doubt some were dissatisfied with their individual experience.

Others recognize that similarities or at least good things can be pulled from both cultures. Doing so requires familiarity with the teachings from each. While the LDS Church makes a tremendous effort to teach doctrine, traditional Navajo culture views many forms of religious knowledge embedded in ceremonial practice as too sacred for the uninitiated to know and too powerful to be handled without appropriate insight. Certain customs like the importance of family, respect for elders, sharing of resources, and other principles of human relations are evident and create a bridge of shared practices. That is what Florence Billy, a former placement student, means when she suggests combining Navajo and LDS teachings by "selecting what's important" and bringing the "good qualities" of the culture to the church.[53] While this helps to reach a middle ground, it does not extend to the far side of the gulf (shared doctrinal aspects between the two belief systems are discussed in the next chapter).

The men and women of this generation of students who experienced placement (most of whom are in their late thirties, forties, and fifties) are fluent in both Navajo and English. It would be hard to find a large collection of young people who fill this bill today, English most often being the language of daily communication. But a fair number of middle-aged adults from the placement era are still comfortable with Navajo and the concepts expressed through the language. From this transitional group come perhaps a dozen scholars on or near the reservation able to converse with medicine people about traditional beliefs on an appropriate linguistic level. Many of them teach Navajo language and culture at a high school or college level and develop a curriculum appropriate for both. In doing so, they are not apologists for the LDS Church. These men and women teach their traditional culture but also understand how the two belief systems are conceptually compatible. They base their beliefs in a deep understanding of Navajo religion.

For example, Clayton Long and Don Mose Sr., who currently reside on or near the Utah portion of the reservation, come from a placement experience, are leaders in their community, and develop Navajo curriculum with a traditional perspective.[54] Both also come from a rich heritage of medicine men (*hataałii*). Clayton's father, Elliot Long, practiced seven different ceremonies—Hózhǫ́ǫ́jí (Blessing Way), Hóchxǫ'íjí (Evil Way), 'Anaa'jí (Enemy Way), 'Akéshgaan (Claw/Hoof Way), 'Iináájí (Life Way), Dził'k'ehjí (Mountain Top Way), and Jóhonaa'éí K'ehjí (Sun Bearer Way)—along with numerous prayers and the practice of hand trembling. This is an extensive amount of knowledge for even the best hataałii: to know two or three ceremonies—

some of which last nine nights—is considered a lot. Elliot actually lived for a year with a Mormon family in Richfield, Utah, and thus knew what he was doing when he and his wife signed the papers for Clayton to go on placement. The experience was positive; but when Clayton returned, he asked his father about perceived differences between the two faiths and how a medicine man of his stature reconciled the two. He received the following answer: "The first thing he [my father] said to me was you have a higher power than I do. I want you to keep that power because you have a fuller understanding of that power. I only hold a small piece of what that power is. If you come back [to traditional Navajo] you're only holding on to the bits and pieces. He's saying you've got the complete power; I want you to hold on to the complete."[55] Elliot was referring to his son's holding the Melchizedek priesthood, a power given to an ordained elder to act in the name of God and officiate in certain priesthood offices and assignments. On one occasion the medicine man compared his abilities to the lesser Aaronic priesthood, which is built upon the fundamental principles of faith, prayer, repentance, and the ministering of angels.

Don Mose Sr., had a different experience but also enjoyed strong family support. When he was a young boy, his family had him herd sheep for his grandfather as the old man grew increasingly blind. Even in his old age, the elder continued to perform ceremonies—the Hózhǫ́ǫ́jí (Blessing Way), Hóchxǫ'íjí (Evil Way), Wóláchíí (Red Ant Way), and hand trembling—as a medicine man. The two were living fifteen miles south of Piñon when Mormon missionaries began teaching them, requiring Don to serve as interpreter. As a young boy, Don could only translate the basics, but he felt that his grandfather understood much more. The missionaries would talk for a while, then the old man would interrupt them, insisting that they were not clear in the details and correcting them. He spoke about "The One Who Stands in the Center of the Universe" (Yá'ałníí' Niníyáhí) and the creation of the world. The missionaries continued, only to be interrupted again with further clarification.[56]

Within two weeks, the grandfather and grandson asked to be baptized. Climbing into an old Ford pickup, the two traveled the long distance to Tuba City to receive the ordinance in "a little homemade pool." Years later Don went on placement, took seminary classes, and began to understand more fully what the Mormon elders were talking about. His mother, who also joined, had a more difficult time. She was a hand trembler and used these powers of divination effectively. Don explained:

My mother, who is a good member of the church, hung on to her culture. My dad was the same way even though he was a branch president [the smallest ecclesiastical unit of church organization]. My mom had a strong belief in cultural ways. She thought maybe God would punish me for her beliefs because she was caught between Navajo culture and the church. That's how she grew up, never to let go of her tradition. She was a hand trembler but was also the one who decided I needed to go on placement. Still, she said: "Don't ever let go of the church because that will be the key to a better life for you. Hang on to your traditions to show respect to your Heavenly Father as well, but don't ever deny the church." [57]

And Don didn't. He went on to serve a mission in the Southwest Indian Mission, teaching Navajo people in their own language, and today develops school curriculum materials on traditional Navajo culture for the San Juan School District.

Lucille Hunt, in contrast, never went on placement and (because she had not) joined the LDS Church at the age of twenty-one. Raised in a hogan with seven other sisters and her parents (ten people in all), educated entirely in BIA schools, and steeped in traditional Navajo beliefs, Lucille eventually attended a trade school in Albuquerque less than two hours from her home. She recalls: "When I went there all my friends were always receiving packages and phone calls and visitors. They were all talking about 'my foster family, my foster this, my foster that,' everybody was foster to them and I thought why don't I have a foster family?"[58]

Soon Lucille's friends introduced her to the LDS Institute (religious education for college-age adults). She began missionary discussions but was disappointed that the missionaries did not provide a foster family. "I don't want these guys to be my foster family. I want a mom and dad and some brothers and sisters, like my friends had. I was disappointed and upset about the whole thing." She continued to receive the lessons and eventually joined the LDS Church, attended Brigham Young University, married an LDS husband, and attends the temple. Through this process of change she felt that what she was learning was simply a continuation of the traditional teachings she already knew. Like Clayton, Don, and others, she depended on the fact, ingrained from birth, that "you are a Navajo. That was the first thing, the number one thing I was taught. . . . But all these teachings from my parents just got opened wider when I joined the church."[59]

From an LDS perspective, these are success stories of people who found meaningful relationships with the church. Statistics are not available to determine how many others had a similar experience, but a large number certainly did not remain faithful after placement ended. Many returned to traditional practices, joined another Christian denomination or the Native American Church, or, like Ella Bedonie, had no strong religious beliefs. My personal observation suggests that well over fifty percent fall into this latter category. Today the wards and branches on the Navajo reservation have far more names on the rolls than ever attend a meeting or participate in any type of activity. The experiences of Jim's brothers and sisters appear to be typical of those who attended placement.

During the height of the Placement Program in 1970–73, Kendall Blanchard investigated the effect of different religious beliefs on economic development among the Rimrock Navajos. In his book entitled *The Economics of Sainthood* he confirms the lack of participation on the part of LDS Navajos. One morning when he entered a church he found approximately 150 people in attendance. Most of them were white and only 7 were Navajos, even though 400 Native Americans were on the church rolls. The exact opposite—120 people in a congregation, only 7 of whom were white—was found in the number of people who attended the Christian Church of the Nazarene. [60] Both faiths aggressively sought members, but Blanchard saw a big difference in their approach. The Nazarenes demanded that new converts denounce their former traditional beliefs and turn solely to the teachings of Christ. Mormons, however, saw conversion as "an extended, educative one, considerably more involved than a simple immediate act, such as conversion or baptism. Most Rimrock Mormons contend that the Navajos who are baptized very rarely, if ever, understand the significance of this most vital of sacraments, and therefore they do not expect radical change. In light of this, the majority of the Rimrock Navajos have never felt the traditional lifestyles threatened by the tenets of Mormonism."[61]

The LDS history of the Navajos of Rimrock is instructive and may be more typical than the church would like to admit. Their history is checkered with periods of increased missionary efforts followed by slumps, experiments with a separate Indian branch that failed, and feelings of white members that the Navajos were opportunistic and interested only in goods and services provided. Separating those who practiced traditional Navajo religion from those professing to practice the Mormon faith was difficult. Blanchard took the approach of "looking at their overall attendance record, and, the crowded membership rolls notwithstanding, very few meet even minimum qualifying standards. Many of those who have been baptized openly admit that they have never once attended an LDS function."[62]

Yet, at the same time Blanchard published his work, the *Navajo Times*, the official newspaper of the Navajo Nation, ran an article entitled "Mormon Church in Navajoland," which proclaimed that "one out of every six or seven reservation Navajos on the reservation is a member of the church and this number is growing at a rate of between 500 and 1,000 every year," with a current enrollment of about 20,000 members, "47 congregations scattered throughout the reservation," and 120 missionaries "spreading the word"—a fourth of whom were Navajos.[63] When the church surveyed tribal leaders, "87 percent of them said that the program did not cause a student to lose his Indian identity, and only 8 percent of the leaders felt that the program could be harmful to Indian culture."[64] Blanchard suggests possible reasons for this acceptance, such as compatibility between traditional beliefs and Mormonism, including a strong interest in divine healing, forsaking the doctrine of original sin, the importance of knowledge as a part of religious belief and practice, a strong stance against alcohol, and emphasis on the family. Still, problems exist in translating Christian terms into the Navajo language and in the way those words affect understanding of the doctrine, a disbelief in sin, and the general fusion of the two religions.[65] Blanchard's concerns are addressed in the next chapter.

Other events brought change to the reservation. As transportation became more convenient, isolation reduced, and dependence on mainstream employment grew, education for all Navajo children increased in scope. Southeastern Utah's experience is indicative, and Jim Dandy played a part in it. In 1958 only 4.4 percent (120) of the students in the San Juan School District were American Indians, while the BIA schools had responsibility for the remainder. By 1974 these figures had changed dramatically, with

Indian students now numbering 1,235 (46.5 percent), 431 of whom were involved in secondary education and 220 of whom were being bused. Studies showed that the high schools were located so that the average Navajo student traveled four times as far as a white counterpart. Many Navajo children spent the equivalent of 120 school days sitting on a bus just to attend classes for 180 days. For students at the end of the longest bus route, which included Monument Valley, these figures rose to 30,000 miles each year and an equivalent of 240 school days on a bus.[66]

Navajo parents from Oljato and Red Mesa chapters filed a lawsuit on behalf of one of these students, resulting in *Sinajini* v. *Board of Education*. Following an expensive legal battle, the San Juan School District agreed to build new facilities in reservation communities: Whitehorse (Montezuma Creek) High School opened its doors in 1978, Monument Valley High School in 1983, and the elementary schools of Bluff, Mexican Hat, and Montezuma Creek were improved. Similar events played out across the reservation as the states and counties assumed a greater responsibility for educating Navajo children while the role of the BIA decreased. The 1970s and 1980s bore the fruit of the ethnic pride movements of the 1960s and 1970s. Self-determination, Red Power, and correcting historical and contemporary wrongs were often tinged with a militancy honed by the past.

Accusations of tampering with Navajo culture became so strong in 1977 that the Interstate Compact Secretariat investigated the Placement Program. Some Native American leaders sought to limit the number of Indian students living in Anglo homes. The final committee report exonerated the LDS Church of any misdeeds. "Native American parents emphatically stated that they, not their children, decided to apply for placement. These parents felt that they were pleased with the program which led their children to happiness and a better economic situation while the children still identified with their Indian heritage. . . . They consistently expressed appreciation to the foster families for caring for their children."[67] Even with this positive endorsement, which allowed the Placement Program to continue, the LDS Church began to limit its offerings. With new and better schools opening on the reservation and a broader acceptance of many mainstream benefits, the need for placement had decreased. By the 1980s only high school students could apply for the program. Ten years later only 500 students actively participated; in 1998 only five students remained, with the last placement graduating in 2000. No others appear to be currently enrolled in the program.[68]

Other important forces of change were afoot—the rapid growth of the Native American Church, Anglo views and values instilled through public education, the increasingly fast-paced tempo of daily life that took mothers and fathers from the home and placed them in the off-reservation workforce, and the burgeoning capacity of instantaneous electronic communication ranging from computers to cell phones. Remembrance of the old days of livestock herding and a 1930s lifestyle faded with the death of each elder. Traditional Navajo religion felt the pinch. In 1992 anthropologist Charlotte Frisbie published her "state-of-the-nation" findings on contemporary Navajo religion. Her report, "Temporal Change in Navajo Religion: 1868–1990," was an excellent attempt to study and quantify a very slippery topic. She summarized her findings as two conflicting trends: Navajo religion is "dynamic and resilient," meeting the needs of its followers by accommodating "outside ideas and internal innovations and . . . changing conditions and problems with new definitions of format and purpose"; but on another level "numbers of knowledgeable practitioners continue to decline, as does the use and transmission of portions of the ceremonial repertoire."[69]

Examples of some of the innovative ways to meet the dwindling number of medicine men include the multiple attempts to establish training opportunities. In 1968 the Rough Rock Mental Health Training Program began, followed ten years later with the Medicine Men's Association. A further attempt to form an association to train future medicine men faltered, began again, and was renamed the Dineh Spiritual and Cultural Society of Navajoland. From the inception of these programs, funding provided by the tribe paid for an instructor to train two apprentices in a particular ceremony in a traditional format. Statistics vary as to how many completed the training. Frisbie states that the first class graduated three men and one woman in 1972 and that by 1983 "there had been 104 graduates, '14 or 15' of whom were women, and '16 to 20' of whom were dead as of November 1983."[70]

Was this attempt enough to stanch the loss? Indications are that the number and type of ceremonials with their practitioners are decreasing. In 1938, shortly before Jim Dandy was born, thirty-five distinct ceremonials were practiced. In 1957 this had fallen to twenty-six; in 1983 "the number is

recorded at twenty-four, eight of which are identified as well known and frequently performed as of the early 1970s."[71] Another way to understand the
impact of loss is to look at a specific study conducted on Kaibito Plateau in
1980. This area, located northwest of Red Lake, is part of the area familiar to
Jim. A longitudinal study covering the years 1860 to 1980 suggests a steady
decline. In 1905 the ratio of ceremonialists to the general population was
estimated as 1:30; in 1980 the figure shifted to 1:175.[72] The study found only
twenty-four medicine men, half of whom were over seventy years old, and
six of whom were not practicing due to health or conversion to another religion. "Of the eighteen practicing ceremonialists, six performed only Blessing
Way and six others knew only the Enemy Way or a single chant way. Only
two medicine men apparently knew two or more chant ways in addition to
Blessing Way."[73]

The author of this study, Eric Henderson, like Charlotte Frisbie in her
essay, ends on an upbeat note, suggesting that Navajo traditional beliefs will
not fade away. True, they may lose their richness in variety, with the Blessing
Way and Enemy Way dominating as the most prevalent ceremonies, but the
Navajo people will continue to call upon their medicine men for healing.[74]
The basic structure of the religion will continue even though increasing pressure from a variety of sources will have its effect.

In terms of Jim's life, many of the events discussed in this chapter have
had a direct impact on his experience. Some are obvious, such as his mother's and father's growing dependence on wage labor, his involvement in the
Placement Program, his role in expanding educational opportunities on the
reservation, and the general loss of traditional medicine men. More subtle
things also affected his life. The reader will find that Jim's greatest familiarity in ceremonies lies in the Blessing Way and Enemy Way, which he refers
to often. The study of the Kaibito Plateau ceremonialists helps explain why.
Jim's strong foundation in culture and language hearkens back to his childhood and the tutelage of his grandparents and father. Jim was able to capi-
talize on this by sharing his teachings through curriculum development, as a
school counselor, and in community activities. His life and work proved to be
a successful melding of the traditional past with events of the present.

CHAPTER TWO

PRAYING TO JESUS, STANDING FOR MONSTER SLAYER

Traditional Navajo Syncretism and LDS Beliefs

Rose Yazzie (fictitious name, real person) sat amid the symbols of her culture. A grinding stone and bags of colored sands lay at her feet, stirring sticks and a fire poker rested in her lap, and woven rugs draped across a nearby chair. She held a small pouch in one hand and with the other pinched corn pollen between her fingers to show how she offered it with prayer. Earlier Rose had talked about her life and the time she had spent on the LDS Placement Program. Avowing faith in the teachings of the Church of Jesus Christ of Latter-day Saints, she spoke with love for the organization, its members, and the generally good experience she had enjoyed since she was just a young girl, sixty years ago. There was no doubting her sincerity. At the same time, she clung to traditional Navajo teachings, as embedded as the yellow pollen in the folds of her brown skin. After a lengthy discussion about both beliefs, she noted that she prayed to Jesus; but if she had to choose only one, "I stand for Monster Slayer," one of the twin gods central to Navajo teachings.

To an outsider, a wide gulf separates Mormon and Navajo beliefs, suggesting that Rose either was untruthful or did not understand the two religions. Nothing is further from the truth. Her syncretistic response, defined as "the attempt or tendency to combine or reconcile differing beliefs," was not new.[1] Native American reactions to Christianity have been influencing traditional beliefs ever since the Spanish set foot on New World soil over 500 years ago. Contemporary Inca ceremonies, Tarahumara rituals, Pueblo dances, and Sioux teachings about the sacred pipe embody elements of traditional beliefs so entwined with Christianity that both religions have been inextricably shaped and reformed into a new image for Indian practitioners.

To most Christians who are viewing this mixing and melding and who were raised with the credo of "One Lord, one faith, one baptism," the mixture becomes blasphemy. Whereas Christianity is based on the principle of exclusion, a cause for dissension among the many sects who derive their faith from the Bible, Native American beliefs tend to be inclusive. With a pantheon of many Holy People, spiritual entities, and powers, adding another—in this case Jesus Christ—augments the potency of beliefs.

Jim Dandy has a somewhat similar intertwining of faiths in which traditional Navajo teachings rest comfortably beside Mormon doctrine. As with Rose, his sincerity and faithfulness to LDS tenets cannot be doubted; but for a stereotypical Mormon from Salt Lake City, the two faiths seem at opposite ends of the spectrum of compatibility. How could a supernatural warrior like Monster Slayer, who traveled about killing evil creatures existing at the time of Creation, be comparable to a historic figure like Jesus Christ? What similarities exist between Christian and Navajo faiths, and how do these similarities or differences play out in daily life? The investigation of these questions would require a book not a chapter; their complexity is immense. The following discussion is a brief analysis to explore possibilities.

Before starting, a few disclaimers are necessary. Above all, the purpose of this study is not to take an apologist approach for the Church of Jesus Christ of Latter-day Saints. In literature written by faithful members, Indians are often categorized as "Lamanites" or descendants of those people found in the Book of Mormon.[2] Historically, the church has referred to Indians in this manner, generally lumping all Native Americans together as descendants of these people. Even the introduction to the Book of Mormon published in 1981 includes a statement that the Lamanites "were the principal ancestors of American Indians."[3] In October 2006 this was modified to read "they are among the ancestors of the American Indians," recognizing that the various groups who made the transoceanic crossings from the Middle East during different periods of history discussed in the text were not necessarily the primary ancestors of all Native Americans.[4]

Due to these earlier perceptions, however, some writers have sought proof that Christ left his teachings with Indians throughout the Western

Hemisphere and that elements within their religion are remnants of those beliefs. This is not the argument here. Instead this discussion compares and contrasts traditional Navajo thought to Mormon beliefs and examines common ground between these two very different religious expressions. Commonalities can be found among most religions. In this case, the similarities that Jim and other Navajo people find is the present concern, with more emphasis placed on Navajo doctrine than on that of the LDS. A broad spectrum of beliefs and attitudes that extends far beyond what is described here obviously exists, much of which by its nature has to be anecdotal. Whenever possible, the Navajo voice and experience are used for illustration.

Recently a few men of the cloth from various denominations have walked a different path, consciously fostering the study of similarities between Indian religion and Christianity. William Stolzman in *The Pipe and Christ: A Christian-Sioux Dialogue* explains how "the two religions fit together" and goes to great length to use the teachings and vocabulary of Sioux holy men to prove the point.[5] Closer to home were the efforts of Father H. Baxter Liebler, an Episcopalian minister, who established a mission to the Navajos on the San Juan River in Utah in 1943.[6] While he incorporated Navajo teachings into architecture, used sandpaintings to explain the Easter story, borrowed music from the Night Chant, and wore a traditional hairstyle embodying important Navajo values, Liebler also learned that there were limits. Sometimes he was too successful, as his parishioners assigned old religious values to the newfound faith. The priest, while interested in the traditional religion as a bridge to Christianity, did not draw upon its deities and the bulk of its religious practices, although he also did not fight against them. He used what he could and respected the rest.[7]

Some Native American groups also have sought a mixing of Christianity with their beliefs, the most prominent for the Navajos being the Native American Church. This organization began to rise among the Navajos in the Four Corners area during the early part of the twentieth century, enjoyed rapid growth in the same years when LDS Placement started, and continues to be widely embraced on and off the reservation today. The teachings in this religion are flexible enough to mix Christianity and Navajo traditional faith, although its fundamental tenets, physical symbols, and meeting structure were derived from the Plains Indians, primarily Comanches and Kiowas.[8]

The peyote buttons used in various forms as a type of sacrament are imported from south Texas and northern Mexico and initially had little to do with Navajo history and culture. As with LDS beliefs, Native American Church practices were introduced from the outside and have proven syncretistic in their approach. Only some generally recognized concepts of LDS teachings and their relation to Navajo thought are discussed in this chapter, without exploring in detail the multifaceted and deep concepts of both faiths.

One temptation to avoid when comparing Navajo to Mormon religion is to select examples from an earlier historical period. Mormonism at the time of the founding of the church in 1830 by Joseph Smith was very different from many of the beliefs and practices of today. Just how different is explained in D. Michael Quinn's *Early Mormonism and the Magic World View*. The chapter headings alone suggest topics where comparisons to Navajo beliefs become possible: "Divining Rods, Treasure Digging, and Seer Stones," "Ritual Magic, Astrology, and Talismans," "Magic Parchment and Occult Mentors," and "Visions and the Coming Forth of the Book of Mormon."[9] Add to this *Popular Beliefs and Superstitions from Utah*, a 400-page work with an encyclopedic approach to folklore and supernatural practices prevalent in the nineteenth century, and suddenly many elements found in traditional Navajo religion do not seem so foreign to an outsider.[10] Superstition is always the other person's religion.

Rather than making these types of comparisons, the focus here is on the fundamental doctrine of each religion as encountered by Jim Dandy. The search for similarities does not suggest that the two beliefs are interchangeable—far from it. Even the Franciscan missionaries working among the Navajos around Saint Michaels Mission, Arizona, during the first quarter of the twentieth century, never made that leap of faith, although their study of Indian beliefs was intense.[11] Few Anglos have ever achieved the depth of understanding of Navajo philosophical concepts that Father Berard Haile did; he stayed at arm's length when comparing the two. His respect for Navajo religion rarely translated into his own system of beliefs. Haile also did not mention what the Navajos thought of his Christianity, although they were undoubtedly studying it as well.

For our purposes, this chapter looks at Mormon and Navajo beliefs encountered by Jim in the last half of the twentieth century. The ultimate goal is to understand possible ways in which the two faiths share common ground. LDS doctrine is found primarily in five places: the Book of Mormon, the Pearl of Great Price, Doctrine and Covenants (D & C), the Bible, and continuing latter-day revelation. The first three are believed to have been received and translated by revelation. The Book of Mormon is a religious history of a number of groups of people living on the American continent primarily between 600 B.C. and A.D. 421. The Pearl of Great Price is a trans-lation of God-revealed passages from the Book of Moses and from Egyptian papyrus scrolls obtained by Joseph Smith. And the Doctrine and Covenants is a series of canonized revelations given to Joseph Smith beginning in 1823 and ending with his death in 1844, with some additional sections added by later prophets. The Bible, as well as being one of these four "standard works," provides a history of the tribes of Israel as well as the New Testament teach-ings about Christ. The fifth source of divine information comes from all of the presidents or prophets of the church to the present, which includes counsel-ors to the prophet and members of the Quorum of Twelve Apostles. All scrip-tural sources are accepted as the word and will of God.

Because these scriptures have been moved from an oral to a written, cod-ified form and are available for all to read, they are different from the flexible oral tradition of the Navajos. Their teachings are derived from a rich body of lore that branches from a main stalk of understanding into various offshoots, giving rise to a variety of ceremonies. Each ritual has its own origin myth, defined as a story filled with power, becoming esoteric knowledge under-stood and interpreted primarily by medicine men. This information trans-mitted through stories has room for moralizing and teaching at their end. Mormon doctrine is different. In their most basic form, LDS scriptures appear in two major categories. First are stories that teach of God's dealings with humanity as found in much of the Old Testament, the four Gospels and Acts in the New Testament, the Book of Mormon, and the Pearl of Great Price. Second are didactic explanations given in the epistles of the New Testament and the Doctrine and Covenants. Finally, instructions for ceremonial behavior are found in Leviticus, Numbers, and Deuteronomy in the Bible. In comparing Navajo and LDS teachings, the practice of storytelling, followed by analysis and reflection, is shared between the two groups.

Still, the large cultural differences in how the stories are told for some people obfuscate what is being taught. Take, for instance, the stories of David and Goliath and the killing of Yé'iitsoh. The plots are similar. A giant has been terrorizing the people, and it is time to stop him. An unlikely opponent challenges and easily defeats him with the help of God(s), after which his head is cut off by the victor. Simple enough. But each story has its own cultural rendering and different interpretations. In the story of David and Goliath we learn that the antagonist came from a line of giants that existed before the Flood. Goliath's armor and weapons were frightening, he had thus far been invincible in battle, and the welfare of Israel hung in the balance. Others had failed to defeat him using normal means. David, however, asked King Saul for permission to represent Israel, which the king granted. The king offered superior armor and weapons, but the young shepherd boy refused. Selecting five smooth stones to use in his sling, David faced Goliath, killed him, then cut off his head with the giant's sword (1 Samuel 17: 1–52). While a number of different precepts can be derived from this story—fight with what you are accustomed to, be humble and the Lord will help, fear not, and so forth—the main message is boldly stated: "I come to thee in the name of the Lord of hosts, the God of the armies of Israel, whom thou [Goliath] hast defied. This day will the Lord deliver thee into mine hand, and I will smite thee, and take thine head from thee" (1 Samuel 17: 45–46). Thus it was man against man with divine intervention.

The killing of Big God (Yé'iitsoh) has its own cultural context. While a number of different versions of this story exist, the basic plot involves Monster Slayer (Naayéé Neizghání) and Born for Water (Tóbájíshchíní), the Twins raised by Changing Woman (Asdzą́ą́n Nádleehí).[12] After visiting their father, Sun Bearer (Jóhonaa'éí), and receiving permission as well as the means by which to kill monsters roving the earth, the Twins returned on a rainbow to hunt them down. Before leaving their father, the Twins promised to let him strike the first blow against Big God, even though he was Sun Bearer's eldest son. The Twins encountered the fearsome giant as he approached Navajo Springs near today's Grants, New Mexico. He drank four times, the Twins and Big God bantered challenges back and forth four times, and the monster shot at them four times with arrows (or four knives or clubs colored black, blue, yellow, and white). But he missed the young men because they followed the advice of Holy Wind (Nítch'i), who warned them of impending danger. A protecting rainbow helped them move to avoid the enemy missiles. Sun Bearer took the first strike with lightning. The young men then shattered the monster's armor with four lightning, sunbeam, and rainbow arrows (or four knives or clubs), killed him, and cut off his head before returning home with his scalp.

A comparison of this story to David and Goliath illustrates some striking Navajo differences. The most obvious are the repetition of elements in a sequence of four, use of the four sacred colors associated with the cardinal directions, the whisperings of the Holy Wind to guide the heroes through danger, supernatural travel, protection by a rainbow, and the Twins receiving permission from Sun Bearer to kill his elder son and their brother. Less obvious is the creation of landmarks—the lava flow outside of Grants, New Mexico, is the blood that came from Big God's mouth, his head is Cabezon Peak near Mount Taylor, and Navajo Springs became important for later ceremonial use.[13] But perhaps most importantly, although David and the Twins are both hero figures, the Twins are fundamental in the Navajo belief system, are appealed to for assistance, and provide healing practices and ceremonial paraphernalia for today's people. They are truly gods, whereas David is a mortal who received divine help but never godlike status.

Rather than pitting man against man, the story of the Twins revolves around supernatural beings and the commensurate power to destroy evil. From this incident derives esoteric knowledge that permeates aspects of traditional religion. Flint, for instance, was Big God's armor and thus enters into ceremonies associated with protection from evil. This type of rock is commonly found around Grants, as is petrified wood, said to be his bones. Lightning from Sun Bearer played a part in killing the monster; the Twins collected certain herbs and plants to protect themselves from lightning's supernatural power, a practice followed today in ceremonies; and when the Twins returned to their mother they swooned from the effects of Big God's spirit, giving rise to the first Enemy Way ceremony that rids warriors of similar influences.[14] Much of this is discussed in more detail in the following chapters, but it is important to recognize the substantial differences between traditional Christian and Navajo stories and the values embedded within them.

Even with these differences, however, Mormons often were relatively tolerant of these beliefs (as pointed out in chapter 1). While they never embraced and hardly understood Navajo tradition, their assumption that this religion initially might have been rooted in early Jewish and Christian practices encouraged them to be slower to criticize than some other missionaries. The Book of Mormon teaches:

> Know ye not that there are more nations than one? Know ye not that I, the Lord your God, have created all men, and that I remember those who are upon the isles of the sea; and that I rule in the heavens above and in the earth beneath; and I bring forth my word unto the children of men, yea, even upon all nations of the earth? . . . For I command all men, both in the east and in the west, and in the north, and in the south, and in the islands of the sea that they shall write the words which I speak unto them; for out of the books which shall be written I will judge the world, every man according to that which is written. (2 Nephi 29: 7, 11)

Later the prophet Nephi explained, "For the Lord God giveth light unto the understanding; for he speaketh unto men according to their language, unto their understanding" (2 Nephi 31: 3). Without belaboring the point, Native Americans played a special philosophical role in the teachings of Mormonism. Though their religious beliefs differed greatly, LDS people who took the time to look often found tangential proof of connections between the two faiths. No doubt Indians also looked at Christianity and found similarities.

Navajo religion has a complexity that surpasses Mormonism. As with most faiths, including the LDS, it is sacred and true to those who believe. An extensive body of literature written primarily by anthropologists details the inspired stories and ceremonies that are foundational for the Navajos. Anthropologist Charlotte Frisbie provides an excellent condensation of the results.

> Traditional Navajo religion is concerned with controlling the multiple supernatural powers immanent in the Navajo world, especially the area bounded by the sacred mountains. The People perceive the universe as dynamic and orderly, and filled with living forces which have complex, dialectical powers that enable them to act in favor of or against human beings. The forces include Holy People—innumerable, powerful, mysterious, personalized supernatural beings—and Earth Surface People, ordinary humans, both living and dead. . . .

It is up to individual Navajos to know and abide by the numerous prescriptions and proscriptions established by these Holy People. Doing so, living the religion on a daily basis by following individual, familial, sacred place, and other ritual practices as well as by displaying other behaviors and attitudes, keeps the self in harmony with other humans, nature, and supernaturals, and helps maintain the delicate balance between good and evil. The ideal state, hózhǫ́, is signified by continuing good health, harmony, peace, blessing, good fortune, and positive life events for one's self and relatives.[15]

From this definition come eight fundamental aspects that are addressed here as common ground between Mormon and Navajo religion: (1) the Holy People (Diyin Dine'é) and the nature of God, (2) supernatural power, (3) a dynamic universe filled with living forces, (4) the spiritual nature of humans, (5) prescriptions and proscriptions established by the Holy People, (6) the concept of good and evil, (7) harmony with humans, nature, and supernaturals, and (8) hózhǫ́.

Mormon and Navajo beliefs teach that there are gods or Holy People who interact with humans on occasion. To the LDS, Heavenly Father is the supreme and absolute being, omnipotent, omnipresent, and omniscient. He directs the affairs of the universe, is prayed to, and has a glorified body of flesh and bones. Jesus Christ, his son, also has a resurrected, glorified body of flesh and bones, serves as a mediator between humankind and Heavenly Father, pays for the sins of others through his atoning sacrifice, and is directed by his Father to carry out His will. The Holy Ghost, the third member of the Godhead, is a spirit personage in human form without a physical body, whose influence can be felt throughout the world, just as the sun is only in one place but its light and power are widespread. All three of these beings are gods, but other Holy People or exalted beings also exist. Elder Bruce R. McConkie, an apostle in the church (1915–85), taught that while Latter-day Saints only worship and pray to members of the Godhead, "There is an infinite number of holy personages, drawn from worlds without number, who have passed on to exaltation and are thus gods. . . . Indeed, this doctrine of plurality of Gods is so comprehensive and glorious that it reaches out and embraces every exalted [resurrected] personage."[16] While Mormons have been criticized by other Christian denominations for this doctrine of plurality, the Bible is replete with examples of ministering angels, the resurrection of the dead following Christ's crucifixion, and the admonition for humans to become like Christ, which includes an eventual deified state.

Navajo religion has a large pantheon of Holy People who possess supernatural power, minister to humans in this world, and affect the outcome of daily events. Mormons pray only to one God, Heavenly Father; Navajo prayers may address any one of the Holy People to provide assistance. Their personality is much more human and earthy, displaying qualities of anger, happiness, beneficence, trickery, sexuality, and other human characteristics, while the deity for the LDS is far more reserved and bent upon setting the right example for humankind according to God's commandments. Both sets of spiritual beings are treated with high respect, according to cultural practices proscribed by the Holy Ones.

Yet medicine men also speak of one God who far surpasses any of the other Holy People; his name is Yá'ałnii Niníyá or He Who Stands at the Center of the Universe. He is credited with being omnipotent and is the one who directed (from behind the scenes) the creation of the world by the Holy People. It is not clear whether this God is a recent introduction influenced by Christianity or whether knowledge of him goes back to antiquity. Regardless of his historical depth, this being is familiar to Jim and other religiously knowledgeable people. For example, Clayton Long, head of Bilingual and Bicultural Studies at the San Juan School District, shared an experience that he had at Diné College with a senior Navajo instructor and medicine man (name omitted). The incident illustrates the role of this superior God as the medicine man shared his teachings with a group of young people. That night, as he taught about clans and the forbidden practice of marrying into the same or related clans, the medicine man paused. He then asked for a show of hands as to how many in attendance had married their "brother or sister," referring to the Navajo belief that clan relations are just as real as biological ties. Clayton raised his hand. The medicine man pointed to him, so Clayton expressed his desire to explain why. He spoke of his initial aversion to dating someone from the same clan but said that through prayer and study he realized that for the LDS "marrying in the temple means not being married by men but being married by God, himself. . . . The temple God was the Father of All."

The teacher looked around, talked for about ten minutes, then commented that he remembered a story about what Clayton had said earlier.

A long time ago there were many, many clans. One clan started getting bigger and bigger, "brother marrying sister," causing concern that all the other clans would become extinct. People began to worry that there would not be any more children. The wise people got together and tried to figure it out, but they couldn't. Finally the medicine people got together and started talking about it, but they did not know what to do. They had always been told that when someone marries into a related clan there would be problems. Everybody was stumped. The people decided to go to the Holy Beings. "They'll know; they are in charge of us." They also had no solution.

Finally, one of the Holy People said: "You know that there is one more person that we know but we do not go to him; we never go to him. He is the one who instructed all of us how to be, how to live, so we don't have any reason to go to him, but here's a reason. We call him 'The Father of All [Ts'ídá Aláahdi Ataa'—literally "The Most High Father/God"].' For all of us, he is the Father of All."

So they went to him, and he invited them in to sit down and discuss their problem. The Holy Beings told him what was going on with the people on the earth, and the Father said: "This is how it will be corrected. If I say it is all right to marry your brother or sister, then it is. Now take my word back down."

That is how everything corrected itself.[17]

When the medicine man finished his story, he said that Clayton had done the same thing by going to the Father of All and obtaining his approval. Next he said: "Now all the rest of you who raised your hand, you're all wrong. If you do the same thing as Clayton, by going to the Father of All, then I will approve your marriage." This was a significant departure from past practices, in which a rigid system of extraclan marriage was the rule.

From this teaching, we get a sense of the subordinate relationship of some Holy People to others and that only one of them controlled the power and right to influence certain activities. This same relationship is found in the Pearl of Great Price's account of the premortal ministry of Christ and the creation of the world. Speaking of this event, Abraham taught:

Now the Lord had shown unto me, Abraham, the intelligences that were organized before the world was; and among all these there were many of the noble and great ones; and God saw these souls that they were good, and he stood in the midst of them, and he said: These I will make my rulers; for he stood among those that were spirits, and he saw that they were good; and he said unto me: Abraham, thou art one of them; thou wast chosen before thou wast born.

And there stood one among them that was like unto God [Christ], and he said unto those who were with him: We will go down, for there is space there, and we will take of these materials, and we will make an earth whereon these may dwell. (Abraham 3: 22–24)

Although the Navajo Creation story is far more detailed and filled with powers and personalities specific to the culture, in both accounts we see Holy People discussing, planning, then creating a world for humans.

In order to accomplish this creative process, power is needed. LDS doctrine teaches that God has provided the ability and power to act in His name and to perform supernatural (beyond normal or miraculous) deeds once a person is ordained by someone holding the proper authority or priesthood. When individuals obtain this power and keep God's commandments, they have unlimited potential to fulfill righteous goals. Priesthood power is also the organizing force within the universe used at the time of Creation. Navajo medicine men, while not calling it priesthood power, use a term that recognizes a similar reality: *álílee k'hego* translates as "according to his supernatural/magical power," referring to an unseen force used to perform either good or evil supernatural acts. For instance, Jesus walking on water, withering a fig tree, or casting out evil spirits is comparable in the use of this power to a Navajo healing the sick, a skinwalker running at superhuman speeds, or a person who can control weather. The power is recognized with reverence and used only by those who understand how to treat it.[18] Many Anglo people such as traders, priests, and anthropologists living among Navajos report its presence but cannot explain how it works.[19] Practices like hand trembling, crystal gazing, miraculous healings, and the effects of witchcraft and counterwitchcraft provide tangible but unexplainable results.

For álílee k'hego to function, faith and prayer must be present. Lucille Hunt, a Navajo woman raised in a traditional environment who later converted to the LDS faith, observed: "When I was growing up, álílee k'hego was the way of spiritual powers . . . and so a true medicine man did things in the way that he has the power to share with his patients or family. Some of those powers could be for protection or healing—powers that an ordinary person does not initially understand."[20] Don Mose Sr., another faithful Navajo member of the LDS Church, also testifies to what he has seen take place at the hands of medicine men. "Many Native people are still doing miracles today. I've seen it. I've witnessed it. I was there. I've seen them work; you name it and I've seen it happen. The thing that does it is faith."[21] Faith and prayer, lying at the heart of traditional beliefs, become concrete when expressed through words and imagery. Gladys A. Reichard, a renowned scholar of Navajo religion, studied prayer and its efficacy. Underlying her analysis in *Prayer: The Compulsive Word* is the Navajo concept that words, prayers, and songs call into power the very existence and sustainability of life. Thus LDS people who believe in the power of the priesthood, an unseen supernatural power based on spiritual principles, can understand how others obtain similar results.

Traditional religion teaches that the control of power is through words, serving as the basis for the creation of this world by the gods; those powers persist today. As Holy People like Talking God, First Man, First Woman, Turquoise Boy, White Shell Girl, and others gathered to discuss life on this earth and establish prototypes of everything from the first hogan to medicines for healing, they created the path for Navajo people to follow. As in LDS beliefs, everything was created spiritually before it was created physically. While the Book of Genesis deals with the Creation in a few short chapters, this is not true for the Navajo account. The development and destruction of the three or four worlds beneath this one and how this world's patterns became established can take entire books to recount. The Bible explains why evil exists, why childbirth is painful, and why men are leaders, as well as God's role in forming the earth; the Navajo account contains a myriad of details about what happened below that affects things above, in today's world.[22] It holds a complete charter for life. Reduced to their simplest form, both versions have Holy People who created the world through words and established guidance for humankind's future long before a physical being ever walked the earth.

The God of the Old Testament said: "Let there be light: and there was light"; John of the New Testament wrote: "In the beginning was the Word, and the Word was with God, and the Word was God. The same was in the beginning with God"; and Abraham in the Pearl of Great Price intones: "And then the Lord said: Let us go down. And they went down at the beginning and they, that is the Gods, organized and formed the heavens and the earth." Navajo teachings contain comparable events. According to LDS theology, Christ in his premortal state was chief among the gods who created this world, a concept captured in the Navajo name for the Creator—Yá'ałnii Niníyá (He Who Stands at the Center of the Universe). Of primary concern in this creative process is the ability to plan, prepare, then form the elements through words, moving them from a spiritual to a physical state. This becomes possible through álílee k'hego or priesthood or the compulsive word.

Preparation to use these words and this power in prayer is an important concept in both religions. The Navajo word for prayer is *sodizin*: *so* means tongue and *dizin* means holy, implying that "my tongue must be holy" before talking to the Holy People. *Tádidíín* (corn pollen) is used in prayers as an offering and is often put on the tip of the tongue as a blessing. *Tá* means knowledge or light, while *didíín* refers to God and holiness. Some people compare the use of corn pollen placed on a tongue to a sacrament, where covenants based on God's knowledge are renewed. That pollen, like the sacrament, becomes a part of a person, physically entering into the blood and tissue but more importantly becoming a part of the person in holy thought and deed.[23]

Just how compulsive words can be is shown in the Creation story found in the Book of Moses in the Pearl of Great Price. The Lord, through vision, explained the creation of the world by saying, "And by the word of my power have I created them [this world and the things upon it] . . . [and] there are many worlds that have passed away by the word of my power" (Moses 1: 32, 35). The creation of night, stars in the heaven, land, and all other things "was done as I [God] spake . . . was so even as I spake . . . even according to my word" (Moses 2: 5, 7, 16). The Lord then explains to Moses: "As one earth shall pass away, and the heavens thereof even so shall another come; and there is no end to my works, neither to my words," connecting the two in the creative process (Moses 1: 38). Later in this same book is the story of Enoch, in which we learn of the power of the word as given to this prophet when enemies besieged his people: "So great was the faith of Enoch that . . . [when] he spake the word of the Lord, the earth trembled and the mountains fled even according to his command; . . . and all nations feared greatly, so powerful was the word of Enoch, and so great was the power of the language which God had given him" (Moses 7: 13). As we read of Jim Dandy's use of faith, prayers, songs, and words—all very much in keeping with traditional Navajo religion—it becomes apparent that many of his experiences are dependent upon similar principles. Much of Navajo healing is based upon prayers and ceremonies where tangible sickness is healed not so much by the physical means used by an Anglo doctor but by spiritual means based on words.

Understanding how Holy People created the world through words leads to the next question: does the physical world still respond to those words? What allowed Enoch to speak to a mountain and move it or Christ to calm the Sea of Galilee? While the beliefs of animism and animatism are prevalent in Navajo religion—where all things have a spirit and power that responds to spiritual practices—Christianity does not often discuss their influence. Most Christian teachings do not view the world as a sentient, dynamic universe filled with animate forces. LDS doctrine, however, explains in part how spiritual power can direct a seemingly inanimate world. First, everything has a spirit. Spirit matter in its primal state was formed from what Abraham called "intelligences that were organized before the world was," which have the ability to recognize truth and light (Abraham 3: 22). "Intelligence, or the light of truth, was not created or made, neither indeed can be. All truth is independent in that sphere in which God has placed it, to act for itself, as all intelligence also otherwise there is no existence" (D & C: 93: 29–30).

Everything, in a spiritual sense, is composed of intelligence; thus it has the ability to respond, which in turn gives it choice. This becomes particularly evident in Abraham's account of Creation, when the Holy People are implementing the plan to create first a spiritual then a physical earth. Numerous times during the process, God says: "And they (the Gods) said: Let there be light; and there was light. . . . the Gods also said. . . . And the Gods ordered. . . . And the Gods called" (Abraham 4: 3, 6–9). Yet the undertaking was not one of total obedience—choice or agency was also present. In forming vegetation that would yield seed and fruit, "the Gods saw that they were obeyed"; but later in other aspects "the Gods watched those things which they had ordered until they obeyed"; and, finally, "the Gods saw that they would be obeyed and that their plan was good. . . . [Indeed] The Gods said: We will do everything that we have said, and organize them; and behold they [intelligences] shall be very obedient" (Abraham 4: 12, 18, 21, 31).

Joseph Smith in the Doctrine and Covenants explained that everything on this earth, in a spiritual sense, belongs to and has within it a kingdom. While today's science categorizes things according to the animal or plant kingdom and so forth, LDS beliefs far surpass these more general physical classifications. Going back to the earth's spiritual creation, we learn: "All kingdoms have a law given; and there are many kingdoms; for there is no space in which there is no kingdom; and there is no kingdom in which there is no space, either a greater or lesser kingdom. And unto every kingdom is given a law; and unto every law there are certain bounds also and conditions" (D & C 88: 36–38). Although the LDS Church today does not emphasize this relationship to nature, it is important to recognize that sufficient doctrine explains how words, songs, and prayers can influence the physical world— "move mountains" as well as heal people. This type of belief and thinking is in keeping with traditional Navajo views of the power of prayer in a sentient world that responds to that power.

A well-known tenet in Navajo beliefs is that everything in the world is either male or female. Rivers, mountains, clouds, trees, and all aspects of the human body are paired with gender. The depth of this understanding is discussed in later chapters. This concept is foreign to much of Christianity and is rarely noticed in Mormonism. It does not seem strange for Navajos to talk about Mother Earth and Father Sky, but to most Anglos that is just a metaphorical concept, a pretty way of recognizing the two. They are inanimate orbs in a solar system—that is, until we start reading LDS scripture. In D & C 88: 45 and 87, we learn: "The earth rolls upon *her* wings, and the sun giveth *his* light by day, and the moon giveth *her* light by night. . . . [and later] the sun shall hide *his* face" (emphasis added). These possessive adjectives shift according to the heavenly body being identified and are similar to the gender used by Navajos to describe the same bodies. In other scripture we read that "the sun shall be darkened in *his* going forth, and the moon shall not cause *her* light to shine" (2 Nephi 23: 10). But the prophet Enoch gives the clearest description of human qualities held by the earth. As the Lord instructed him, this prophet looked upon the land and "heard a voice from the bowels thereof, saying: Wo, wo is me, the mother of men; I am pained, I am weary, because of the wickedness of my children. When shall I rest, and be cleansed from the filthiness which is gone forth out of me? . . . And when Enoch heard the earth mourn, he wept" (Moses 7: 48–49). Indeed, "all of the creation of God mourned; and the earth groaned; . . . [until] the day shall come that the earth shall rest" (Moses 7: 56, 61). Eventually the earth will die, but until then "the whole earth groans under the weight of its iniquity" (D & C 88: 26; 123: 7). Thus Mother Earth and Father Sky as discussed in Navajo beliefs find limited companionship in LDS thought.

Another tenet of Navajo belief is that because all things were created spiritually before physically each has an inner form, called *nítch'i hwii'sizíinii*, meaning the "In-Standing Wind Soul," glossed as the "Inner Form That Stands Within." The complexity and role of this spiritual form is open to various interpretations, but at its most elementary it is a spirit that enters the body at birth and departs at death.[24] Often referred to as a wind or winds whose essence gives individual character to each person, it also has qualities common to all. We should not confuse this with the type of wind (*níyol*) that brushes against people's faces. This is a spirit with power and part of the general concept of *nítch'i* (discussed below). Anthropologist Maureen Trudelle Schwarz writes: "As it did in the creation of the first [Holy People], air plays a pivotal role in the animation of every contemporary human being. Wind gives life and breath to Earth Surface People [humans]. In the Navajo view, the entrance of air into an infant marks the beginning of life for every person. . . . The individual nature of the specific winds that enter a child after birth determine what kind of personal characteristics he or she will have. There are many different kinds of winds that may enter a child."[25] Comparable in function to the "spirit" discussed in LDS beliefs that is within the body at birth, learns and grows during life, and departs for another realm at death, the inner form is individualistic, with a personality all its own.

A second form of spiritual being, a member of the Godhead, is the Holy Ghost. Believed to be a noncorporeal being whose purpose is to communicate with the spirit within, the Holy Ghost instructs, warns, and protects. Likewise, Nítch'i to the Navajos is a deity, a force that functions in a similar manner. James McNeley in his ground-breaking study *Holy Wind in Navajo Philosophy* writes, "In order to emphasize the latter aspect of the Navajo concept [differentiating between *níyol* and *nítch'i*], the phrase Holy Wind has sometimes been used although Spirit or Holy Spirit could perhaps as well be used."[26] Its purpose and function is clearly defined, and unlike other Navajo deities, it always tells the truth. It is also capable of informing not only humans but also other animate and inanimate forms because of their "Inner Form That Stands Within."

Nítch'i is a common persona found throughout Navajo mythology. The Holy Wind constantly warns the protagonist in a myth how to avoid trouble by whispering in his ear. Perhaps the best-known example is the role it played as the Twins—Monster Slayer and Born for Water—journeyed to visit their Father, Jóhonaa'éí or Sun Bearer (see the discussion above).[27] The two boys not only avoided all of the evils encountered in their travels, knowing how to pass all of the tests that their father gave them to prove that they were his sons, but also succeeded in killing the monsters inhabiting the earth, including Big God. In each instance, it was Nítch'i that guided them. Just as the New Testament is filled with examples and admonitions to listen to the Spirit to avoid pitfalls, Navajo beliefs contain a voice of protection and help.

By now it is apparent that Navajo tradition and LDS doctrine contain some comparable elements. One of the most pivotal narratives for the Navajos is the story of the Twins and their mother, Changing Woman. This fundamental main stalk with its leaves branching out provides the origin for many Navajo ceremonies and practices of daily life. Briefly, Changing Woman, the most beneficent of all deities, is bathing one day and becomes pregnant with the Twins by the all-powerful Sun Bearer through a mystical union of sunshine and water. Light and moisture, symbols of life, are the catalyst for this virgin birth that produces two exceptional sons. But monsters roamed the earth and lived by eating Navajo people, innocent young children in particular. These monsters came in many forms, but all were created through impure sexual practices and evil design. Changing Woman hid her boys from the monsters by putting them in a hole and covering it with a flat rock, giving the boys the name of Raised Underground (Łéyah Nolyání).

Eventually the youths asked their mother who their father was. She told them that he was Sun Bearer who lives far away and that it was impossible to go to him. The Twins decided to go in search of him anyway; with supernatural aid primarily obtained through Nítch'i, they ascended to the heavens and met their father. He did not believe that they were who they claimed to be and so put them through a series of tests, which they passed with the help of the Holy Wind. When Sun Bearer then asked what they wanted, they replied weapons: four different kinds of lightning and sunbeam arrows to kill the monsters. After he granted their wish, the Twins returned to earth and set about destroying the evil that had beset their people. At the completion of the monsters' destruction, only four remained—Old Age, Death, Poverty, and Lice.[28] Seeing that their work was done, they buried their weapons and purified themselves.

This story has many variations, but the framework remains constant. Some of the more obvious points to consider are the role of Changing Woman and Sun Bearer. As a chaste and benevolent woman often equated with the earth and its nurturing capacity, Changing Woman conceives through a magical, mystical union comparable to a virgin birth. While LDS teachings about the Virgin Mary are limited primarily to the birth of Jesus, the Mariolatry of Roman Catholicism could be compared to Navajo teachings about Changing Woman made manifest in the kinaaldá ceremony. Her husband is a god and holds significant supernatural power. Though he is not viewed and does not act as the Christian God who is perfect in all, Sun Bearer's humanlike traits never overshadow his all-powerfulness. He is the one who moves mountains, controls destructive forces, grants protection, and enriches life. The only way that the Twins could overcome the obstacles standing in the way of reaching their father was through the assistance of the Holy Wind, who whispered in their ear and warned of impending dangers.

The Twins had the task of ridding the world of evil, destroying its many forms to make the land safe for the People. Guided by the promptings of Nítch'i, the Twins killed the monsters plaguing the Navajos. Only the four who could enrich people's lives remained. Old Age made it possible for young people to enjoy their youth by adding a sober look ahead to the future; Sickness fostered appreciation for health; Death made room on the earth to prevent overcrowding; and Lice created compassion and the need for people to serve each other.[29] Christian doctrine, while taking a different approach as to how to deal with these concerns, recognizes that these maladies were ordained by God from the beginning for a purpose. And it was Christ, born by supernatural means, who came to the earth to destroy evil—not by shooting physical monsters with lightning, but with the power of thought, word, and deed given or approved by his Father.

How then do we cope with these problems when they enter life—sickness, in particular? As the Twins went about killing the monsters, they received new names. The one often referred to as Elder Brother, a title used for Christ in LDS literature, became known as Monster Slayer; Younger Brother received the name Born for Water. Monster Slayer energetically went about the task of killing the enemy. He was the adventurous "dominant male" side of the pair, who developed the plans and executed them successfully. As his name implies, he was the one who performed the deeds. Born for Water was the calmer and more reflective of the two, in many of the stories staying behind to offer prayers and play a supportive role for his brother. He participated in some of the adventures, but more as a companion with strong spiritual values as compared to his brother, who aggressively waged the war.

Sin, as explained in Christianity, is a matter of breaking commandments or teachings given by God, who holds each person accountable. In the final reward or judgment an individual's good or evil deeds will be recognized and rewarded or punished. While the Christian concept of individual sin is foreign to traditional Navajo beliefs, the Navajo world definitely contains good and evil forces that can influence an individual. Rather than viewing right and wrong as a battle between cosmic forces of light and dark vying for an individual's soul, the Navajo world is circumscribed with powers inherent in an object or situation that can be turned either to help or to curse a person. The correct behavior is to appeal to and then utilize that power for protection and well-being. Evil is to turn that power against an individual. Chapter 11, on the light and dark sides, shows just how powerful these forces can be in both helping and hindering a person.

In discussing this struggle against evil forces, some people go so far as to suggest that Monster Slayer—even with all of his trickery, deceit, and bloody deeds—assumed a Christ-like role as he went forth to save his people. While he is far from the contemplative, peace-loving Savior portrayed in the New Testament, if we equate the monsters to a metaphorical personification of sin or evil, then that sin was not tolerated and was destroyed. As both purified the world in their own way, they were doing so with the assistance of their

Father. In a similar light, some Christian Navajos interpret Born for Water as John the Baptist. While this may be stretching the point, it cannot be denied that Monster Slayer is the one Navajo people appeal to when in need. He is central to ceremonies like the Enemy Way, Evil Way, and Protection Way, to name a few. His symbols are found everywhere—from the bow and arrow that hangs over the doorway as a defense against evil, to the "precious stones" (ntł'iz) used in male offerings, to the flint (béésh) of his armor used in ceremonies for protection, to his actions as a warrior. Monster Slayer is the most important example of proper behavior and protection for males, just as Changing Woman is for females. His power is the one invoked when people need help.

At this point we should ask: what is the final outcome desired by both religions? Do perceived similarities lead to the same goal? After all, Mormons have a strict ethical code for daily life that provides the criteria by which they will be evaluated in a final judgment by God, after which they will inherit a kingdom commensurate with their spiritual growth and accomplishment. Navajos, in contrast, have a different set of values, are not concerned with sin in the Christian sense, and fear the afterlife. Although no final judgment will occur, all people will go to a not-so-pleasant spiritual realm someplace to the north, where they will remain forever.[30] The apparent disparity between the two seems large.

A Pharisee lawyer, in an attempt to trick Jesus, asked what was the greatest commandment. The reply: "Thou shalt love the Lord thy God with all thy heart, and with all thy soul, and with all thy mind. This is the first and great commandment. And the second is like unto it, Thou shalt love thy neighbor as thyself. On these two commandments hang all the law and the prophets" (Matthew 22: 37–40). The Navajos have two terms that encapsulate similar ideals: k'é and sq'a naagháii bik'e hózhǫ́. In these two teachings lie many central values of traditional religion.

K'é, in many respects, is comparable to "loving thy neighbor as thyself." This word identifies the ideal relationship that the individual should strive to achieve with people and the world in general. Encompassed in this term is the meaning "compassion, cooperation, friendliness, unselfishness, peacefulness, and all those positive virtues which constitute intense, diffuse, and enduring solidarity."[31] Also inherent is the thought that all people are related, a feeling that is expressed through bonds of love and assistance. Navajos use kinship terms to describe this relationship, just as Mormons refer to church members as "brother" and "sister" even though they may have no genealogical link. These kinship terms show respect, so people do not address individuals by their "street names," as is done in Anglo society. Kinship with its accompanying responsibilities becomes the basis for all relationships. The closer the biological kinship, with the mother-child bond being the strongest, the more intense the feeling and commitment. Vincent Denetdeal described k'é this way:

> If you and I were sisters, I would sincerely love you as a sister. I would try to please you, make you happy. I wouldn't say harsh words. I would be honest. We would listen to each other. You would take my advice. If I told you not to drink, you'd stop just like that. When you needed help, I would know. You wouldn't have to tell me. I would take the initiative to take care of you. You'd just go along with it. This is where respect comes in. It would be the same way in a marriage. It would be the same way with other siblings or relatives.[32]

Feelings of k'é should begin at birth and be nurtured through childhood, as an individual is taught about caring and respect in a holy home. Talking God, in one of the twelve hogan songs, sings: "I have come upon a holy place. . . . You have created a holy place. Look around and be nurtured. Isn't this a beautiful place?"[33] The thing that makes the home holy is not the dirt and logs but the relationships that play out as well as the presence of the Holy People within. The word *dilzin* means to keep something holy, with k'é being a primary concern. John Salabye and Kathleen Manolescu expressed it this way: "When we consider something holy or sacred, we have particular sets of expectations about how it should be looked at and treated. The expectations are based on knowledge and the practice of respect, or how to treat something as if it is precious."[34] As the child learns and is disciplined, the foundation of the teaching is stressed through terms like "son" and "daughter," showing that the reason for the teaching is the bond of the family to which the child belongs. Discipline becomes an act of love and acceptance instead of rejection and anger.[35]

The practice of k'é extends beyond the family to all other beings as they adopt this code of behavior. Social interaction of this nature produces harmony and brings people into a bonding relationship of peace, love, cooperation, and a state called *hózhǫ*, a term described below.[36] Even beyond these feelings between humans, the ties of k'é can be expressed toward Mother Earth, a flock of sheep, the mountain soil bundle, and other objects or physical entities referred to as "mother." Thus "the symbols of motherhood and k'é solidarity which they represent pervade Navajo culture and provide the patterns and sentiments which order Navajo social life."[37] Very much in keeping with the injunction of Christ to "love thy neighbor as thyself," k'é is the Navajo expression of just such an ideal.

While this explains the second commandment on how to "love thy neighbor as thyself," a far more complex series of thoughts addresses the first commandment of how to love the Lord with all of your heart, soul, and mind. This ideal is encapsulated in the term *sǫ'a naagháii bik'e hózhǫ*—a state of being that puts the individual in tune with the powers of the universe. This feeling is difficult to describe. Indeed, anthropologist John R. Farella wrote an entire book, *The Main Stalk: A Synthesis of Navajo Philosophy*, trying to do so. Any attempt to explain it here—when leading scholars such as Washington Matthews, Berard Haile, Gladys Reichard, Gary Witherspoon, and a number of Navajo medicine men and women do not totally agree as to its comprehensive meaning—can only be incomplete. What follows is a bare synthesis.

From the beginning, the Holy People established this way of being as an end state or goal to achieve—both in mortality and after. Witherspoon cites Reichard as saying that this phrase is the synthesis of all Navajo beliefs as well as human attitudes and experiences. Reichard glosses *hózhǫ* as "long life" and "happiness" as well as "in-old-age-walking-the-trail-of-beauty," "according-to-age-may-it-be-perfect," and "according-to-the-ideal-may-it-be-achieved," while linguist Robert Young believes that it "represents the capacity of all life and living things to achieve 'immortality' through reproduction."[38]

Everything living and inanimate is infused with this power to be. The goal for a Navajo is to arrive at old age having lived the precepts of sǫ'a naagháii bik'e hózhǫ, the "central animating powers of the universe, and, as such, they produce a world of hózhǫ, the ideal environment of beauty, harmony, and happiness. All living beings, which include the earth, sacred mountains, and so on, have inner and outer forms, which to achieve well-being must harmonize and unify with [these powers]."[39] Evil, in its many forms such as witchcraft and other antisocial behavior, disrupts the process of obtaining goodness. To end the downward spiral of sickness or affliction, the person must be restored to health and well-being through ceremonies that take that patient back to the time of Creation, when goodness and positive power first formed the earth and triumphed over evil. The Holy People who initially performed these worthy acts are there, participating in the ritual, using their power to restore goodness and beauty. As Witherspoon notes: "In doing so, I would describe są'a naagháii bik'e hózhǫ as the generating [power] plant or sources of animation and life for the inner forms of all living beings. The Holy People are supernaturals because of their closeness to these power sources and because of their knowledge of the ways (rituals) to connect and harmonize with these central power sources."[40] It is the ultimate origin of good in the universe.

In addition to thinking of this principle as power, it also represents completeness. For humans, this is part of the process of life in which an individual moves toward greater selfhood. Farella believes that the idea of restoration, expressed during ceremonies, is part of that process. Until the ritual is completed, the patient is incomplete and has not achieved the state of są'a naagháii bik'e hózhǫ, which "is to become complete, and perhaps to become more than you were before. It is not to return to the same person. The overriding theme of this discussion and all of the stories is the creation of a way of life that will last."[41] A medicine man has the responsibility of inviting the Holy People to participate in a ceremony and therefore must be in a state of beauty and peace or hózhǫ. Saying prayers, performing in the sweat lodge, gathering ceremonial materials, and achieving a tranquil mind-set are all part of the preparation. And when a person dies in old age, completeness is achieved by returning to the powers of the universal beginning.

Mormons tie in to similar universal forces. They view the priesthood as an eternal power through which the world was formed, which, in connection with deity, not only can heal the sick but can create binding covenants for this world as well as the next. The similar belief of są'a naagháii bik'e hózhǫ parallels this doctrine. If both of these powers are dependent on one guiding principle, it is state of mind or worthiness, or, as Mormons say, "being in tune with the [Holy] Spirit and God's will," that allows the power to be activated. While LDS priesthood holders may not envision Holy People per se when entering into a room to heal the sick as a Navajo medicine man does, they certainly feel that the Spirit is present and directing the event. This power was present at the beginning of the world; Christ during his ministry modeled its use. It exists throughout eternity, and a righteous person who has lived a good life (comparable to hózhǫ) is able to utilize its powers now and in the world to come.

As older Navajo medicine men pass away and few others take their place, we might ask what will happen to these traditional views. This is a real concern today among Navajo elders, as numbers continue to shrink across the reservation. The old ways and deep knowledge disappear a little bit more each time one of them dies. Clayton Long recalls:

[My father] says there will be a time when the things that I had will be so small that people who think traditionally will try to find them but they can't. Our medicine men say it all the time; you hear it across the reservation, "The medicine men are going. There is no more to replace them. Nobody is picking it up. We are losing what we had." That is what my father is saying and when it is gone, the people will hunger for something to hang on and live by.[42]

Long and other LDS people, many of whom experienced placement, suggest that Navajos will gravitate to the LDS Church to find comparable beliefs and powers that lie in traditional concepts. Whether or not this is true, certainly both religions have served their people well over time.

One final question: how many Navajo people have embraced some of these syncretic elements? While it is difficult to determine this aspect of individual thought, we get a general impression that those Navajo people who understand and respect both traditional teachings and LDS doctrine are comfortable in moving between them. For both religions, the question of how much is understood always arises. Some people are more philosophical and contemplative, while others care more about doing and stress the pragmatic, without a deep theological understanding. Others are just there because that is how they were raised. How many people really understand the LDS sacrament or a priesthood blessing well enough to compare it to the Navajo use of corn pollen; look at participating with Holy People in a ceremony as similar to performing a temple endowment; think of the white-painted Yé'ii Bicheii as equivalent to Christ's apostles; believe that the Holy Wind functions the same as the Holy Ghost; see the Twins' role of slaying evil as comparable to Christ's mortal ministry; or take the stories from one and transpose them over the other, as Don Mose's grandfather did? All of this is dependent upon the level of understanding of the individual, but it occurs regularly where knowledge and acceptance of both exist.

In summarizing this chapter, it is important to stress again that its purpose is not to claim that Navajo beliefs derived from "Lamanite" origins or that aspects of traditional Navajo and LDS religion are interchangeable. We hope that the reader has gained respect for both religions and a better understanding of how certain beliefs, while set in extremely different contexts, share comparable elements. A medicine man, familiar with ceremonial knowledge, stories, and language, would be more at ease in this type of discussion than many Navajo people unfamiliar with traditional teachings. In Jim Dandy's circumstance, where he is conversant with both worlds, he has no problem going between the two.

Rose Yazzie, introduced at the beginning of this chapter, is also such a person. When she prayed to Jesus but stood for Monster Slayer, her inclusive approach did not demand excluding one for the other. The metaphors or teachings used in Navajo beliefs are different in their outward form when compared to LDS theology but can be comparable in function. The two become wedded through descriptive Navajo vocabulary that delineates how they work and what they mean. Concepts central to LDS beliefs such as the Godhead, priesthood power, sacrament, prayer, spiritual assistance, and the creation of the world have their counterparts in Navajo teachings. Are there major differences? Certainly: they are rooted in different stories and metaphors that may point people in different directions. What is comparable is their breadth, flexibility, and underlying principles. As Kendall Blanchard pointed out after studying the impact of Mormonism and another Christian religion on Navajo converts:

The converts are synthesizing elements of their customary thought patterns and implicit philosophical premises with selected elements of the new doctrines. This accommodation legitimates certain new behaviors without, in most cases, seriously modifying traditional belief systems. Therefore the event of a Navajo's rejecting traditional religious activities and joining a Christian congregation is actually not as "radical" or "surprising" as some anthropologists have previously suggested.[43]

For Jim and thousands of other Navajo people, this is truly the case.

JIM DANDY'S LIFE

CHAPTER THREE

JIM'S EARLY YEARS

"Only a Stick Is Left Standing"

Cora Shorty guided the horse-drawn wagon toward the hogan. Her sheep camp, located between Kaibito and Navajo Mountain, rested in the midst of a high country desert of grasses, sagebrush, juniper, and piñon. A strong, sturdy woman, she had been ranging over the barren land for firewood and water to bring home. Her mother and father, concerned about feed for the sheep, cattle, and horses, were seeking other spots to graze their herds, leaving their pregnant daughter with her two small girls to handle routine chores while they were away. Heavy exertion had its effect. Sharp labor pains bespoke the obvious; it was time to bring new life into the world.[1] Cora's daughters were too young to be of much help, so she prepared for the task alone. In the distance rode Ruth Whiterock, a relative who was in search of wood with her uncle when they spied Cora's shade house and hogan. Turning her team to the camp, Ruth began to hear the faint sounds of a woman in labor. As the wagon came to a halt, Ruth alighted from the seat, assessed the situation, and tied a sash belt from the hogan's cedar beam for Cora to grasp as she squatted and pushed over a small hole filled with clean sand on the floor. At times, birthing women feel intense pain that may cause them to choke or harm their teeth, so Ruth placed a part of the belt in Cora's mouth. The young daughters huddled in the corner, not knowing what was happening or what to do but sensing their mother's pain. Ruth, however, did understand. Washing her hands, cleaning the area, and coaching the mother, she delivered a small baby boy.[2]

Symbols of protection were all around. With a sharp arrowhead, Ruth cut the umbilical cord, tied the remnant in a loop, and pushed it into the baby's belly, after hitting him on the bottom. The arrowhead or a flint knife serves

On the way back from the Red Lake Trading Post, 1947. Albert and Lillie sit side by side
with Zonnie and Jim in the back of the family wagon that Cora drove the day of Jim's
birth. He later recalled, "We hauled everything in that wagon and were always on the go."

as both a tool for cutting and a means of defense.[3] Just as First Man and First
Woman were the first to use them in the preexistence, setting the pattern for
the Five Fingered Beings (humans), so Ruth used them now. The flint point
ensured that goodness—whether in butchering animals for food or in the holy
act of bringing forth a child—returned to the arrowhead to protect against
hunger and harm. A few days later, when the end of the umbilical cord dried
and fell off, Ruth placed it in a special spot, determined by the sex of the
baby and the family's desire. Perhaps she wedged it in a young juniper tree
with healthy leaves so that this part of the person would return to something
that is growing and strong. It may have been buried close to the family corral, so that the thoughts of the newborn would come back to the home and
its livestock in later life. Or it may have been placed under a yucca plant, a
cactus, or a sharp stick to keep evil at bay. Jim was never told.

Ruth marveled that the baby wailed so loudly: "I know you are going to
be a good leader and out there." She did not forget this, often reminding him
later: "Grandson, I am the one who brought you to this earth. I'm the one
who made sure you are alive." She wrapped the infant in a Blue Bird flour

sack, a common type of cloth around Navajo camps, used to make clothing and light blankets. Entering into the sunlight, Ruth walked to the north, the place where ashes from spent fires are laid to rest, and scooped up a handful of black soot. Pronouncing, "I want this boy to be strong," she patted the refuse on his bottom. Ash both cleanses and protects. Just as his grandmother would later have him take out the ash from a spent fire to cleanse what was within the hogan, this act cleansed what was within the newborn to prepare him for his new beginning. Like a ceremonial arrowhead, it created a barrier against evil and sickness. Later Ruth washed the child with a soapy solution made from yucca root and cedar leaves swished in water. The cold liquid made the baby strong to greet the rigors of life.

Ruth had other things to do. She calmed the two sisters, taking care of their needs and introducing them to their little brother. Her uncle now entered and assisted. Men are not excluded from all of this activity. Usually the blessing, singing, and ceremony can be done by either a man or a woman. Often a medicine man sings to relieve the pain during birth and gathers plants taken internally or placed on the stomach.[4] Ruth also cleaned up where young cedar leaves had been warmed in a hot fire pit after the ashes had been removed. These had been taken out and applied to the expectant mother's stomach directly and in hot water, which served as a lubricant before rubbing it around the torso and waist. This relieved the pain and decreased the trauma of childbirth. The baby came easily.

Cora directed that a sheep she had raised with a bottle from infancy be butchered in celebration of the event. The time was right to introduce the newborn to traditional foods like mutton stew. Ruth later teased: "I would just put a little soup on my finger and in your mouth. You would try to open your eyes to see." But the experience went both ways. "When I left that little place I was so happy; all that week I was lucky with everything that I did." This was in 1940. Ruth continued to live in the Red Lake/Tuba City area for a long time and died at the age of ninety-five. How fortunate that she appeared for this event— as Cora testified, "That woman really knows what to do."

So did Cora. The little baby who grew to be a man named Jim Dandy remembers his mother, also known as Hastiin "Elay's" (Eli's) Daughter, as a strong woman. Born on July 26, 1920, and raised in a traditional Navajo family, she embraced the tasks of herding sheep, weaving rugs, and performing

camp chores as part of everyday life. At the age of ten, she attended the Phoenix Indian School and progressed through the eighth grade. Shortly afterward an arranged marriage to Albert Dandy, known as Many Yellow Mules'
Son, changed her life. This was in 1938. Born in 1910, Albert now stood over
six feet tall, wore a size five-and-a-half shoe, and was a perfectionist who
demanded the best from his young wife; she felt totally inadequate in this
new relationship. His desire to excel landed him the last name of Dandy from
his white employers on the railroad construction crew. "Oh, you are doing
a good job; you're doing a dandy job." He passed the name on to his three
brothers, but his four sisters never took it.

As with Cora, Albert's early life centered in the livestock industry. His
family ranged sheep from Kaibito and Inscription House to Black Mesa, with
a base homestead in Red Lake, all in Arizona. His home was at Rat Spring,
a place named for an artesian well that erupted into a rat's nest. The site
received its name during Albert's grandparents' time when they faced starva-
tion. The only food available was the pack rat, which helped them survive.
The older folks still respect this animal for assisting them through their difficult trial. Their camp, located four miles northwest of Red Lake's Wildcat
Peak, served as a base for their limited livestock operation.[5] The family built
a corral near the pile of sticks that formed the pack rat's nest, cleaned the
water, and used it for home and livestock. Albert grew up dirt poor, raised
primarily by his grandmother. With seven sisters and brothers, he considered
himself lucky to have a tin can for a dish. Eventually, a trading post entered
the area, which opened his eyes to a world of wealth that he did not know
existed. Perhaps that is why he worked so hard all his life to obtain the things
that he had never had growing up.

Although his family camp was in close proximity to Cora's, Albert did
not speak to her until his father and mother arranged the marriage, Albert's
second. He had left his first wife in Tuba City. The parents were happy with
future prospects, Albert somewhat unsure, but Cora knew she was just too
young. Still, when the families decided it was proper, the young couple had
little choice. Just as poverty-stricken as before the marriage, Cora feared
entering into the relationship. She eased into it by living apart from her new
husband and bringing food prepared at her grandmother's camp to his hogan
after he returned from herding sheep. Two months later she felt that she had

gotten to know him better and started staying with him. Albert translated his drive for excellence and hard work into the marriage. He was pretty rough with Cora, making her train horses by standing in a wagon in a corral and roping the ones that had not yet been broken. She was not afraid, having survived a difficult childhood in a traditional Navajo setting, but she also valued her white education and experience, later encouraging all of her children to pursue their own. People recognized her for this type of openness and kindness as well as her generosity to those in need.

As if this early life had not been hard enough, Cora and Albert strengthened each other through physical and mental training. With the first snow covering the mesa, the young couple arose early and rolled in the blanket of white then stood under a cedar tree to shake the fresh powder off the branches and onto their bare chests. Like a whip cracking across the skin, the cold knocked the air from their lungs; then they ran.[6] Jim recalls: "Dad was pretty rough, worse than John Wayne, but he was not mean or hurting, just taught her discipline. My mother would really laugh about what they did together. They were both very good parents."

Albert was just passing on the way he had been raised. Discipline was harsh. He had to be alert all the time with little sleep, sometimes staying up all night, because no one knew when they might be "attacked."[7] Many of the great-grandparents who lived through the Fearing Time urged alertness and were strong people, physically and emotionally. Every time there was some type of disturbance or war, the People prepared. The elders taught: "I won't sleep a lot. You also must learn to be up early in the morning to be prepared and strong." One of his grandmothers consistently woke Albert up well before dawn with a long stick, saying:

Wake up, wake up. You'll never get rich; you'll never survive; you'll always be crippled; your life will not have anything. Like me, I don't have anything. I'm just a poor person with no wealth. You're always going to be a slave and never learn how to work or raise a family. We're teaching you now because you will have to be strong to survive in this world. The only way is to be able to beat the Holy People who come early in the morning. If you run early in the morning, you will be strong, talented, and smart. If you do not, you will die in your sleep.

Cora, Marie, and Jim, 1951. Jim: "When I think about how I grew up, I remember my mother was always there—even though my grandparents raised me. Mom was close to her parents and we were always happy to see her come."

That was what his grandmother and great-grandmother taught, two very strict, tough ladies.

Albert was in California working for the railroad and was not with Cora when she gave birth to Jim. She moved back to Rat Spring and awaited her husband, who decided to remain with her to provide assistance. But Jim did not stay with his family for very long. Navajo custom allowed grandparents to select a child to raise, and Cora's parents selected him when he was not even a year old. Cora and Albert agreed with this decision because they needed to leave the reservation in search of work. The couple handed the baby to the maternal grandparents while Marie, his sister, went to Jim's paternal grandparents. Mother and father started on the road, a pattern that continued for years, while the children lived a traditional life with the elders. His mom and dad returned to Rat Spring infrequently to visit their child.

Jim was not the first to have such an experience. One of his sisters, Zonnie, who was a year older, lived with her father's parents. The grandfather's Navajo name was One Who Gambles with Cards, and his wife, Sarah Zonnie, was known as Lady with No Eyes because she went blind. Her other name was Mildred Many Mules. One Who Gambles was a very powerful medicine man, who performed the Red Ant Way and taught it to his son, while his wife was a medicine woman who healed with plants.[8] Both worked hard raising crops and herding livestock, but it was not enough to keep them together.

Zonnie recalls:

My grandmother's husband left when she lost her sight at the age of twenty-two. My dad was in a cradleboard at the time, and her two daughters were herding sheep. When One Who Gambles deserted her, he took one of his sons, put him in a bag on his horse, and rode to Ganado, where he married another woman. I never saw my grandfather.

My parents just dropped me off as a baby to be raised by my aunt and my blind grandmother. I didn't really miss them because we were raised to be tough. I felt at home with my grandmother, my aunt, the sheep, and horses. As a young girl I was told to get up before the sun rose and be in bed at sunset in order to get enough sleep. I awoke in the dark at 4 A.M. because we were taught that there could be a war at anytime; the Utes used to attack the Navajos in the past when my grandmother was growing up. So she felt that war was always possible. We prepared. Grandmother got us up early in the morning, sang songs, then had us run about five miles.

After Grandmother could no longer see, she identified medicine plants by feeling them. Through a sharpened sense of smell she could tell a lot about her environment and its vegetation while her hearing became more acute. Rug weaving was another talent. A helper would lay down rolls of yarn and tell her what color they were so that she could select them as she sat before the loom for hours. At night, when not herding sheep, she kept the children busy carding wool while constantly teaching traditional ways. Lady with No Eyes rewarded her helpers with candy, which she bought for them at the trading post. She kept it hidden in her things or under her feet while sitting. When the time was right, maybe once a week, Grandmother would give us a little piece of candy. One day my brothers and sisters told me to steal some from her so I crawled quietly into the hogan. She was sitting there working with her hands as I crept forward. Out came her guide stick and swish, she struck out at me, depending on her sense of hearing and smell for a direct hit. You could never outfox her, but she kept the family together.

Grandmother raised Zonnie near Wildcat Peak at Gopher Springs. Although completely blind, she was often alone with only Zonnie and another child to help with the sheep. The granddaughter did not complain, remembering the times when:

We didn't have a home but put a shack together wherever we camped for the night. We all slept in a small space. There were no tools to make a hogan, so in the winter we dug a hole, stacked juniper boughs on top, and lived underground. Inside we built a fire, Grandmother always having a round sandstone rock with a hole in which she put a sumac spindle with cedar bark beneath to catch a coal to start a fire. Oak also works well for a spindle. Once we got the fire started, we had to keep it going. During the war [World War II] government agents told us not to have fires at night. After it rained we hung all our belongings in the wind to dry. Everything got wet. I remember I was taught to lead my grandmother around and that was why my dad put me with her when I was between the ages of two and six years old.

We didn't have a wagon, only a donkey to move our things as we herded the livestock. Wooden saddles with crossed sticks on the frame [aparejos] were used for riding and packing our donkeys and horse. We didn't get a wagon until Jim was born. For our mattress we used sheepskins finely tanned with sheep brains. Our blanket on top was made of goat skins sewed together with cow tendon thread. This was my bed in both summer and winter. Sometimes lambs would freeze after they were born, and so Grandmother made shoes out of their skins. She sewed the hides together like a sock that went up to the middle of my calf then sewed the other end at the toes. The skins hardened on our feet. That was our shoes. She taught us to sew our skirts together from flour sacks.

It was terrible how we lived. We didn't have a frying pan so we cooked and ate in an iron pot a quarter of an inch thick, nine inches in diameter, with no cover or legs. We had two or three of them, which we stuck in the coals of a fire to heat. For carrying water we wove jugs of sumac and covered them with pitch on the outside. There were two metal pots, one for each donkey. Sumac for the woven baskets grew in the corners of the canyons and on the mesas where water collected. Not only did it provide basket-making material, but it also had sticky, sour berries that once sweetened were added to corn mush.

Water was very scarce, so we did not wash a lot. In the summer we traveled to Red Lake and near Black Mesa to plant corn. It rained frequently, about every month, so there was always enough grass and vegetation for the sheep and other animals. During harvest time we picked corn, drying it and also lots of squash for the future, but always herding sheep and gathering plants. There were over 250 sheep, so we moved a lot.

My grandmothers and aunts on both sides of my family knew how to make cheese, which they cooked in ashes. We also had prairie dogs. To catch them, we blocked off all the holes then poured water down a few of them. When it rained there were lots of puddles around the prairie dog towns from which we filled our jugs and poured the water down the holes, leaving about three of them open in different places. The prairie dogs surfaced, so I hit them in the head with a stick to knock them out. Jackrabbits or cottontails were also taken with a rock or club. If they ran in a hole, I put a stick down it, twisted it into their skin, and pulled them out.

Grandmother had us move every month so that our sheep, goats, and horses could find grass. Even at night we slept with the animals. As shepherds, we ate mutton all the time. Grandmother taught me how to butcher them. As small as I was, I had to herd sheep by myself, taking them to water without being told because I knew where the waterholes were. Every three days I took the animals to drink. We did not drive the sheep to the waterholes too much because it was usually a long distance, perhaps seven miles away. I had to herd them all the way early in the morning and then get them back before night.[9] Nowadays our sheep want water all the time. Everything is different.

In 1954 grandmother died, most likely from appendicitis, because her side hurt. We had no vehicle to take her to Tuba City and the mail truck was not around. I was still very young [fourteen] when she left us behind. Before going she told me to take care of my little sister, to stay away from colored [black] people and Mexicans, but she did not say anything about whites. She didn't like Mexicans because they were mean and took a lot of relatives, long before my time, during the Long Walk.[10] The night before she died she asked us to take her out somewhere, but my aunt told her no.[11] She knew we would bury her if anything happened; and so when she passed away, my aunt went to the trading post on horseback and got boxes. We dug a hole in the middle of the hogan, painted her all over with red powder, and let her hair down.

My aunt and I and two small children had no one else to help, so after the burial we moved everything out of the hogan behind a hill to the south, spent four days there, then washed before leaving.[12] No one is supposed to come near you. My dad came just after we buried her. At the time of a funeral nobody drinks, nobody eats, and everyone does nothing for a whole day. Then they burn the hogan with the dead inside. Sometimes they just leave the structure as it is. After the fourth day everybody washes with water, yucca roots, and juniper leaves. We moved back to our range at Gopher Springs. Later, when Dad became the Red Lake Chapter president, he gave up the land where my grandmother was buried to use as a graveyard. Another part he turned over for a school.

My dad had finally returned. He and my mother had traveled around a lot as they moved from job to job off the reservation. My mom spoke English; my dad was uneducated, so during World War II they went to Belmont, Arizona, where my mother put her schooling to work for the government as an English-Navajo translator while my dad made munitions. Jim was in a cradleboard at the time when he was given to my mother's mother, Mildred Shorty. I rarely saw that side of the family because they lived near Wildcat Peak about five miles away. These grandparents also took my older sister Lillie because they have a huge number of sheep too and traveled just like us. My aunt worked hard to make the little money she received for our food.

When Mom and Dad went to Belmont they learned to make wine and whiskey, which brought money in to our family. Upon returning to Red Lake, they came back with equipment and tubing so Dad could go into business. We moved to Preston Mesa behind Wildcat Peak. He also brought a rifle and an ax from

Belmont and began teaching his sons to hunt. Another memory I have of my dad is when he bought an old truck in Utah and learned how to drive it. He did not want to just get something for himself, so he took his relatives, a lot of them, to the Grand Canyon. They camped for about two weeks picking piñons, so those he had given rides to presented him with a bag for transporting them. They picked a lot, truckloads, and brought them back to the store.

Jim's experience with his grandparents proved just as formative. His mother's father, Eli Shorty, was named for being a messenger or Elias, which came from the Bible. Because he was a medicine man, Navajos frequently summoned him, sometimes in the middle of the night, to perform over the sick and dying. He never said no. For three or four days he performed a sing then returned home across the mesa with his pay—driving six or seven sheep. At that time, a lot of people did not have money, so livestock served as cash. Jim often helped herd them, once he was older; when he did, Eli gave him a sheep. At other times the medicine man brought back a bracelet, necklace, silver belt, or horse for his healing work. Jim apprenticed with his grandfather to learn the songs and practices, but it was a lot of effort, especially if the patient was very sick. On their way to perform a ceremony, they would stop their horses to gather herbs and other necessities.

Jim's grandparents instilled respect and hard work into the young boy. His grandmother warned him that things were changing and that survival and success were achieved through hard work and vigilance. Life was only going to get harder, things more expensive, so prepare. If the children disrespected the hogan or were rowdy and did not sit quietly when it rained, she disciplined them. She usually kept a fire (the heart of the hogan) burning, especially in the winter. Grandmother arose extra early to pray for everybody by using ashes.[13] After she cooked, she put the food away and prayed again through the ashes. The ground within the home was very sacred as a part of Mother Earth, while the sunray that came through the smoke hole at the top of the hogan was a part of Father Sky. When a person opens the door and the sunlight streams in at dawn, that is when the Holy People are just outside. People should be out before the Holy People, so that they can be just like them. Doing this makes individuals holy and, if they go out running, in good physical condition.

Perhaps that is why Grandmother Shorty was rich in sheep: over a thousand head—and this was after the livestock reduction era of the 1930s. Her mother, Gambling Lady, who lived with them, also had a large herd. When combined with the sheep of Jim's mother and other relatives, their traditional Navajo prosperity was obvious. Although livestock reduction was a thing of the past, Grandmother Shorty lived in fear of it occurring again. When the government sought to reduce Navajo herds, in some cases by half to meet the carrying capacity of the land and prevent overgrazing, the livelihood of most families and dependence on the herds ended.[14] This not only terminated the traditional way of life but forced Navajos into an off-reservation wage economy.

Jim's father explained why this happened. In his view, the Navajo people became too wealthy and greedy. He compared them to the Anasazi [Ancestral Puebloans], who in traditional Navajo teachings were a wealthy, talented people who did not pay attention to their prayers, failed to listen to the Holy People, and no longer held their songs sacred. The gods destroyed them. Before livestock reduction, the Navajo people walked the same path. "They were so rich they turned the world." People gambled in card games, their horses' bridles and saddles were heavily decorated with silver, and Navajo thoughts became consumed with greed. As a knowledgeable people they knew how to do many things but became too smart for their own good. The government stepped in to change all of that. This perspective on livestock reduction in traditional Navajo teachings, an event often compared to the Long Walk and incarceration at Fort Sumner, explains why things turn bad and society is punished, a belief that extends into the future and the end of the world.[15]

This is also why traditional Navajo culture stressed self-control. During Jim's early years all of his relatives helped enforce strict discipline. Starting with his grandparents, all the elders played a part in teaching a child in their own way. Jim's grandfather disciplined with love and left the stick to others. His grandmother, however, believed in a sharp reminder. She would take a stick about two feet long and swat their legs to get the children moving. Children reach a certain point in life when they understand what is right and wrong and can choose on their own. When the children were slow to work, his grandmother would chide: "You should have already learned what your chores are and what you're supposed to do. We don't need to be here telling you what to do. We have already taught you all of that and you should know." That's the way the grandparents were.

Jim remembers:

My father didn't beat us to death, but he was strong. He might talk to me twice about something I needed to do, but the third time he made sure it was done. My great-grandparents, some of my great-uncles like my grandmother's brother or my father's brother, or some relative would come to our home and made sure I was behaving. The parents did not allow their children to be abused, but there was never any time that my parents would defend me from a relative either. Dad did not, and my mother would never say to leave me alone but just stayed out of it. My uncle disciplined me in his own way.

When someone talked to you, said they needed something and to go get it, you did. You are scared and believe what they said is going to happen. One of my grandfathers used to say, "I'm going to cut your ears," then take out his pocket knife and pretend that he was sharpening it on his pants. "I'm going to cut your ears if you don't listen." That is when I would scurry off to do whatever my grandparents said. When he spoke, I did it and hoped that he would not come after me; but if he did, I then hoped that his horse tied to the wagon would be too tired. As I grew older I had less fear and more respect for these people. I never hated them, and now I can say I'm glad they did that to me. I am glad they took part in my life and provided discipline. They always encouraged me to be strong and not give up. They took me to the sweat lodge, where they taught songs, prayers, and the things I needed to know to be successful as a real man.

Still, there were times when I did not want to herd sheep. Grandmother, as usual, was up early one morning and said, "Grandson take the sheep out of the corral, get them ready to move to pasture, then come and get something to eat." After I left the homestead, I hid behind a nearby hill and let the sheep graze the tufts of grass amid the rocks, without taking them any real distance. Old Man, one of my great uncles, rode up on horseback. Somehow my grandmother knew that I was just over the hill, and he came to get me. He was scary! "Come over here. Look!" Drawing a big gunnysack from the back of his saddle, he threw it on the ground. "Put it on"; so I did. "I'm going to leave your shoes here; you won't need them; now you're coming with me."

Once I was inside, he fastened the top with a knot, threw me on the back of his horse, and away we galloped. He threatened to take me to see Yé'iitsoh [Big God—a monster] and his people. "If you're not going to behave and listen to your grandmother, then you're not going to listen to your mom, so you're coming home with me. I'll make sure you work." I cried all the way as I bounced up and down to the rhythm of the horse's stride, but he just kept telling me to stop fussing. Finally he reined in his horse a mile and a half down the road and I stopped bawling, fearful to know what was next. He dismounted, took the burlap bag off his horse, untied the opening, then sat me on the ground. "Grandson, the next time I come and you're not behaving, doing what you're suppose to do, I'm going to take you to my home for sure." He sent me on my way over the blistering hot sand. Without any covering, the bottom of my feet burned as if they treaded hot coals, but there was only one way to get home or at least reach the comfort of my shoes. I'd run a little ways then stand on low brush or get under some shade before starting off again. It seemed like a long time before I reached my shoes and the protection they provided. From then on, I listened and was always afraid Old Man would come around. That is how I learned discipline.

Jim's brothers and sisters also learned discipline from their dad. He never seemed satisfied with what they had accomplished, always urging them to do more and to do it better. Family members categorically use words like "hard," "strict," and "tireless" to describe him, but they hold him in great respect and are grateful that he "pushed" them and "helped" them. Albert became notorious with his children for insisting that they do things that were normally left for adults to do. He would tell them not to ask somebody else to do it but for them to try, because that was the only way they could really learn and experience it. Zonnie felt that he wanted his children to know everything. "He'd put us on a wild horse with no harness or saddle and tell us to just hold onto the mane. We kept riding until we either trained the horse or fell off, but if we were bucked off, he got mad and pushed us back on after we got a whipping. 'You can't fall off and don't ever quit. If you give up, that means you're weak.'"

The same principles applied to herding livestock and every other thing they did. They had to learn for themselves; if they needed their mind straightened out, Dad helped them with a two-foot greasewood switch that stung when it hit the back of their legs. Then they went back to the task until it was mastered. Zonnie's reaction: "It's not beating you. He was mean in the sense that he really wanted to train you and to get you ready for the hard things in life. . . . Dad loved his boys. He had Jim out of school to travel with him and

Albert and Cora, 1970s. Jim: "My father was a great role model for us children to follow. He knew a lot about the People, was a great story-teller, and taught a lot about plants and animals. Mom was a real advocate for education and encouraged all her children to learn."

he loved his daughters too. He did everything good for me. He was a good man." Charlie, Jim's brother, remembered that before he got married his dad talked to him, saying: "I would hate to see you just lying under a wagon with your wife out there herding sheep. You might as well be a baby-sitter."

Albert as a child had spent a lot of time with his great-grandfather, a medicine man. Although he was not officially apprenticed to become one himself, the boy went to the sweat house with his elders and listened. He did not ask questions; but as they sang, they also explained the songs and what to do or not to do. Familiar with the Blessing Way and Yé'ii Bicheii ceremonies, Albert specialized in the Enemy Way ceremony. He was also well known for healing livestock. People came to him when their animals were sick; he prayed over the animals and gave them medication. He used his hands and pine gum to heal. One time a man named Sam Black came to Albert for help. His horse was lying on the ground and apparently infected. Albert cut a gap in the horse's hoof and into the soft part underneath. He packed it with pine gum, which he molded into the hoof with a lot of pressure. It removed the pain and kept infection from developing inside. People liked and respected him as a good horse trainer and for assisting as a medicine man.

Albert never received an education but encouraged his children to, once he saw that a better life could be obtained by learning from white people. He recognized that times were changing: although people in his day were viewed as rich because of ceremonial knowledge or livestock, school opened the door to a better and happier way of life for a family. He had his eye on the future. Still, Albert was also interested in teaching traditional beliefs. As a medicine man, he knew the Enemy Way ceremony and took his son Charlie with him to study and participate. Charlie learned mountain songs as they sat side by side traveling to or performing in a ceremony. Sometimes Albert arose early in the morning to show what he wanted to teach. He took his grandchildren to the cornfield before dawn to plant and instruct. Today the family still works the same field every spring and summer, just as Albert had for years.

These traditional ways are now embedded in daily practice, tying the children to a rich heritage in an impoverished landscape. Cora added to these beliefs through loving care and her own teachings. Jim recalls:

My mother always told me how each child was born. She said I was the loudest and slowest of all the children when it came to getting on my feet to walk. The others got up quickly to walk then run, but I was a month or two behind. When I stayed with my grandparents, I would see my mom and dad at least a couple of times a year and stayed with them for about a week. I do not really know a lot about what it was like for Dad when he was off working on the railroad, but when he came home, we all got clothing—his money bought us a hat or shoes and my father would buy a saddle. Mother tagged along with Dad so they bought a tent to live in.

Dad did not know how to drive a vehicle so the railroad people came to pick them up and sent them to places like California and Idaho. The amount of time they were gone depended on how long the railroad kept them working. Sometimes they were traveling the whole summer or the first part of fall. During the winter my parents returned to Rat Spring, where Dad kept busy. He did a lot of arts and crafts, making hackamores and bridles to sell, or hauled wood or performed some kind of ceremony. One time he took Zonnie and three other young girls to Grand Junction to play a part in a John Wayne western. They dressed up like little girls and sat in a wagon with a female actor playing the part of a Christian lady. The girls received twenty dollars for their part then handed it over to Dad. He also played a part. With hair in braids and skilled in horsemanship, he was well-known among the movie makers and helped others to get employment as well.

In 1951 Albert received a serious injury when he was building a hogan at Red Lake. He and my uncle had been drinking and were hauling some beams, and somehow the wagon with its heavy load of wood ran over his neck and chest. One side of his lung collapsed and part of the other was destroyed so that he had very little left. The doctors at the Fort Defiance Hospital told him that he should no longer work, but he never listened. He spent about a year in the hospital after the doctors removed half of both of his lungs because they were so crushed and infected with tuberculosis. I was just a little boy at the time. They told him that he could not work anymore, but he never gave it up. He just kept on but quit traveling with the railroad because of his health. His tiny lungs continued to work; the doctors could not believe his persistence. It seemed that the harder he pushed himself, the stronger he became. Still, he had a pretty tough time getting back into life with Mom and eventually drifted away from her after a few years. Later they got back together until he died in 1987.

It was really hard on Cora when Albert was away, because she had no income. At one point he left his wife and married a younger woman near Kaibito. Jim remembered this as a very sad time. From the outset Cora provided for her family, at first by weaving rugs on a loom. By 1954 she realized that she could not continue this way, so she decided to work for the BIA, went back to school, and graduated as a teacher from Fort Lewis College, Colorado. Cora became the first combined principal, teacher, and cook in a small trailer under a cottonwood tree at Red Lake. Soon a black woman joined her, and they worked together to bring education to the local children. "Mom was both a good teacher and a good cook." Later, when the BIA established a new school at Cow Springs near the old trading post, Cora transferred there. Through the years the government sent her to a bigger school in Kayenta and later to Shonto, from which she finally retired. For about six or seven years Albert was gone, but then he began to come home often. Cora would not give up her job and told him to stay away and leave her alone, but he never gave up. He just kept coming home, so they finally got back together. He never left until death separated them. She died in 2006, having lived a life of service.

Like her husband, Cora was tied to Navajo traditional practices to the end of her life. Unlike her husband, she put her educational background to work but never lost sight of the roots of Navajo beliefs. Central to the welfare of her children and their posterity was the mountain soil bundle that she passed on to Charlie.[16] The ties to his mother were close; he seemed best prepared and situated to assume control of this medicine bundle that brought the blessings of the four sacred mountains not only into the home where it resided but to the entire family. Charlie spoke of his relationship to his mother and the importance of his family heritage:

I learned a lot of things from my mother, like her songs. Because of this rela-
tionship and the things I had learned she asked me to keep the family mountain
soil bundle, which has been passed along from generation to generation to keep the
family together. Mom wanted me to keep it for my brothers and sisters because I
knew the songs for it. That is what holds us together now. Whenever there is some-
thing going on and we need to work as a family, all of my brothers and sisters
come to help. That is what the bundle does. It also blesses our homes, the horses,
cows, sheep—everything that lives and is under our care. I think that is what
makes our family strong.

When she handed it to me I said that I was not the right age and that she
should give it to my older brother or older sister, but she told me, "No you're here;
you're not in Blanding or some place and you know the way and the songs for that
bundle." My father held it for all the children; but when he died, Mom was the
only one who knew all the teachings and songs. Every three years or so, the bundle
has to be opened, blessed, and retied to keep it safe and well.[17] It should never be
dropped but always treated in a sacred way just like a baby. Every once in a while
I prepare and care for it, praying and keeping it safe. That is what she told me to
do. My mom and dad both taught us to respect these things.

Jim is like that too. Born in a hogan, raised with the teachings and practices of the elders, rooted in a Navajo experience, he understands the importance of tradition. The hogan where he was born is gone. Only a small stick
poking through the rocky, sandy soil remains, and the remnants of his umbilical cord have joined the elements. His thoughts return to his place of birth,
however, to family members departed and forward to his own children. The
teachings of the cord and bundle hold power in his life.

CHAPTER FOUR

LEARNING OF NAVAJO CULTURE

Teachings of the Hogan and Life

When Jim was less than a year old, his parents placed him in the care of his maternal grandparents. Many of Jim's earliest recollections are of his life in their hogan, sitting around the fire receiving instruction. One of Grandfather Eli (pronounced Elay) Shorty's first tasks was to bless his grandson in preparation for a life lived on the edge of survival. Accustomed to working hard, practicing self-discipline, and leading the life of a medicine man, Shorty knew what he needed to do to prepare his grandson for what lay ahead. Jim recalls what happened:

I just barely remember a little bit about the first day when my grandfather took me outside as the sun arose, just as Ruth had done when I was born. Grandfather prayed as he washed me in the sudsy water of the yucca root then dusted me with white corn pollen for protection from evil so that I would grow strong.[1] When he was a young man at the Grand Canyon, a bear attacked and almost killed him before he was able to kill it. From that bear he took some of its fur, which he kept in his medicine bag for protection.[2] Now he ground some of it into a fine powder and blessed me, recalling that he knew that one day he would have a grandson who was strong. "Nobody's going to wrestle with you and win. You're going to be tough," he said. It was around that time that I received my name. He called me Yinney instead of Jim. Others called me "Yellow Mules' Son" or "Half Nose" because it was so flat with not much of a point; to him I was "Strong Yinney [Jimmy]."

Grandfather was a very good horseman and sheep owner and had experience working at the Red Lake Trading Post. Even though he had only a little education, he was not afraid to communicate in his soft-spoken way. I never saw him get angry, abuse a child, or fight with his wife, even though she controlled everything

Grandfather Eli Shorty, accomplished medicine man and teacher. An excellent horseman and veterinarian, Eli taught Jim a lot about traditional culture but encouraged him to get an education rather than become a medicine man.

that happened in the home. He was a very kind man but always busy. Sometimes I went with him to look for horses or to hitch up a team to a wagon to get wood or water or go to the trading post. Even though we worked hard he was a really fun person. He taught me not to argue or run around or wrestle in the hogan. Grand-mother taught us how to stay clean and pick up after ourselves. She made us either fold our sheepskin bedding or hang it outside to air. We never had a really good bed with sheets and so we slept on sheepskins until we got a goatskin. That was really warm so we fought over it, until she got one for each of us.

My mother's mother was the one who really raised me. As a medicine lady, she knew a lot about herbs, especially those used to control pain. She assisted young women in labor struggling to have a baby. Special herbs for the birthing process helped them deliver the child and manage the pain. Her grandfather was also a very intelligent medicine man, who I watched heal people. He knew a lot, and Grandmother learned from him. She always had many visitors who stopped by when coming from Red Lake in their wagon. There always seemed to be food and hot coffee on the stove so no one left hungry. She is remembered for being very kind and taught us to always be willing to help. She would say: "When somebody comes to see you or needs help, don't just stand there, either help them or get them something to eat."

My grandmother and other elderly Navajo women were toughened by hard-ship. A family story shared by my father tells of one of his great-aunts and her experience during the Long Walk period in the 1860s. She was fleeing with some Navajos from a group of soldiers and their Indian scouts. These scouts were greatly feared because they killed people with their guns or arrows and showed no mercy. Once they captured a person, they enforced silence or else killed him to prevent him from crying and giving away their location. My great-aunt was walking along with her cousin when word reached them that the enemy was approaching. She became frightened and wondered how they could escape. Family members drove in a group of horses, and she selected a very strong stallion that had never been rid-den. She was a spiritually powerful young woman who talked to the animal and said, "My horse, please, I don't want to be here. I want to go home, back to Navajo Mountain. Would you please save me?" She and her cousin mounted their horses and rode a long distance, leaving the army on both sides of her shooting as they fled. Her horse carried her up a canyon that nobody knew and safely out of dan-ger, helping her to escape, but not before her cousin was either killed or captured.

The young woman made her way back to Navajo Mountain only to find that all the homes were burned and the place deserted. Eventually her family found her and left that area by traveling across Copper Canyon to the Henry Mountains then the Bears Ears, behind Blue Mountain to the La Sal Mountains, into Colorado to Mount Hesperus, where they fought with Indians from Laguna [Pueblo]. Next they passed through where the Jicarilla Apache Reservation is today [northeastern New Mexico], made contact with members of the Santo Domingo pueblo before making their way to Ramah [New Mexico] then across to Flagstaff [Arizona] and the Grand Canyon, where they homesteaded for a while. This great big loop took them hundreds of miles through hostile territory, during which they lived off the land in every season of the year. Eventually they returned to the Navajo Mountain area then settled near Red Lake and Black Mesa. My ancestors were tough, tough people.

As a child I was raised in a hogan and learned at an early age about its teach-ings. My grandparents taught not only about how this structure came about but also proper behavior and how to treat people with respect even when living in such a small space. Grandmother, especially, had extensive knowledge about this that

Eli Shorty's shade house with a female hogan to the right. This picture was taken from a car window in 1959; nothing remains today. Jim: "I lived there a long time and have so many memories of this place, which is not far from where I was born." During ceremonies, food is cooked in the shade and brought into the hogan for the participants.

reached into many aspects of my life. These teachings helped me understand the world of my grandparents. Starting with the building, maintenance and care, then philosophy about the hogan, I learned to respect this dwelling as my home.

In traditional Navajo culture there are two types of hogans—male and female.[3] Male hogans usually have very sacred teachings and healing associated with them. If one is not available for a ceremony then a round female hogan can be used. The male hogan is so sacred a place that there are some things discussed and performed there that are not done in the female hogan. For example, if someone is dying of cancer, the ceremony performed for the patient is powerful enough that it should not be overheard by those who are not participating and so is often performed in a male hogan. The Holy People designed the first male hogan in the beginning of the world for ceremonial purposes, while the female hogan is mainly for family and daily life. Just as with a Mormon temple, the strongest teachings and powers are associated with it because it is male power. Continuing the comparison, women's power is more like what goes on in the local LDS church. In Navajo culture it is said that a woman is the leader of the family, but in order to get things corrected you go back to the man, just as in white society. This sense of greater power is comparable to the teachings about the difference between the male and female hogan. The sweat lodge has the same shape as the male hogan, with its posts coming to a point. The female hogan is built by overlapping logs and has a calmer power because it is not pointed. Family activities like the shoe game are usually done in a female hogan, although sometimes they can also be held in a male hogan.

When building a female hogan there are six main posts, while in a male hogan there are five; but in each instance the four cardinal directions are represented. These logs are partially buried in the ground with prayers for protection and assistance before anything else is added to the structure. This is called "addressing the mountains," where each post represents and is blessed to hold the powers of one of the four sacred mountains. Each of the four directions has a mountain associated with it: to the east is Sisnaajiní [Blanca], to the south is Tsoodził [Taylor], to the west is Dook'o'oosłííd [Humphrey in the San Francisco Peaks], and to the north is Dibé Nitsaa [Hesperus]. There are two poles for the door that faces east. These posts represent wealth on each side of the door and bring all kinds of good things to the people living there. The east posts in the blessing song always represent wealth. The foundation or the legs and other logs at the bottom of the structure are aligned with the four directions and represent the whole hogan. There are an additional twelve posts in the female hogan, symbolizing the twelve people who compose the main part of the foundation, forming the circumference of the home. They are Holy People, the same ones involved in the Yé'ii Bicheii, who serve as primary deity, participated in the creation of the world, and represent different things such as water, colors, and teachings.

In building a female hogan the four posts and two door posts are put in first, while in the male hogan the five posts that create its tepee shape and entryway are the primary posts, representing the mountains. In the male hogan there are three main posts made from forked trees that are intertwined at the top and correspond to the south, west, and north. The two doorposts serving as the entryway act as one connected entity associated with the east. Remember, when you bless the door, the whole structure becomes one person with two arms that hang down. In the female hogan the four sacred mountains are always posts, and the next two are people who assist the mountains. Those are the two doorposts.

The door in both types of hogans always faces east, while the place for a person of honor to sit is in the west, the woman's area to the north, and the man's

A male hogan with an extended entryway. Its conical shape is not as spacious as the shape of the female hogan but is believed to add power to the ceremonies held within. The Navajo sweat lodge is much smaller but also conical. (Courtesy Milton Snow Collection, Navajo Nation Museum)

area to the south. In the old days the woman's activities and storage area for dishes, cooking equipment, etc., were on the south side, but now when there is a ceremony or wedding the man sits on the south side, the medicine man who is conducting the ceremony sits to the west or sometimes in the center, while a person being healed is to the north. The reason for this is because a sick person is affected by something evil that needs to be removed and sent to the north. Sickness, harmful things, and death belong in that direction. For instance, weapons, knives, and other sharp objects associated with harm, death, or witchcraft are also kept to the north, where their strong powers can be controlled. When a person dies, her spirit travels to the north, and so the family moves to the south away from that spirit. In the same sense, once a patient is healed in a ceremony, he moves from the north to the east by leaving the hogan and receiving the blessings from that direction.

My grandfather was a pretty quiet man and did not get after us unless we really did something wrong. He did not say a lot, but he was very knowledgeable about sacred things to do with ceremonies and healing. My grandmother, on the other hand, was more outgoing in her discipline and taught about things around the home. Whenever we entered the hogan we had to behave ourselves. She taught us a lot, and I miss that. One of her teachings was about how the hogan is compared to the body, with the fire being the heart of the home, the floor like a person's back, and the opening of the smoke hole symbolizing a person's navel. She also taught about the four directions and how to do things in a respectful way, especially during a ceremony and the blessing of a hogan. Each one of us had our turn to learn. There are other practices to be followed when playing the shoe game. The game goes between the south and north with people sitting on either side. If someone is ill and needs to be healed, she sits in the middle between the two sides facing west so that when the morning comes and the door is opened, the light comes in and with it the Holy People. There is also the sunray that comes in from the top through the smoke hole, and that is the sun opening the way for the patient.

The hogan represents life. A person comes in from the east with birth, goes to the south, which is life, enters old age to the west, and ends with death and spirit-travel to the north. While life starts in the east, west is where the heart sits. When a person follows a circular direction in a hogan, he follows the path of growth through life. When handing out food at an Enemy Way ceremony, it is blessed and presented with an offering before handing it to people in a clockwise direction. This shows respect for what is taking place. A medicine man blessing a hogan always starts by the southern door post on the east side and moves around to the south then west. The blessing on this post and the other main posts associated with the cardinal directions is done when the structure is first built, and so the blessing of these areas that is performed for a later ceremony continues and strengthens the power. When the medicine man goes around the hogan with his corn pollen, he moves to the door post on the north side but stops there and does not complete a full circle where the blessing initially started. This is done twice, with everything circulating in a clockwise manner, but the circle is never closed all the way because the door is open to let the evil out. So the medicine man starts with the east door post, goes to the south, west, and north, stops at the doorpost, then goes back counterclockwise around the hogan for the continuation of the blessing of the structure. A woman who brings in food during a break in the ceremony is not to double back but goes all the way around and then out.

There are many other teachings about the hogan. When someone enters, she moves clockwise, especially when a ceremony is being performed. If there is a stove, you always put the food either on it or in the center of the hogan in front of the medicine man to show that you are going to be feeding the people. Nowadays *people have separate plates and bowls, but in the past there used to be one big bowl in the middle that all ate from. Everybody eats and sings who participates in the ceremony. Usually the ones who are eating are mostly men because at night they are the ones who sing. Very seldom did you see a woman eat in the hogan, because she brought in the food but returned to where the cooking was done.*

Fire, like a grandparent, is a provider and must be respected.[4] Every time my great-grandmother cooked, she would stir the coals with her fire poker (honeesh-gish), pray, then place in the fire any food that was left over so that the fire, too, could eat. She thanked it for being a Holy Person, a great-great-grandfather who provides. When my grandparents prayed it was always addressed as a male in the prayer, thanking it for its help. Another way we showed respect was not to play with fire, especially at night. Sometimes a person would get a long stick, light its end, then swing it around in the dark. That is wrong, causes nightmares, and could bring a curse to that individual. Fire is very powerful and when someone plays with it, that person may have hallucinations because the fire's image has entered the mind. The picture becomes permanent if he continues to do it. The only people who play with fire like that are skinwalkers or ghosts.[5]

The fire is in the center, and a person should walk behind the medicine man instead of between him and the fire. Traditional people talk a lot about this issue. Some say that it is always possible to go around behind, but I have never seen people go behind, but instead go right between the medicine man and the fire. A lot of times medicine men do not want you to go behind them, but I do not know why.[6] They say to just walk right straight through. If there are two fires, a person cannot walk between them but may go beside them. The medicine man gives directions on what to do, but I never heard any of them say to go behind. I used to help a lot in performing ceremonies, having done it since I was a little boy, but I do not do it much anymore.

The fire poker, like the fire, is a help and guide.[7] Just as Moses in the Bible used his staff to show the power of God, the fire poker is also important and holds sacred powers. There should be one in the hogan at all times; a person should not live without one. There are two different kinds—one is used for cooking, the other for ceremonies. The same is true with moccasins—one for daily work, the other for night ceremonies. The fire poker used for cooking is female; the one for ceremonies, male. They are shields that protect the home and must be cared for as living beings.

The cribbed roof of the interior of this female hogan is made of peeled cedar (juniper) logs that add to the brightness of the interior. Traditional teachings compare it to an inverted wedding basket, a bird's nest, the sky projecting up from the earth, and the womb, all of which represent peace and security. (Kay Shumway photo)

Grandmother started with the ground inside the hogan and likened it to the Navajo wedding basket. When the hogan is compared to an upside-down basket, the point of communication and connection is the smoke hole. The logs in the cribbed roof become smaller as you move closer to the top; they become smaller each time, step by step. The rainbow is like the inside of the roof as it surrounds above and arches over the people below. You cannot go beyond its sides, but on every sacred mountain the rainbow reaches over it, just as the roof inside the hogan does.[8] So the rainbow for the hogan goes from the floor up to the smoke hole and down to the floor on the other side.

The stove or fire with its opening is in the center. There are the mountains that are the upright logs, the roof like the rainbow, with the sky and clouds above. The roof beams are similar to a ladder that leads step by step to heaven. When the sunlight comes in the top through the smoke hole, it is a part of the heavens entering. The outer rim of the wedding basket is like the dawn that goes around it with the two stitches on the rim that gets bigger, the same as when you move closer to the floor of a hogan. Beyond that point a person does not really know what is there. When building a hogan there is always to be an opening [smoke hole] just as in a basket.[9] It represents the knowledge you receive from the heavens, and so this hole for learning should never be blocked. The same is true when making a rug; there should be an opening somewhere in it. You do not just put a rug together without a string or a pathway to keep the rug open so that you can learn a lot about what is on the other side, beyond the object. People do not usually talk about these things, and when they do it has to be in certain seasons of the year just as with Coyote stories. It is not talked about during the summertime because all the animals are listening to you.

A hogan is usually blessed at least once or twice a year. A family will live in a hogan for between six to twelve years and then a new one is built in a different place. When it is the twelfth year, the dirt can be removed and the logs taken apart and set up in another location. If there is a stove or fire pit a lot of black smoke and soot accumulates inside. It is cleaned off and the hogan reblessed, just as it is reblessed once a year. A long time ago, if there was a crack in the hogan, people would not live in it and not try to fix it but would just take it apart and rebuild it elsewhere. The belief is that the crack in the hogan did not happen accidentally; someone who had evil intent was behind it. People became suspicious about the structure. Yíiyá [Scary]. Even when a glass window is cracked, this may be a sign of evil penetrating the home; if dishes are broken or badly cracked or chipped they should not be used. The reason for concern about cracks and unwanted openings is to keep undesirable things and evil out.

Additional coats of dirt are added once or twice a year, depending on how much rain and snow there has been. Maintenance is a constant concern. If a person leaves her hogan for a while, taking her sheep on an extended absence, then when she returns she has to make sure there is no light from cracks, birds' nests, or anything else that has made its way into the home. If birds build a home inside, it means bad luck. There should be no spiders, especially in with the dishes. They should stay out all the time; put them somewhere so that they cannot come in; otherwise you will be wondering who sent that black spider to bother you. Snakes should also remain outside; but if one comes in, take it out and kill it.[10] Do not leave it alive; get rid of it, but spiders can just be set outside. Do not kill them if they are not bothering you.

Anything like lizards, snakes, and mice must be kept out of the hogan. If you see a snake in the distance, leave it alone. If it gets mad at you, get rid of it. If a snake is found on a blanket, the blanket is discarded. If a mouse builds a nest in a home, it may bring in a bad spirit. Mice can go into a graveyard, dig beneath the ground, connect with the dead, chew on their clothing, then bring a curse into the home. Anything like your shirt, coat, pants, or socks that a mouse has nibbled should not be worn and is often burned. A tarantula is said to have big, long hairy legs and walks like a hand grasping, which is different than a spider. These are also left alone.

A person should never write his name on a hogan or make other marks because it is disrespectful. To do that is similar to writing on your hand, which is like putting a curse on yourself. The only people who do that are the dead people. Somebody can secretly take that name and put it under a rock or take it to a graveyard. Whoever does this will not want to be known because she is working against an individual. A hogan is also like a person; when the mud comes off, it is like your skin peeling. If there is no fire, it is as if the heart has stopped and the hogan cannot stay alive and functioning. It should be cared for just like a human.

My grandfather started his teaching about the home by saying, "I'm afraid I'm not going to live forever. Your grandmother has taught you that as she cooks she prays for you as part of your life. By doing this the fire becomes your grandfather also. When she sings about you there is a light involved in that process and the fire, as the great-grandfather, keeps everything alive in the universe inside the hogan. As with the sun the fire sits there, where there is moisture and air and everything that makes you alive is found within the hogan. The fire represents the sun because everything that is cooked for you becomes a part of you. When your own fire dies out you will be just like your grandparents and pass on. It is our job to share these teachings with you to carry on. Keep the light going all the time; that is your responsibility, and as a father you should teach your children."

The Navajos are clean people. When they cook, they are careful to have a clean work space. I know my grandmother kept her hogan clean. When we got up early in the morning, she would take us outside and give us some tasks, making sure we checked around our home to pick up any trash. Sometimes we would chop wood, not throwing the chips away or leaving them on the ground but bringing them inside to use. After the fire had died out, we removed the ashes and were careful not to just trail them all the way to where they were dumped to the north of the hogan. Ashes are a very sacred thing. You have cooked your food on them and so you do not just leave them lying around your home. They are placed where they are supposed to be.

Left to right: Jim, sister Marie, aunt Sarah Tohannie, sister Lillie, and mother Cora.
Marie, raised by her blind grandmother, eventually received a master's degree in
education; Sarah was a strong medicine lady and hand trembler; Lillie served on the
Arizona Board of Education and on school committees in Tuba City. Little wonder Jim
said of Cora, "She is my hero, a very strong lady."

*Cleanliness is particularly important when a woman is menstruating. When a
young woman has her first period, there is a small ceremony that is performed, but
with her second, there is the kinaaldá, a major four-day one. She should already
have been instructed as to how to keep herself clean and prevent harming others
with her blood, which is considered a type of poison.[11] A woman having her period
should always keep her hands clean and make sure that no one can be affected by
its presence. Women must be careful, disposing of their napkin by digging a hole
and burying it so that it is not left lying around. If a man comes in contact with the
smell, he may develop a hump on his back, have problems with arthritis, or stunt
his growth. This teaching goes back to the time of Creation when one of the Holy
People named Begochídí encountered this problem.[12] This is why at the end of the
kinaaldá ceremony, people line up before the young woman, who gives a blessing through Begochídí that they will grow taller and have good health. A woman
having her period also cannot participate when a ceremony for others is being*

performed, especially the Enemy Way. She also has to be careful when around children. Much of this is taught during the time of the kinaaldá along with other aspects of womanhood like cooking, hair care, and proper behavior.

When living in a hogan, the traditional value of modesty is maintained. This modesty is seen in the clothes women wear—skirts that go down to their ankles and blouses that extend to their wrists. But in a small home like a hogan, there might be five or six children plus a mother and father living together. Individuals may change their clothes when they go out to the bathroom or when no one else is in the home. The adults would tell us ahead of time that our sisters or the women were going to change, so we would go outside and do something until they were finished. When I was growing up, I slept in whatever I wore every day—the same socks, shoes, and pants. I seldom changed. We all shared this small space, with my mother sleeping on the south side with my sisters and the boys sleeping with my father on the west or north side. We were being taught that we were male, there was a different role for us, and that we needed to respect those differences and our family members. Sometimes Mom and Dad slept together and we learned that they were married, but we could not sleep close together as brothers and sisters.

Boys never kissed their sisters or held their hands, but hugging was just fine. We knew that love was in the home. The boys could never look at their sisters in a sexual way and were not supposed to stare at them. The word yíiyá is used to describe having evil thoughts about your sister. We were told that if we saw our sister's private places or anything like that we would go blind. If we started inappropriately touching our sister we would go crazy, just like a moth that flies into a fire and kills itself. To do so was a curse. I remember that I did not think anything about a woman being topless in a ceremony, as ashes were placed on her. We had already been taught that a woman was just like our mother and so we did not think anything in that way. Now they leave their bra on, and it is a woman who usually performs that part of the ceremony on the lady, not the man. When this is going on the men should not be there if it is their sister or else they could go blind or crazy.

Another way we showed respect for our brothers and sisters was to avoid calling them names. A person can tease their aunts, maybe some cousins on the father's side, but not on one's mother's side. As with the sisters, you did not touch a brother. I remember my sister teased me, but we never touched each other or called names. The teaching of this closeness was an important part of what our *parents wanted. When my father was on the railroad, my mother or grandmother was always there with the children, teaching us how to show respect to a female. We were told that they were the image of our mother and so should not be abused. My sisters and other females were no different, my grandmother would say, so you should show that same kind of respect. The same was true of the boys and their father. It was my father who taught us never to touch, tease, or look at our sisters inappropriately. So even though we were raised in a small home, we really respected each other. I think that is the reason Navajo people were so closely knit.*

Another important aspect of traditional daily life, in addition to the hogan, was livestock. My grandmother was known for having many sheep and in the [1940s] my grandmother's mother, Gambling Lady, was also alive. She had a large flock, too, so when all the family lived together and pooled their animals, there were a lot. Close relatives like sisters and brothers also had sheep, which added to the number. My great-grandmother won much of her livestock through gambling or from people who sold them to her for money. She always seemed to have large piles of Spanish silver and coins. She even hired a silversmith to make a large concho belt from this silver.

At an early age I understood the meaning of sheep. I was a shepherd. When we were young, we learned responsibility and how to work with these animals. Sheep bring wealth to a family who use every part for food, medicine, clothing, and rugs. Our elders told us not to waste any part of a sheep. If a family has them, there will always be more income because they are a valuable resource. This was true at the beginning of the world and still is today. Caring for them is still an art taught within a family, where there is valuable knowledge about herding to be gained. This task provides physical conditioning so that a person lives longer. When I was a young man my parents observed families with young women who had sheep. If they knew of a family with a well-cared for flock, my father would go and ask about the daughter and if she was available for marriage. The herd was an indicator of the teachings of the family and their work ethic. The more livestock, which included goats, cows, and horses, the more capable the people were and the more likely they were to work hard and excel. The young man will grow up to be a leader who understands what life is about.

When we took the sheep to Red Lake for dipping, there would be at least five or six of us to herd around them to make sure that they would not go into some-body else's flock.[13] *It was hard work. If you do not take care of them, they will mix with the other animals and have to be taken out individually. Bringing them to good feed, especially in the springtime, meant a lot of walking. I started to build my own flock at a young age. Every spring when it was lambing season, my relatives gave me two or three lambs that were especially earmarked for me with a "v" notch in each ear. If I had worked hard herding or shearing sheep, I would get a new pair of shoes or a hat. Grandmother would take us to the trading post, where we chose what we wanted like a pair of Levis, shirt, T-shirt, or socks. Even when I got only two shirts and socks, it meant so much and was appreciated because I had looked forward to it. Today we are spoiled and want to have everything we can get a hold of. But at that time receiving something was based on earning it or how well behaved you were through the year. I had to get out and help a lot with the sheep in order to get something. People watched you.*

A person pretty well knows which lambs are his; Grandmother knew how each one appeared. She could look at the flock and say, "Oh, run up to that sheep," and call it by name, especially the ones she had raised with a bottle. She named them by how they looked and their color. If a sheep had lots of wool she might call it "Curly," another that did not grow much by another name. If its wool was very white or thin or the sheep had a thick bunch of wool around its neck or had a black face or lots of meat—each one got a different name. In Grandmother's flock, there were usually about seven hundred animals, and if one was missing she knew it.

Women use wool to make many things, such as rugs, clothing, rope, and blankets. A person taught to weave will always survive. Even our bedding was made from sheepskin. Wool insulated our boots and pants during the cold winter to keep us warm. Women spun the wool to make string for children hand string games. Rugs, clothing, purses, pillows, belts, head bands, and saddle blankets were fashioned from wool, as was the tie for the traditional Navajo hair bun. It was also used for a baby lamb's bedding because it soaked up liquids. My grandparents told me to never touch a lamb because the mother sheep would not want her baby. Often we rubbed the mother sheep's wool on her lamb so that she would recognize and feed it.

When you butcher a sheep, all of it is used. The tendons are stripped for thread to make shoes and clothing. The intestines and stomach are cleaned and dried to serve as a water bottle or purse. Bones turned into a digging stick when planting a garden or when cut four to five inches long and threaded with rope

"Sheep are life." The Dandy family depended heavily on their livestock for food, clothing, and money to provide the necessities of life. The animals also taught responsibility to the children who herded them and provided an opportunity to start their own economic resource. (Courtesy Milton Snow Collection, Navajo Nation Museum)

through a hole served as hinges. Shined bones can turn into children's toys, dry hardened elbow joint cartilage into buttons, and the fat when mixed with red clay heals or prevents sunburn. During ceremonies, fat with ashes is used for body paint. Brain or bone marrow softens and waterproofs leather to keep feet dry. A sheep hide is soft and when used as a saddle blanket prevents injury to a horse's backbone. The tanned hide provides gloves, belts, and arrow quivers, while a family might take the extra ones to the trading post to sell.

The person butchering the animal takes great care to do it properly. Almost every part of the sheep turned into food. For large family gatherings, we roasted a whole sheep in an underground pit. The first step was to dig a hole and insulate its sides with rocks after placing a big flat rock on the bottom. The people cooking next built a fire and heated this oven for a whole day before removing the ashes, laying the meat on top of the rocks, and covering the food so it did not burn. The meat cooked from the bottom up. Some people started the fire the day before and at night opened the pit, lay the meat in, put wet sand on a cloth spread over it, and covered it again with dry sand. At times the hide was left on, its wool singed, [it was] cleaned, then the entire sheep was laid in the hole to cook. I think the best way to eat sheep meat is fresh, sliced off while butchering, then fried.

Underground storage pits held dried food for the winter. These were cool places that prevented meat from spoiling. In the summer we dried meat by keeping it in the shade so that it would last a long time. Some ways of drying meat are to slice it into thin strips, put it in a gunny sack and hang it, lay it on chicken wire, or just thread it on a string and leave it in a shady area. Sheep intestines must be cleaned before cutting them into small pieces to fry or boil. Blood sausage and blood pudding are mixtures of blood with cornmeal to which potatoes, liver, and other things are chopped into small pieces and added. The bladder, eyes, and private parts are not eaten. Navajos believe that if they eat sheep eyes their own eyesight will be affected later in life.

During lambing season we loved to drink sheep or goat's milk. There is not much difference between the two. In the evening we would put a mother sheep alone in a pen and spread manure on her teats so that her lamb would not suck. The next day, her bag was full and ready to milk. We boiled the milk then used it in a number of ways, including cheese. At an early age family members instructed that sheep were valuable and no part should be wasted. To do so brings poverty. If mutton is served and a person does not eat it, he is considered disrespectful. If someone wastes it, he is considered greedy.

Sheep products also play a part in religious ceremonies. The person receiving the ceremony wears clothes made in certain ways with specific colors. In the Enemy Way and Mountain Way ceremonies, participants put on these special garments for the last day. The dyed wool colored with black, red, and white is woven into a dress. Women who carry the sacred stick as part of the Enemy Way use yarn made from this wool.[14] *During the ceremony white sheep fat, free from blood, is applied as a healing cream to a person's face while sheep meat is fed to participants. We are taught to share this food with all relatives and people who participate. Products from sheep are also used for clearing out a person's congestion or cough. You inhale the smoke from wool mixed with herbs to cleanse the body. Chips of sheep hoofs or goat horns can be burned with mountain tobacco in a pipe so that the smoke clears the lungs. Livestock that are sick also inhale the smoke from a ground horn to remove illness. During the summer if there are lots of flies, wool is burned to keep them away, while sheep fat mixed with yucca makes soap.*

People who do not have sheep in their family have no wealth and are in poor physical condition. Herding sheep helps a person live longer, like my great-aunt who is over one hundred years old. She still herds today. My grandparents lived a long time and had lots of sheep. People moved around often to find good grazing areas. In the lambing season, I got up early to check the animals and again at midnight. To lose a lamb is a bad sign. I remember my parents telling me that if I worked hard in the winter, the toughest time to work with livestock, they would buy me a new pair of shoes or some clothing. They gave me lots of praise, telling others of my hard work, which made me feel good. They said, "My son is good with sheep," which was especially uplifting in the cold winter months when sheep raising was so hard. I learned to work and appreciate this kind of family unity.

When I was growing up there wasn't very much soda pop or anything sweet. At that time I had never heard of a heart attack, diabetes, cancer, or stroke. Sometimes I wonder why people in the past were so healthy. It was probably because they were on the go all the time, herding sheep and walking, but I also think it was their diet. In the morning, we were lucky to have some corn mush, maybe some potatoes and onions. Very seldom did we eat fry bread, but there were a lot of tortillas and a type of roll made by putting the dough in the fire, covering it with hot ashes, cooking it for a while, then dusting it off. There were also blue corn dumplings. Seldom did we use white flour, which is so slick that we called dumplings made from it k'inéesh bízhii náldzidígíí, meaning "wild dumpling," because it was hard to hang onto and slippery, while blue corn meal dumplings were easier to handle. We ate very little meat; but whenever we killed a sheep, there was reason for a feast and family gathering. You could count on family members coming over once the word was out.

When Grandmother went on horseback to the trading post in Red Lake, I stayed home with the sheep and horses. But I knew when she came home she would have Cracker Jacks for me, which meant a lot. I might take a whole week to eat them, a little bit at a time, hiding them from my cousin sister whose mom had died when she was just a little baby.[15] She was always looking for my Cracker Jacks, so I put them somewhere she would not find them. I still loved her, and it was fun to watch her grow. She lived primarily on goat or sheep's milk, but when someone went to the store they might get her two or three little cans of milk. Sometimes I helped by getting up early in the morning and milking all of the goats and coming back with two or three brimming buckets. The next problem was keeping it cool. Our family had a little underground pit for storage and refrigeration. This was made by digging a hole in the ground fourteen feet long, six feet wide, and six feet deep. The sides were lined with stones or cedar posts or packed with mud. Some people suspended a line from the roof to hang dried meat on to keep it cool, especially in the wintertime. Then milk froze a little and lasted a long time.

As I grew, I started to go places with my grandfather as he worked as a medicine man. I wanted to be like him. Sometimes in the middle of the night someone would arrive on horseback requesting help, and we would saddle our horses and leave right then and not return for three or four days. At that time many people did not have cars or pickups, but occasionally someone would have one and came and got us. One of my tasks was to collect what was needed for the ceremony, such as herbs, some of which we picked along the way as we traveled. This is how I learned a lot from my grandfather, who performed healing rites for people around Kaibito, the Gap, Cedar Ridge, Tuba City, Red Lake, Cow Springs, Shonto, and Navajo Mountain. After the performance, if we had gotten a ride in a car and received sheep for payment, I would herd them toward home while he went back, got a horse, and met me halfway.

Grandfather was well known for his ability to heal using very sacred ceremonies. Often the parents or relatives did not let anybody else know about the performance, keeping everything quiet. One of his most powerful ceremonies was the Evil Way (Hóchxǫ'íjí), in which a spirit is cast out of an ill person cursed by contact with a grave or the dead.[16] I had to gather certain plants like rabbit brush and desert grass, the same kind used as a hairbrush, then burn them on a flat stone. The ashes are scraped together as a fine powder, mixed with mutton fat, and applied to the body. This covering cleanses and keeps evil away, acting like a shield, while the singing that takes place all night heals. The songs that they sing just before early dawn at the end of the ceremony are particularly powerful for protecting a person and for having her walk in beauty with health and wealth. I have learned some of these songs and can assist a medicine man. Your voice is real and must be strong; I do not know why medicine men do not lose their voice as they perform. I think it comes from a lot of practice. They also rarely sleep at night. Maybe once he is through in the morning or on the last day, he might sleep, but usually he is up and about. At the end of the ceremony, when the patient is washing, I would go out and dig yucca roots to wash the hair and body.

Grandfather often said, "Grandson, a long time ago when people knew that they were dying, they also knew that a song and prayer would heal them." So he taught me parts of these songs, which I needed to carry with me all the time. I learned a little at a time, and today I use some of them. If you follow along with the song they are not hard to learn, which is good. During the ceremony I listened closely, and when it was time to take a break, I prepared the sweat lodge for the men to go in and rest. I went in with them and listened, rarely asking questions. But Grandfather would either tell me something or sit down and sing a song slowly so that I could follow along with him. The next time I came in, he wanted to listen to the song I had learned. I repeated it and if I forgot a part he would sing it to me, making sure this time I remembered it.

Knowledge is power. One time a man came to us in Red Lake looking for a medicine man. He was very depressed and badly stressed. I watched grandfather use his power, which was amazing. The two walked out behind a mesa where he sang a chant for the young man, who was ready to die. Grandfather put his hand on the back of his shoulder and placed his other hand in the middle of the head. He sat there and massaged him a little bit then said to me: "Come here, Grandson. Sit right here. I want you to rub this a little bit more." I really felt weird, standing there and rubbing in a clockwise motion. He said not to go counterclockwise and to do it just a little bit. With one hand on the chest and the other straight on the back, he told me to put a little pressure on the back. Soon the man began to relax, then suddenly he opened his eyes and looked around. He told me that I had done something that really made him feel good. All of his problems had left. "I was so down. I felt like something was choking me and couldn't breathe when suddenly you hit me and popped that something out of me. I feel weak but so good; I felt empty and am now perspiring." I was perspiring, too. Grandfather said that if I was going to be a medicine man, I would have to do things like this often because this is what it took to make somebody better.

Another time when I was a teenager, my aunt was having a baby so one of my brothers-in-law and I had to go find Grandfather, who was performing ceremonies in various places. This was the first time I had ever traveled in an automobile, and we got stuck in a blizzard. The night turned bitterly cold, the snow two feet deep, and all I had on was a T-shirt. My pants were wet from my knees down from walking in the mud and snow and I had no blanket, while my brother-in-law wrapped himself in one and wore a coat. I stayed up all night huddled over a fire, but the next day my knees were frozen all the way to my toes. Once we located Grandfather he was in a hurry because my aunt was in labor, but by the time we returned to our shade house (we had no hogan), she had already had the baby.

Grandfather warned me not to put my legs by the fire, just to keep them in the sun.
My feet were so swollen from freezing, he cut the back and side of my shoes to get
them off. Both sides were frozen, but he would not let me by the fire. He just had
me sit where it was not too hot. I thawed out all day. Sometimes I looked at my
frost-bitten feet and wondered. As they thawed, there was no burning sensation
and they got better. I guess that is why my grandfather told me not to go by the
fire. I was lucky that somebody knew what to do.

One day a woman sick with stomach cancer came to him to be healed.
Although we did not know the cause, she was throwing up blood and could barely
move. Grandfather sang all night, then the next day we went to the mountain on
the other side of Page [Arizona] to gather the plant used for mountain smoke.[17]
We picked it with some other herbs, which he had me boil and prepare to give to
the person a few drops at a time. Back then there used to be these old coffee cups
made of copper not aluminum. I drained the herbs into one of these cups and took
a little stick about four inches long with a small hole in it. I sucked the juice into
the stick and then dripped it into the lady's mouth a little at a time. About every
fifteen minutes she received two or three drops as I sat there for at least two hours.
When we left, I thought the lady was going to die that very day, but she lived. It
was a miracle how we cured her of stomach cancer. The same thing happened
more recently when a man from Monument Valley brought his sick wife to me. She
also had cancer. He said that he had gone to a lot of Christian people but that it
did no good. He asked me to heal her, and so I sang some of the sacred songs and
gave her a blessing. From the prayers that I had learned from that previous experi-
ence, I knew that she would get better. To this day she tells me, "Jim, it's amazing
that I don't have cancer now."

Another power that my grandfather had was that he could speak to animals.
One time we lost the key to a hogan door where we stored things. Grandmother
needed some wool for weaving, and so grandfather got a bucket, tied a rope on it,
and lowered me down through the smoke hole and onto the floor. As I removed
some of the wool from a pile in the corner, I felt something strange. A sense like an
electric shock went shooting through me as I picked up a rattlesnake that had been
resting at the bottom of the wool. I threw the snake and wool up in the air almost
to the top beam of the hogan. When it hit the floor it was mad, rose up about two
feet, and charged. Grandfather saw from above that it was trying to corner me
in one area so he spoke to it and the snake suddenly stopped and dropped. I had

already opened the door and run outside. He told me to go back in and bring the snake out, chop it into pieces with a shovel, put its remains in the bucket, and dump it on the other side of a nearby hill. A powerful medicine man can make things like that happen just through using powerful words. It was a miracle. He told me of a time at the Grand Canyon when a similar thing happened. He met a big mountain lion face to face, spoke to it, and it dropped until Grandfather was safe then got up and left. He had just talked to it and it went to sleep, because he did not want to kill it.

As my interest in becoming a medicine man increased, Grandfather counseled me in a different direction. He warned: "You need to get an education. You don't want this. I can't give this to you, Grandson. It will be better for you to get an education. Eventually there will be no such thing as a medicine man because this knowledge is going to fade out. There may be people out there, quacks, who say 'Give me your money and I'll heal you,' but they will not understand the power." He was also concerned with my becoming a medicine man because part of their knowledge, in order to cure people, must also involve evil. "You have to have some experience with evil before becoming a medicine man if you are really going to be able to help someone. You're going to have to do some evil things. I can't do that to you, Grandson. A real medicine man has to deal with some evil things because that is what you are going to be working against. You at least have to know what to do or not do. If you try to help a person who has been cursed by witchcraft you have to know what the evil person is doing and who it is. Without this kind of knowledge, you can't work well. In order to perform a ceremony you have to know a little bit about evil things that have to be overcome." Grandfather did not want to see me get deeply into that side of healing but rather wanted me to stay on the good side. Some sacred, powerful things are difficult to work against. I believe he was afraid of my getting involved in situations that I did not understand, thus putting myself in a dangerous position. Now all of the strong medicine men are gone.

My father, grandmother, and great-grandfather each approached my becoming a medicine man very differently. Father was willing to let me learn about all of these things, but the older folks were very touchy and did not even want to talk about it. Sometimes they would get really superstitious about this topic, but I do not know what they were afraid of. It seems like when a person is being taught to become a medicine man, he learns a lot of things, but the teaching also shuts off, not really giving a clear idea of what is there or what they are presenting. In other words, a person would learn up to a certain point and then the information stopped. That is why I admired my father. He always shared things that he had learned and was not afraid of anything. My mother was totally different and a little superstitious. Normally, she would not talk about these types of things, but there were certain times you might say something and she would answer. I still go out and help with medicine whenever anyone wants assistance, and I do it with my own family. I also try to teach them as much as I can.

Grandfather encouraged me to go to school and was pretty much in favor of the LDS Church. Even though he was not baptized as a member, he told me one day that it was best to stay with that faith. He thought that this education was better than becoming a medicine man because soon not very many people were going to believe in traditional ways. In his words, "What I have and what I practice is going to phase out and once I go who will take over?" He told me that I should stay with what I was learning and live by the church's teachings. He did not tell me to get rid of Navajo culture but to respect it. I think it is a good thing that I've learned a little bit about the tradition because I can help Navajo people learn about their roots.

CHAPTER FIVE

BOARDING SCHOOLS
AND PLACEMENT

Education in the Dandy Family

Jim stresses the role of education:

Education has always been important in the Dandy family. Early on my father taught that as Indians we were not in a position to outsmart the white man, so we might as well get used to the fact, live with them, and get an education. If you know how they think, then you are better prepared and stronger. That is why my father put every one of us in school. Without him I don't think we would have gotten the education that we now have. He always said that we were going to school and that our grandparents would not have a say in preventing it. My grandmother was very disappointed with him for this, but my father had his way.

Part of this attitude came from his experience. He always talked about how he wished he had gotten at least two or three years of education, but he never went to school. He blamed his mother and father and grandparents for his loss. When he was growing up, they hid him every time a government vehicle approached their home. One day a car with government officials came looking for children to be placed in school, and his family hid him in an underground pit where they stored wool. They put him in a large burlap sack used for shipping wool on wagons. Dad hid in there as the officials looked for him and other young school-age people. If they had found him they would not have said anything but just taken him. Still, Dad blamed his grandparents and mother and was very unhappy that he did not get an education. He always told me he would have been a lawyer sitting in Washington, D.C., with his own office. Dad was a hard worker, and people looked up to him even without an education because he was pretty smart. As a chapter president, he helped and encouraged a lot of young people to get theirs.[1]

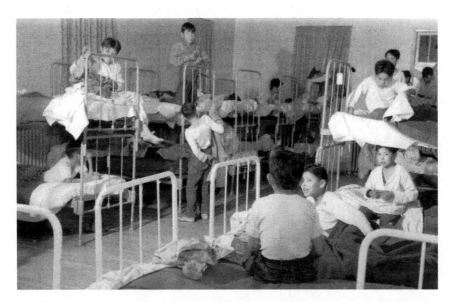

Boarding school, with its strict discipline and enforcement of Anglo ways, was a difficult experience for many children coming from the traditional environment of the reservation. The Dandys were no exception, sometimes harboring a rebellious attitude. (Courtesy Milton Snow Collection, Navajo Nation Museum)

Zonnie remembers her introduction to education. Relatives also took turns hiding her and other children from school officials. The little girls crouched in a dirt hole lined with a sheepskin while only one or two were given to the government agents seeking students. BIA officials persisted in tracking her and others until, at the age of fifteen in 1955, she went to school at Tuba City and later Anadarko, Oklahoma. Jim, while staying with his grandparents, had a similar experience. Whenever a government vehicle came to their camp, they hid him in a pit by the corral where they used to load wool. He remained there until the people left. His grandmother refused to send him until he was nine or ten, and his father demanded that he enroll in the Tuba City boarding school. His grandmother and grandfather argued that they would give him more attention and care than the school, but Jim's father insisted and he went.

I remember when my father took me to Tuba City in the wagon I was a really strong, healthy young man. For some reason I could not enroll at that time, which was fine with me; I was happy to get home to my grandparents, who rejoiced. Father had bought me a sombrero, a really big wide hat, so I felt content. I resumed life with my grandparents herding sheep, helping around their camp, and traveling with my grandfather to ceremonies. The next year, 1952, however, I returned to Tuba City and this time the school accepted me and my younger brother Charlie as well as my sister Lillie. Charlie, who had been very close to mother and father, was lonely and cried all the time. Everywhere they went he went with them, and he loved to ride horses. Now that had ended. For the next year and a half I was locked into the boarding school education system, which was hard. Almost all of the children, with the exception of a few Hopis, were Navajos. We were all there to learn English and writing. Dorm life was particularly difficult, centering on strict discipline. Occasionally, maybe three or four times a year, our parents visited us, but most of the time you saw only school employees.

With the younger children, the administration stressed always speaking English. They punished you if you did not, but if you spoke English all the time, nobody bothered you. I walked around nervous because somebody was always looking. I had to watch my step in whatever I did. One thing that was difficult was for me to look at my teachers. When Navajo children are little they are taught to never stare at people because the elders, especially medicine men, are very powerful with their eyes. Even white people are said to have this power. This practice comes from the teaching that at one time there was a monster that stared at people and killed or cursed them with its eyes.² I was very stubborn because I was taught never, never look directly at a person for a long time, especially an elder. So when the teachers told me to look at them, a lot of the other children and I would not do it. After class the teacher came up to me, grabbed my ear, twisted it, and kept telling me I had to look at him. I just could not because I was not taught that way. Then they would send me to the dorm, where I would stand with a chalk eraser on top of my head for a long time and if it dropped I got a kick in the butt. They treated us with disrespect, trying to force us to become like the Anglos.

The administration was never on your side. They would support the teachers or dorm attendants. Sometimes they placed high school–aged Navajo leaders in the dorm, which got out of hand. They forced you to do things, twisted your ears, hit you in the head with their pocketknife, or kicked you for no reason, and you had to live with that. They were the worst ones because they did not care what they did and would beat you up. There was nobody to back the younger children; so when you told on them, you got punished worse. The head dorm people were the ones who made the decisions, and they gave full support to the high school students.

Nobody said anything, but if they did they were called tattletale and embarrassed. That was enough to prevent me from doing it again. If they caught me doing something then I might end up with a chore where I had to work until late at night. One punishment I especially hated was scrubbing walls with my toothbrush. I would be on my knees all night scrubbing and washing. If I did something bad, I had to stand in line in the corner or somewhere with soap in my mouth. Any time, when you least expected it, you would get kicked in the butt. They did many things to discipline us, and there was nobody to protect you. It happened, believe me. It was bad. There was no love or affection; they did not care if you ate or not; and there was discipline all of the time.

My family became involved in other things from which we learned. During Dad's era people acquired the knowledge of how to make alcohol. He had some experience brewing his own whiskey from corn he grew. Our family did not have a very large income, so he supplemented it by charging for alcohol. We would go to a social gathering sometimes and sell whiskey in pint-sized bottles. Then we began to see what damage we were doing and how it hurt the people. There were some really good families that we could have destroyed. We knew it was wrong, so we quit. From then on, Dad encouraged us not to get into it. My mother and aunt never drank and were totally against alcohol. That was a really difficult experience for me when I realized that this was not the road to take.

Zonnie recalls her experience in this family venture:

My aunt taught us how to take care of our distillery. Making bottles of alcohol was exciting. First we ground the corn a little bit. The Hopis always raised grapes at Moenkopi, so we mixed grape juice with the corn in a big drum or pot and kept a fire going underneath. A tube fed into a jar that caught the boiled whiskey. There was plenty of corn available, so the real work was keeping the fire going. I really got into trouble with whiskey-making one time when I was a little girl. Grandfather Eli Shorty used to store alcohol in a wooden barrel with metal bands in the rocks on a hill near Wildcat Peak. My cousin and I were herding sheep and goats nearby; they were hungry and curious to know what was inside the vat. We climbed up to the site, since the goats were already there, and braided a rope from yucca fiber. We tied it around the barrel and attached the other end to the saddle's cross pieces. She pulled the horse while I watched the barrel, but it toppled, flipped open, and spilled everything onto the ground. The goats enjoyed themselves and we were thirsty too, so we drank some. Three hours later I awoke to find my cousin

5.2. Following livestock reduction and the end of government programs like the Civilian Conservation Corps and war industries, Navajos worked in the wage economy off the reservation at the end of the 1940s and 1950s. The Dandys were a part of this lifestyle, which introduced them to a different environment, including the LDS Church. (Courtesy Milton Snow Collection, Navajo Nation Museum)

crying under the rock where she had passed out. I got up and looked around. Some goats remained, wobbling around like they were lost, but the horse and sheep had vanished. The search started; quite a way off I found the horse, brought it back, and put my cousin on top. Any other animals I found lying around I herded over to Wildcat Peak then told my cousin to take them back home. I ran to another place on the peak, found the rest, and herded them back that night. For two days we did not get caught, but one of the men tracked us and told Dad, who had to pay a large sheep for what we had done. I will not forget the whipping.

Jim continued:

When school was out in the summer my family traveled about doing odd jobs. We might be clearing the land of juniper trees for white people living in Blanding, Monticello, Moab, or Dove Creek. We also planted and weeded sugar beets for large farms. My father took the whole family to Colorado to work in the sugar-beet fields. We all went in the wagon to Tuba City, where some large canvas-covered cattle trucks picked us up with other workers. We traveled to Grand Junction and began to work. The owners of the fields were waiting for us and anxious to get started. This was the first experience that we had as a family off the reservation. Next we transferred to Wellington near Price, Utah. Charlie was just a little boy, too young to work, and my sister Ruby was in a cradle.

One day the family was hoeing weeds when an elderly couple serving as Mormon missionaries stopped by to give a lesson. They didn't teach us very long before my mother decided that she and all of the children who were old enough—me, my two older sisters, and a younger sister—should be baptized. Charlie and Ruby were too young, and my father refused because he was a medicine man. I was about fifteen years old at the time. Soon after that the family went to Richfield to work, but there were no missionaries to visit us at our new camp, so when the work ended we came home.

Following her baptism in Price, however, Zonnie remained with a woman named Schwartz for a short time at Sunnyside. She considers this her experience in the LDS Placement Program. As Zonnie looks back on this time, she also realizes how little she knew about the faith and that her staying there was a functional thing to get her into school. She remained for only a month before a traumatic event sent her home far worse for the experience. Zonnie and her foster mother and father had attended church in Salt Lake City and were returning when they encountered a train wreck. The exposed bodies of the accident victims lay about. Mrs. Schwartz, not understanding Navajo beliefs, "chased" Zonnie out to the scene and insisted that she help. "I was scared but had to do it. My foster mom was mean, because the smell of blood from the accident got me sick, but she made me cover all the dead bodies. Following this train crash I fainted the next day at school, because I was a very traditional Navajo person."[3]

When Zonnie's father received word of his daughter's situation, that she was constantly fainting, he brought her home for an Enemy Way ceremony that removed the spirits of the dead. "Then it stopped. I got healed. I never went back on placement. After the squaw dance [Enemy Way] I stayed home because I had a ruptured appendix followed by surgery in Tuba City. When I awoke, I remember my dad crying and my grandfather and his uncle singing and then their using herbs; I healed quickly." They took Zonnie to Flagstaff, where she stayed with the wife of a trader friend from Tuba City in order to attend school for four or five months. In summarizing these experiences and feelings about the LDS Church, Zonnie says: "I go to church sometimes and I believe in the LDS Church. I always say I'm a member, but if I am asked I say I am traditional. I don't see a conflict between the two. I stand for Monster Slayer. I always say LDS is my church, but my heart is with Monster Slayer on my traditional side."

The next fall BIA officials visited the Dandy home, lined all the children up, and sent them to various schools. Ruby went to Kayenta, Marie to Shiprock then Brigham City, Zonnie to Anadarko, and Jim and his sister Lillie to Shalako, Oklahoma. For the two and a half day trip they tossed Zonnie on a bus, where she "just cried and cried." Once there, school officials separated her from all other Navajo children and put her with Indians from the Oklahoma tribes. BIA employees told her not to speak her native language, only English. Tacked on her door was a sign "Speak English"; since she did not know the other tribes' languages anyway, the children just smiled at each other. For about three months Zonnie tried to get used to the different people. They taught her English; although her dorm aide was friendly, she was also very strict. Each of the children received a set of clothes—a skirt, blouse, socks, shoes, and panties. Every evening they had to wash their underclothes in preparation for the next day, but halfway through the year they received another set. Workers cut off Zonnie's traditional bun and clipped her hair into bangs: "I looked terrible." Zonnie, small in frame and shy, felt tiny and totally unprepared for this life, but her supervisors started her in the seventh grade and made her one of the cooks for the school.

Three years later, the unfamiliar had become routine and the shyness worn off. Zonnie had made a lot of Oklahoma Indian friends and began attending powwows with them. Tired of the environment, she ran away with some of the Navajos and other Indian students—twenty-one in all—and went to a dance. At the powwow they received shawls and necklaces and had a wonderful time, but the next day, Sunday, school officials caught them and brought them back to Anadarko. The adults were furious and told them that they would have to stand all day long.

We were sleepy because we had danced all night. One of the boys said, "Don't let the white man put you down. Let's keep our traditions." He was a leader and told us to make a circle, the boys on one side, the girls on the other. We stood with our arms linked, holding hands to make it look like we're just standing there, but we were sleeping. We all slept and nobody fell, but I do not remember how he taught us to hold onto each other. That evening the officials thought that we were worn out and brought us supper. They were still mad, and so the next day after school we had to do the same thing, then a third and fourth time. They also had a stick to hit your shins real hard with. It hurt. I was told to never be rebellious again, and I obeyed.

Jim had his own problems at Shalako, where there seemed to him to be about a hundred and fifty different tribes represented.

Talk about prejudice—that was the worst place I have ever been. None of the tribes seemed to get along and the Navajo students were usually quiet and alone. They did not go around as a group causing trouble, whereas the Utes, Blackfeet, or Comanches were always together. They constantly wanted to challenge me, so that is where I learned to protect myself. At that school it was survival. I got into trouble so many times I just wanted to leave the place. One time I ran away with some friends, but we all got caught as we neared home. Another time I ran away and was picked up in Oklahoma City. A counselor at the school was very concerned, so he brought me into his office, where there were one white and two or three Navajo lady counselors. Instead of helping, they treated me as if I was ignorant, saying, "Jim Dandy you're just no good. You'll never learn. This is not the place for you. We're just going to have to do something, send you somewhere." There was no warmth in anything they said or did. After they told me that I would never succeed in school, my behavior changed and I was in trouble constantly. It really bothered me to think that I was no good and that I did not belong there. I still have in the back of my mind that I can't learn. I had completed two years at Shalako, but the third year I started a different program.

It was during this time that I had further contact with the LDS Church. There was a town in Arkansas not too far from the school where a missionary couple lived. They used to come on campus and hold a short church service. I made friends with Chester Yazzie and another young man who ate dinner with this family. The couple also invited me to eat at their home in Arkansas; and since I was attending a number of different churches at that time, I decided to go. I began participating in church with them a few times, but I never was really introduced to the gospel. They continued to invite me until the administration at Shalako removed me from the school and put me in a five-year vocational education program. I left the area and was more on my own.

This job training provided a place to work while earning credit. I moved to Kansas City, where I learned the trade of a cobbler, fixing heels and hand-stitching or machine-stitching seams in boots and shoes. Next I did leatherworking, making wallets and belts and, after I got good, working on saddles, bridles, and hacka-mores. I decorated them with hammered stamp designs. Then the government sent me to Tulsa City, Oklahoma, where I became involved with construction, concrete, and brick laying. All of this broadened my experience and was enjoyable.

I worked my way to Amarillo, Texas, where I got into trouble with alcohol taking over my life. My drinking got heavier and heavier. Every weekend I ended up in jail and had to be bailed out. I struggled with drinking and got to the point where the only thing to do was to go home. After I came home, I did a little bit better and began working in Williams, Arizona, on the railroad with some of my friends. We traveled to a lot of places, even as far as Idaho, but alcohol was still part of my life. Grandfather saw what was happening and contacted some of the older people. Medicine men are usually straightforward and very good in their counseling. He gathered a number of them as well as chapter officials and some ladies from the community to counsel me. They left no doubt in my mind that drinking was wrong and stressed the importance of the family, who love and care about you in the healing process.

A strong family is there to help, not to discourage or hurt. They may yell at you, but Navajos teach that everybody in the community is there to assist and lis-ten. I still hear their voices sometimes. They know that drinking destroys people, and so they used examples of grandparents who have never touched alcohol. They also pointed out that a lot of the chapter people do not have problems with it. Navajo religion taught that even at the time of emergence from the underworld there would be problems with it, but there were never any teachings provided to handle those issues. Now I see others with similar problems and am so thankful that I had good friends who were honest, strong medicine men and leaders. They counseled that drinking was wrong and I should not be involved but rather be a good example in the community and help young people.

I remember when a lot of those elders sat me down and talked. They warned: "Listen to your dad and your grandparents because they have more experience and knowledge of all the teachings. Listen to the older people whether they are your close relatives or not." They laid down the law, which was really good. The lead-ership in our community was a source of strength and guidance, but today these old people are not used anymore. In those days someone from your family or an elder really got after you, and they did not hold back. A lot of these old folks disciplined me, while my mom and dad never defended me but were always there to help. They were happy that somebody really cared enough to correct my behavior. They did not go out and get somebody who had a degree but thought of each other and who could best solve problems within their community. This is rarely done anymore. I honor those elders for helping me.

My father once talked about his understanding of alcohol. He had a lot of experience with counseling and wanted us to avoid drinking. He said a long time ago the Navajos were very wealthy and independent. They were talented in arts and crafts, making their own saddles, silver jewelry, and whatever else they wanted. Gradually people started in a new direction. They began with gambling. Playing cards came out, and people held games at a lot of different places. Card games appeared at ceremonies like the Enemy Way, at social gatherings, and at trading posts. Alcohol followed. The whites introduced all of this to the Indians. Father taught that white men are smart and when they drink they know how to handle themselves. But Navajos do not know anything about it so just get in, like flies, and don't even know we are in it. The people lost everything—their jewelry, handcrafts, and employment. Alcohol and gambling destroyed whole families and was especially harmful for young people, who had a long life ahead. The elders tried to teach children not to drink and to stay away from people who did.

Welfare was another thing my father talked against. People refused to work anymore and just sat around, waiting for their paycheck. Everything was free. Now a lot of young girls want to become pregnant and receive money for having children. The more children there are, the more money that comes from the government. That is what he talked about. Before this time people were protective of their daughters. Whenever they attended a squaw dance, the mother was sitting right there to make sure the girl did not disappear. Once welfare came, it seems to have really affected the people. Today nobody farms, raises sheep, owns horses, or exercises. To me, people now just give their children away.

During one of those difficult struggles with employment and alcohol, I had just barely returned home from jail. By chance I attended a local chapter meeting where an LDS Placement Program case worker, Tom Hadley, came by looking for somebody to interpret. One day after we got back from my showing him where some of the children lived, he was about to go but bought me a soda pop and some crackers. I was standing there and asked him a little bit about the program. After a while he told me that I was a smart young man who should stay in school. I was around eighteen or nineteen and thought it was too late, but he said it was never too late to get an education. I explained that as far as school was concerned I was not very smart, but he replied, "Oh, you shouldn't say that. Never. Think that you are one of the greatest students in the world. I guarantee if you go back to school you'll do fine."

At first Tom was not sure that I could get in because the school year had already started and the program had all of the students it had homes for. My mother had already signed for Charlie and Marie to attend, but I just lived in hope and helped the Mormon elders pick up children who were going. I pawned my saddle and Mom brought some money to me in Tuba City, while the trader at Red Lake told me he could sell all of the saddles that I made. Things just seemed to work out. Even though it appeared too late, Tom said he would do everything he could and to wait and see what happened. He told me to come to Tuba City in about five days to see if my name was on the list. Father had just barely bought a truck, so he gave me a ride after the time passed. Sure enough, my name was on the list. All the others were typed, but mine was in ink. It was a miracle; I never dreamed of going back to school until now. Tom had told me when I first met him: "I want you in school. You could be a top-notch individual." I got thinking. Teachers always told me I would never learn. That got me down, and in my head I felt like I could not. This was my chance.

My grandparents, who had mobilized community members to help me through my difficulties, had been praying. Now they were so happy. Grandfather wanted me to go back to school and become something. His advice was very strong, and he knew that the LDS Church did not believe in drinking and gambling. He was very supportive of my being in this church, agreeing with its general values. I had no knowledge of what the placement program was, but there were a couple of kids who had gone out from our area and it seemed all right. At that time I was so interested in going back to school, but I just did not know how to do it. I soon found out how lucky I was.

I went to Plymouth, Utah, and the dry farm of my foster parents Jess and Bertha Lamb. They were a good, close-knit family who did everything they could to help me. My foster dad, Jess, sometimes stayed up at night and talked to me about things that I could do in my future. He always said that he wasn't a smart man but

Jess and Bertha Lamb, Jim's foster parents in Plymouth, Utah. Jim felt the same closeness with his adopted family as he did with his family of birth. Both had a sincere desire to guide him to be a productive member in both the Anglo and Navajo world. Jim attributes much of his success to these loving relationships.

that he had worked hard for where he was. Looking at his children, my brothers and sisters, they have all done well, too. They taught me a lot and treated me like one of their own, which helped me to get an education. I learned how much they cared during the first year I was on placement. Initially, when I started the program no one had any idea what grade I should be in. Since I was older, they just kept it quiet and nobody said much about age or eligibility. But eventually others learned how old I was, and the church determined to send me back to the reservation. My foster dad would not hear of it. He told the case workers that if they did, he would form his own agreement with my family. "I want to raise this young man. He's a hard worker and he's doing so well that I am going to make sure he graduates." The church changed its mind and kept me on placement. They even sent children having a hard time in other foster families to him to keep them out of trouble. Both my foster mom and dad were hard workers but made it enjoyable to live with them. They were just like my own parents.

The Lamb family always kept me busy, with no time to sit around. They taught me to be responsible and that if I really wanted an education bad enough, to "keep your chin up, walk straight, you'll never fall back; you'll always succeed." I knew all about Jim Thorpe and wanted to be like him, a go-getter and top athlete.[4] I began to think that way and work toward goals, but I was far behind in school and it took a long time to catch up. With their help I did it. Every activity that I was involved in, they supported me and were there all the time. They thought that I was one of the best workers that they'd seen as a young man. My foster dad always said how lucky he was to have me in his home, how he would never forget

5.4. Left to right: Jim, foster brother Don Lamb, foster mother Bertha Lamb, foster sister Donna Lamb, and Apache placement child Marilyn Dasla, 1964. Jim: "Don has always been a role model for me and been there when I needed help."

this experience, and how he had learned a lot from me. I think this is true. It is amazing how different this was from my other school experiences and how much I did because they loved and trusted me.

Life on the farm was good and offered a lot of variety. Sometimes I might be out fighting a fire, another time using heavy equipment or helping with dry farming. Every night Don, my foster brother who was about my age, and I drove to the mountain to feed the cows and haul water. We had an old jeep, so we spent a lot of time traveling, catching turkeys, working on the irrigation canal, and roping and branding cattle. There was always something to do.

One time after school I hurried home to the old jeep. I had never driven before, and Don offered to teach me. I was driving up this steep hill when suddenly the jeep stalled. The gear was bent, and so Don crawled underneath to get it out and then put it back in. Somehow the brake slipped a little, and I tried to hold the vehicle in place but could not. I heard Don hollering all the way to the bottom as the jeep dragged him over the dirt and rocks. He was pretty shaky by the time I got it stopped and he let go of the back brace where the spare tire rides. That was probably what saved him.

Senior graduation picture, 1964. Jim: "Everything that happened to me there [placement] was a miracle—especially that I graduated." The pin on Jim's lapel represents four years of attending LDS Seminary religious instruction. This picture sat on his mother's bureau; whenever Jim looked at it, he felt: "I will not end it here." Subsequently he served a two-year mission for his church and continued with his education.

Another time Don was lying in a pickup reading his homework. I got a bucket of water and splashed it all over the windshield and into the side window, getting him wet. He leaped out of the truck and sprinted after me. I jumped a barbwire fence then waited for him to spring over. Just as he did I pulled some of the cut wire up and caught him on it, putting him into a somersault. He was so mad I took off until he cooled down. After a while I came back. He stomped his feet a couple of times and swore he would even the score with "Shash" or "Bear," the nickname he gave me because I was a good wrestler. He waited until I had forgotten all about what happened. A few hours later I was sitting on the trough and thought he was in the pickup truck. He sneaked up behind, grabbed me, and pushed me down totally underwater in the tank. We used to wrestle a lot, but there was no contest this time. Don was a big boy, a good football player and wrestler, and loved to challenge me because I was lighter. He weighed about 185 pounds to my 120. We had other wrestling matches where I made him really work hard for a win, but he got the best of me then.

My foster family is still my family, and I love those brothers and sisters as much as my own. I am still very close and miss them. When it was time for me to go home for the summer, my foster dad drove down to visit with my mother and father. Mom thought a lot of him, and Dad enjoyed talking to him because he was so outgoing. They got along well, my father saying I was lucky to have such a good foster family. Don and I still get together sometimes at Thanksgiving. He knows a lot about my brothers and sisters.

When the LDS Church ended the placement program I was upset. There were a lot of things said about it that were false. People accused the program of doing away with Navajo culture by removing the young people from it. That is not true. A lot of the people I know who were on placement are now principals, school superintendents, and in other leadership positions. They have sought out their culture, understand it, are good Navajo speakers, and continue to learn. Still the Navajo language, in general, is being lost. It was amazing what I saw, even on the reservation, working in education. A lot of the children coming from very traditional homes today cannot even speak Navajo. Some of them are raised by their grandparents, but very seldom do you find a child who is really fluent or knowledgeable about her own culture. There are just not that many. But a lot of the placement students who went through the program have done well in both worlds. It is sad to see this program gone, because a lot of children now do not have a place to go, especially if they come from broken homes. If they had the program, it could help them along as it did me.

Jim is not alone in his feelings about the placement program. To give an idea of how pervasive it was in his family alone, Jim's wife, Betty; his brother Charlie and his wife, Virginia; and their daughter Corilyn have all been on it, had a positive experience, and still hold to traditional beliefs as well as speaking the Navajo language. Each person's involvement varied in detail but followed the same pattern. For instance, Betty was raised in a traditional Navajo home near Gallup, New Mexico, by her mother (Angeline Watson), whom she characterized as being quiet and caring, and her stepfather (Warren Yazzie). She never knew her biological father, but both her parents were kind and loving. They also both fell into the trap of alcohol.

Betty's family followed many traditional Navajo practices in their home. Her grandfather performed a ceremony for her welfare, her grandmother taught her weaving and basket-making, and her mother schooled her in daily traditions. She now wishes that she had continued to weave but found basket-making totally frustrating and had little patience for it. Spinning and carding wool, making blue corn meal mush, kneel-down bread, and other traditional foods, and butchering sheep were part of her daily life.[5] Prior to Betty's reaching puberty, her grandmother often asked if she had yet had her first menses. Betty did not realize that she was supposed to tell her when she did; but once her grandmother knew, she insisted that there be a kinaaldá ceremony to celebrate reaching womanhood.

Although Betty's family lived and practiced traditional ways, they never commented on what she was to believe or provided strong direction as to right or wrong. Few Navajo or Christian teachings were ever given. With alcohol increasing as a problem in the home, the children went to boarding school near Twin Lakes, not too far away. Betty felt sad as a child to see her three brothers and five sisters removed from their home. The children lived totally at the boarding school, because the family did not have a car to pick them up for the weekend. Betty went there for two years, starting at age seven. Unlike Jim and Zonnie, she was able to speak Navajo in class, but the school also required English. She did not get into trouble and encountered no degrading forms of punishment like the ones they endured. Betty's wildest fling was "throwing peas under the table because I didn't like them. But I love peas now."

During the summer Betty returned home and was there when an elderly couple, the Ottleys, knocked on her door. They were Mormon missionaries, who began visiting regularly in the evenings to teach about their religion. Betty interpreted for her mother but had no idea about who these people were, where they had come from, or anything about their church. At the age of nine, she did not understand a lot. The couple sensed that the children were in a difficult environment because of the drinking and explained the placement program to the mother. Betty thought that they were social workers trying to help the family until they said they were serving an LDS mission and explained that she had to do certain things to be in this program if she wanted to go. Betty had no religion at the time, but what they taught she believed. Both her mother and father saw it as an opportunity that would give their children a chance. Every time they came to the house, the couple taught a new lesson. "I think they thought my family had a problem and that we did not belong to any religion. Finally they stepped in and taught us that there were things right and wrong, which is something we really did not know. I think it was best for us to go somewhere to a lot better environment so that we could do something with our lives." Betty, two sisters, and a brother ended up going on placement.

The more Betty thought about it, the better it seemed. Her baptism came quickly and placement followed, which lasted for nine years from elementary school through high school. She recalls:

When I first went on placement I thought, "Where am I going? Where are they going to take me?" I cried because I did not want to leave home. It was my mom and dad who wanted me to go instead of me saying it was a good idea. I couldn't say anything; this was what my mom and dad wanted, so I said okay. When I first arrived in Provo, I saw these huge mountains like I had never seen before. They made me feel really lonely. Once I got off the bus, they [placement workers] had us go into a building to take a shower, check our hair for lice, and put medicine in it. They did this to all of the children. Then we had to wait for our foster family to come and pick us up. It seemed like all of the other kids were taken before my family came and got me. I was really lonely, but this is what I had gotten myself into.

At first I was afraid and cried that I wanted to go home, but day by day I became accustomed to it. The first year I lived in Vernal with Mabel and Orlo Goodrich and their five daughters. The school was really small and very different from boarding school, where everything was kept simple. Here the classes were far more challenging. I really had to study and do my homework, but on the reservation we didn't have to do anything that I can remember. I was comfortable at boarding school because all of the other kids were "John Browns" or Navajos. The really hard part of placement was that suddenly you are put in a sea of white with different nationalities around you and no Navajos. I spoke Navajo well, so when I saw another Navajo, I would break into our language. I was not ashamed to say hello. Nowadays kids struggle with the language. A lot of them can understand it but can't respond. When I was in school some were ashamed to use their own language, but I was not. It was good to see them because there were not that many at the time.

I remember getting lonely and feeling Vernal was a really desolate place with nothing around. It just did not feel right. I liked the family I was staying with, but I could not feel comfortable there, although I still do not know why. So the next year I wanted to go somewhere else and ended up in Salt Lake City. I lived with Daniel and Vondra Dipo and another foster girl. Initially, there were just the two of us. My foster parents really cared, loved, and helped me, treating us both equally. I stayed with them for the rest of the time until I graduated from high school. I continued to see my family on the reservation every summer while I was on placement

Vondra and Dan Dipo, around 1971. This couple became Betty Dandy's foster parents on placement. They were educational and spiritual teachers who assisted Betty in making good choices.

and enjoyed being with all my brothers and sisters. They were also happy. Grandfather, before we returned to school and when we came home, always butchered a sheep as part of a celebration. He was glad when we were there. But if I had a problem I would go to my foster family. Even after I graduated from high school, I would see my family on the reservation but just to visit. As far as family was concerned, I called the Dipos more of a family than those who lived on the reservation. I visited my mom and others, but my real ties were in Salt Lake City. I continued to live with the Dipos when I went to beauty college, staying with them until I got married. They were happy with me and the success I had achieved.

My younger sister, Karinda, also joined their family, but in a different way. When she was about a year old, she developed a health condition. I told my parents that I wanted to take the baby back with me because I did not think they could care for it with its health problems. She was no longer nursing and could be fed by

a bottle, but I knew I could not take her on the placement bus. My foster parents
agreed to take care of Karinda, and my parents felt good about the arrangement.
She never would have survived if she had remained on the reservation. The Dipos
drove to my home and picked her up with the understanding that they would care
for her until her health improved but would not adopt her. She would return to my
family when she was better. It did not end up that way.

My natural family struggled financially; Karinda did not want to return to the
reservation so asked to be adopted when she was old enough. My natural mother
and father felt all right about it and never said they wanted her back. They died,
however, before she was adopted. The Dipos raised her in Salt Lake City, and she
now owns the home that was theirs, the Dipos leaving all their property to her. She
now has a big house and works in a flower shop that keeps her busy doing what
she likes. She will probably never go back to the reservation, since she never has
visited and does not speak Navajo.

The placement program provided a very positive experience for me and my
sister. The main reason that I feel this way is that my mother and stepfather never
taught me what was right or wrong, but my foster parents did. I believed in the
gospel of Christ and was converted. I cannot explain what made me think that it
was true, but what and how things were said gave me a feeling I had never felt or
known before in my life. My foster family said I had to pray about it to know if it
was true and what I really wanted. I did and felt that it must be the best way to
live. Something came over me, like a really good spirit, and I felt very happy.

In spite of Betty's strong attachment to the LDS Church, she still sees
power and value in traditional Navajo beliefs. When her daughter reached
puberty, Betty felt that it was important for her to have a kinaaldá.[6] The
young woman did not want to have the ceremony performed and felt embarrassed that she had physically reached womanhood. Betty did not push the
issue: "I was embarrassed too, but that's what my grandmother wanted. It
was good for me. I wanted it done for her. She wishes now that we had done
it." Having just come off placement, the daughter struggled to understand the
teachings about what and how a woman should be, the combing of the hair,
and the "smoothing" of a girl with a weaving batten, all of which is steeped
in traditional values. "I didn't really have any conflict even though I lived
some of the traditional ways. There's nothing wrong with that because this
is part of my first belief. Even though the church is different, it also seems
somewhat similar and both are good. It's good both ways."

Like Betty, Charlie had a positive experience on placement. He first attended boarding schools in Tuba City and Kayenta. He feels that he learned obedience, to respect people, and did not see himself as being abused or mistreated. While some people said it was cruel, "I don't think so. It was a teaching. All those people who went to boarding school are making a good life now. They learned about hardship from that experience." When he was in the sixth grade, his parents sent him on placement.

Mom and Dad wanted me to go. My dad said, "You need education and you can't get it here. These white men will help you a lot more than I can." That was one of the reasons I went on placement. Another was that while I was going to school in Kayenta there was a missionary who later became my foster brother. He asked me one time if I wanted to go and live with his mother and father in Morgan, Utah. I did not know what it was like, but I thought it sounded all right. The missionaries drove us from Kayenta to the church in Blanding, which was the only place to get baptized. That was when I was in the fifth grade; a year later I was at a squaw dance when they came and got me, put me on a bus with fifty other children, rode to Provo, then started my placement experience with the missionary's parents. Seven years later, in 1967, I graduated from Morgan High School.

During my senior year, I decided to go home, so I just left and went to my mother in Shonto. She really got after me for that, told me I should go back, and my family came down and returned me to Morgan. My foster parents urged me never to forget my language. "What you know as an Indian, you keep. It's a gift. Your second language is English; your first language you should treasure." I never lost track of my roots and never forgot what they said. Both my foster mother and father have passed away, but I still have contact with my foster brothers and sisters and their children. One of my children, Corilyn, also went on placement. I think the program is a teaching. I learned a lot about respect and things like that.

Virginia Adakai Dandy, Charlie's wife, went to Fontana, California, for her placement experience for three years, starting in the ninth grade. Before she left, her view of the world was limited to things close to home. As she described it: "I hardly went to Flagstaff. We didn't even know what was beyond the big hill close-by. We just knew around Tuba City where we went to school and Kaibito for church, but otherwise that was as far as we went for all of those years." It was culture shock going from the Navajo reservation to a community that had a preponderance of white and black people, although she felt it was a good experience to see "what was out there." Virginia lost her parents during her senior year, and her foster family offered to adopt both her and a younger sister. Her grandmother said no, afraid that she would lose the children permanently.

Even though I was worried about my brothers and sisters who stayed with my uncle, I came back because I wanted to play basketball. There was no competition over there so I played half of my twelfth grade year, but it was my choice to come back. I think that placement was a good experience. I was able to be independent and think for myself, while my LDS family did not force their teachings on me. At that time I did not understand very much about it. I really enjoyed my foster family and got close to them; now I've lost touch. I would have been happier if I had lived with someone my own age, but all they had were younger children and my main chore was to help care for and clean them. In general, the people Charlie and I know personally felt placement was a good experience and learned a lot. Many of them married and now live in white society. One of my daughters went on placement, but I wish I had not sent her. It was a nice experience for her and she lived with a nice family, but with my other girls going to school here, we knew exactly what they were doing. They played all kinds of sports and earned scholarships. Corilyn probably would have gotten a scholarship if she had stayed here, but there is more competition off the reservation.

Corilyn agrees that she missed the sports. She started placement in the fifth grade class in Willis, Utah, as the church-wide program decreased, graduating in 1992. Her foster parents had two foster boys and two girls, with a big gap between the youngest daughter and the other children. Corilyn felt that the parents wanted someone as a companion for her to grow up with, so they filed with the placement program. She wanted to go to Utah, but in order to be eligible she had to live in the state for a year. Blanding provided the opportunity of living with an aunt before going on placement. After the bus ride and her lice shampoo, Corilyn remembers sitting at the collection point, waiting to be matched through the picture that her foster family had received. She was so scared at this initial meeting that when her foster mother handed her a box of peaches, she ate them all but would not talk. She recalls: "It was nice. I was really quiet. They just really made me feel at home." While she seemed to enjoy the family, she missed her own and the familiar surroundings of the reservation. The small town of Willis did not offer a lot of sports until high school. Corilyn missed that part of life terribly.

It did, however, have a band, directed by her foster dad; everybody in the family played an instrument, so she took up the clarinet but had little enthusiasm for it. Corilyn felt as if she did not have much of a choice but solved that problem by running in track year-round. She never felt pressured to attend church. Halfway through her junior year, her foster mom had health issues, which required Corilyn to return to the reservation. She still keeps in contact with her foster family and visits them each year. In her words: "It was a good experience, other than the lack of sports. Now I feel like I have another family out there."

Having had family members in placement from its beginning to end, Charlie summarized the Dandys' perspective best:

I think going on placement taught what was right and wrong. As Dad used to say, there are really two roads—you choose the bad one or the good one, but if you choose the good, it is hard work. I think people who went on placement learned that. You understand life is going to kick you in the ass or else you're going to make it. I know what is right and wrong. I do not know where I would be if I had not had the opportunity of placement. A lot of friends my age are no longer around because this was a kind of education they never received and so went in the wrong direction. Even in my own family, as I watch my children, some go this way and some that. I look at it and think maybe I should have sent them all on placement.

Virginia chimed in:

I think placement was good and wish they still had it. I remember there were some kids who just didn't like it because of the religion or some things they were told they could not do. Before they went on placement they were able to do anything like drink and smoke. I think that's why they later became rebellious. Today there are a lot of children who need direction and the experience of being away from home. Everywhere I go there are kids who do not feel loved and do whatever they want. Their parents are always gone, rarely give counsel and not much love, just things. I say that because Navajos traditionally never said, "I love you" to their spouses or children. They just did something for them to let them know. They never said I love you. That's what I found.

Charlie continued:

Mom and Dad never gave up on us. They wanted us to be better so gave us a lot of support. Some people complain that placement brainwashed them and took away their culture. Dad would never turn around and criticize. He would say that what a person has accomplished, even through a little experience, means a lot in a lifetime. That's the way I think, too. There are a lot of returned placement students on the reservation who are very successful. Teachers, principals, government administrators, and others have done a lot for their people. They are very successful in their jobs. Dad always reminded us that if you are going to compete with the white man, you have to know a little bit about how he lives. That's the way I look at it.

CHAPTER SIX

OF MISSION, COLLEGE, AND MARRIAGE

The Ties That Bind

J im recalls:

During my time on placement, I attended church regularly, blessed the sacrament, learned in seminary, and even went out with a companion and taught people about the LDS faith. There was a lot to learn and I struggled to understand it all, but I became increasingly knowledgeable. Once I graduated I returned home and continued to attend church. At first I helped Dad farm but later got into a construction company from Phoenix, building the boarding school and teacher housing in Kayenta, where my mother lived. One day a man arrived with a load of lumber and asked for people to help. A large group of us spent the day unloading the truck, and by the end he asked me and another man to stay with him. The pay was good; I eventually joined a labor union but still felt something was missing and waited for my foster dad to come and pick me up.

One fall morning after the children had gone to school I sat eating breakfast and said to my mother: "What do you think I should do? What do you think of me going on a mission?"[1] She thought it was a great idea even though she knew I had a good job. She wanted me to do something like that to improve myself and felt that it would be good for my foster family, too. My father also was highly supportive. I would not have the temptations of alcohol, would become a teacher, and would follow good Christian values. Dad was traditional but told us, "Some day the Navajo way will be gone, replaced by that of the white man. You will live better if you know their language. I don't think you will learn all the traditional ways of living now that you are on your own. Whatever you want to be, follow that road." Once I became an elder and a strong church member, my father was

Jim flanked by two LDS missionaries who befriended him while he worked construction in Kayenta. His jacket indicates that he lettered in wrestling, football, and track—sports in which he would later coach children and teenagers in various schools on and off the reservation.

proud.[2] He never disliked anyone Christian and would ask them to pray for his family. When elders came to his home, after they prayed he would congratulate them for doing a good job and say, "Teach my kids your story."

I went to work and sat down with my construction boss, telling my plans and that I wanted to go back to Plymouth. I explained a little bit about the church and my boss decided he wanted to help me, so he did—a lot. He had been in construction in Phoenix much of his life, understood what this decision meant, and was happy I wanted to serve a mission. So I drove off and went straight to my foster home without even calling my foster dad. I knocked on his door early in the morning, walked in, and there he was as surprised as could be. I said, "Dad I'm ready to go out on a mission," and that I resigned from my job and wanted to do something for myself. He was so happy, he hurriedly dressed and we went to see the bishop. Once I submitted my mission papers it did not take long; but while waiting,

I worked for the sugar factory in Tremonton and accumulated quite a bit of savings to help pay for the mission.

I spent two years in the Southwest Indian Mission. My first companion was George P. Lee, a Navajo man who eventually became a general authority in the LDS Church. We both worked hard, starting in Gallup, New Mexico, teaching both English- and Navajo-speaking individuals. I did not know as much about the gospel as he did, so I really respected him and felt he was a good companion. My mission took me to Tohatchi, Canyoncito, Ramah, Window Rock, Fort Defiance, Crown Point, Inscription House, Shonto, and Navajo Mountain as well as to the Mescalero Apache reservation. My last assignment was in Tuba City, right near home. When I transferred to Canyoncito to reopen that mission, people were nice, but the chapter president was against the church a little bit. There was an old chicken coop that we cleaned out to live in with old pop machines for coolers. Life as a missionary on the reservation could be very primitive. Later I trained other missionaries, helping them to understand Navajo culture and to improve in their use of the language. Every month I'd have some new ones to help with their problems. I really enjoyed my mission, was well supported by both my families, and had a lot of good companions, families, and friends. People treated me well.

At the beginning of my mission, I spoke mostly English and did not interpret the lessons in Navajo unless the family only spoke that language. I focused a lot more on the English side of the Mormon stories, but there were times that I used Navajo beliefs to show how some interpretations are similar. Navajo examples and language helped the people to understand and form a stronger bond with the church. In some areas like Canyoncito there were a lot of very traditional people, so my companion and I tried to bring the two teachings together. For example, we based one of our discussions on the two sticks—one is the Bible and the other the Book of Mormon.[3] There were Navajo stories that we compared to those in the two books for our lessons. As much as I could, however, I used teachings straight from the Book of Mormon and the church. Sometimes the very traditional people had many questions, so I did a lot of interpretation to make sure they understood. It helped to know my culture's beliefs because the people understood them well. You really need to know a lot about both to be a good teacher, especially with the elders, because sometimes I got in a corner discussing some church lessons.

George P. Lee, my first companion, on the other hand, loved to debate with any minister or church, but I tried not to do that.[4] I will not force people to believe.

George was very demanding, telling people that they were wrong and that he belonged to the true church. What he was saying is that we should be really strong in our church, but debating and telling people they are wrong was not the best way. That was one of the reasons I thought I needed to respect my culture as well as the other churches. George eventually, when a man, became a church general authority but later fell away. He is no longer involved with the church. I think when the church stopped teaching the Navajo language in the Mission Training Center, President Spencer W. Kimball passed away, and George became involved with other things, he left the church and started worshipping on his own.

Spiritually, there is no way that I would go against another person's beliefs. I hold two beliefs, and it is very sacred to me to have both LDS and Navajo teachings. There is no way that I would turn around and disrespect my culture. I know that the Lord has helped me a lot, and that might serve as a way for some of my folks to come back into the church. Some people may reject my thinking and say, "How come he goes to the LDS Church and now he is having a Navajo ceremony?" That does not bother me; I just say they are both mine. If I believe that it is helping me, if I know that I am a good person, then I will be blessed. I do not see any conflict in that. During a Navajo ceremony, I take off my garments and do not use them again until after the four-day cleansing period.[5] Then I get cleaned up and put my "armor" back on. This is just the same as a person going to the hospital, where they take their garments off. I do the same.

My sister Marie provides another example of how Navajo spiritual gifts can be used by a person who is LDS. Her power of hand trembling came unexpectedly. One time her hand started to ache and shake a little when she was with a person who had come to her home to do a hand trembling ceremony for her. Suddenly she became a hand trembler when her hand started to work by giving signals. Navajos call this Tiníléí, a spiritual power from God given to a person to diagnose what is wrong with a patient.[6] Other people use a crystal to clarify their thinking and knowledge. My sister is not the only one to do this; most of my sisters are also involved in it. One time Marie used this power to find a person's keys. They were lost and nowhere to be found. She performed hand trembling and then told the family that the keys were out on the playground. One of the children had been playing, taken the keys, and put them underneath a slide. Sure enough the adults went to this place and found them under the slide, sticking out of the ground. Somehow the holy being Talking God communicates through the Holy Wind to the

Canyoncito, 1966, while Jim was serving during the first year of his mission. Jim both proselyted and trained Navajo and Anglo missionaries as they opened new teaching areas on the reservation. He is in his room holding a traditional dance outfit given to him by a Shoshone friend while on placement.

person using this power just as the Holy Ghost speaks to us. Marie said that it is really hard sometimes because the power can get so strong. My sister Lillie is also a medicine lady and does hand trembling. Both she and Marie are strongly into traditional religion but were also members of the LDS church at one time. Two other sisters, Ruby and Rosy, are still interested in the LDS Church, but I am the only one still heavily involved.

When comparing LDS teachings and those of traditional Navajos, I go back to the Twins' journey to their father.[7] They wanted to know who their father was and how they were born. Some Navajo beliefs are comparable to those of Christianity with an earthly mother and Heavenly Father. The Twins and Jesus, the Son, had supernatural powers they inherited from their parents. In both the stories, the earthly mother became pregnant, and the child's desire to know more about their fathers is similar. In each, the young men had to return to their father for help. There was evil on the earth killing people for no reason, and they needed assistance. That was one of the points when they learned who their father was, requested help, and took advice from their father.

I also taught about the four worlds beneath this one and this, the Glittering World, and compared them to the three degrees of glory. Just as there were four worlds before this one there will be four worlds after this earth life is complete. Moving through the darker worlds to the Glittering World is similar to what will happen at the time of judgment.[8] When the end of the world comes, people will be judged in the dark world if they do not make changes. Navajos started in the Black World and moved upward, and we believe that we are going back to the Black World. We will return there if we do not learn anything or if we do things wrong like killing people. The happy world is going to be the highest or the Glittering World. There were also twelve holy beings who led the people, just as we believe in twelve apostles who are also important leaders.[9] Sometimes we talk about the sacred mountains and how they are probably where the Lord stood when he taught the gospel. Holy mountains where people go today are still sacred. Navajo teachings are very similar to those of the Mormons. If you really get into them, they are very similar.

There are a lot of Navajo teachings that can be compared to LDS teachings and seen as compatible. For example, Talking God, a very powerful holy being, communicates through the Holy Wind people who speak to a person's spirit. It is through this that thoughts and impressions are put into your spirit. The spirit that is inside of you cannot be seen and is like what we are made of.[10] When we think about the air, we compare it with the wind; this is like the air that is inside of you, which is alive. The air inside a person is that person's image. Trees and mountains, rocks and water—everything, even things that are not viewed by Anglos as living— have this spiritual makeup.

Corn pollen used in blessings is like the sacrament but can also be an offering for help. It helps to give an offering, my sister always told me, to those things that can assist you. For instance, I have hearing problems, so she told me to find a beehive. Those little bees make a round nest from clay. My aunt taught that if a person had a hearing problem, he should take some pollen and give it to the home of the bee. The pollen plus a prayer to that little beehive will heal hearing. The bee nest is comparable to the ear with the eardrum and ear holes. By giving the bees the prayer and corn pollen and anything that guides you, you will heal. Every prayer and song is an offering for help from Mother Earth. Corn pollen is used to assist people, to help yourself, and to aid your immediate family. If a person has a really serious illness, she goes to a healthy plant, say a juniper tree, then gives it an offering and states that she wants to be healed.

My father and grandfather felt that I should stay with the things I had been taught in the LDS religion. There were teachings at that time that they did not want me to get involved in. To become a very knowledgeable and powerful medicine man, one has to experience evil in order to help others overcome it. There are a lot of things that hold power and must be controlled. Medicine men usually do not talk about the power that they have, just as with the temple; there are things that are not talked about outside of it because they are so sacred. Father said that in order for me to sit and listen, I would have to come back to the hogan or the sweat lodge to be taught, just the two of us. He did not want to be heard by others who have similar knowledge in what he had learned and then be tested or cursed by that person. Medicine men do not like to pass on to others some of the things that they have received.

My father said that where I was at the time was just fine and that I should remain with what I believed. "You are strong in that faith so better stay with it. There are things that you might otherwise practice that might hurt you." There were teachings that they were afraid of and did not want to pass on. It is said these teachings cost human lives. What is sacred may be given to others, but it can harm a person and that is why it is only mentioned under certain conditions. Even when I teach cultural things today, I have to be very careful with what I share with children. Some ceremonies can curse a person, bringing sickness or shock, and every song or healing can hurt you. It is so powerful in some ways that some medicine men are afraid it curses a person. If you stay with what you believe then you are fine. Father believed that there would not be any more real medicine men who knew a lot; soon the truly knowledgeable ones will be gone and the whole practice will phase out.

My grandfather worried about these things when I told him I wanted to be a medicine man. He knew that I would have to have experiences that were not good for me. In the Navajo culture there are teachings about both evil and good, and medicine men are the same way. There are some evil ways of a medicine person and some good ways. I think it is based a lot in what they are trying to accomplish. If you really have a testimony of the church and faith, you will be strong in the church; it is the same with Navajo religion. Their prayers were given to these medicine men and their herbs and medicines are good, just like those of a medical doctor. I think that's the same knowledge that a lot of Navajo medicine men use to heal the sick. Many of them can heal or help a person. This understanding prepared me for the church.

Other religions tell their people to get rid of all their traditional beliefs and practices and never go back to them. Some churches, when you become a member,

Just outside of Gallup, New Mexico. Jim: "I was a happy young man during those days and ready to teach the Gospel."

encourage a person to throw away his culture and strictly believe the Bible, then try to discourage the convert. They say, "How come you're a believer in the church and you're doing all of this?" There were a lot of challenges from other churches. People often asked me how I could quote a scripture where the Lord said there should be no other churches. I tried to teach but at the same time have respect for other's beliefs. I did not condemn them for being different, but they seemed to be living on the jealous side.

I have also noticed that parents do not want to have their children learn anything about traditional teachings and culture and the Holy People. I look at it this way. Why would the Navajo people be given this healing way of life, know what herbs to use, and have knowledge to help people if it was not good? They have survived this long and been a happy and peaceful people. There must be something good in it. My father always said that even one song or prayer could heal a very ill person quickly, right there. Today when somebody gets sick, all they do is put her in an ambulance and take her to the doctor or a hospital.

My father, even though he was very strong as far as his own culture and religion, taught that just because people have their Navajo culture, it does not mean that they cannot believe in the church. He felt it all came from the Lord and there was only one way, that the people have been blessed and healed by it, and that the very sacred songs cure. There was no conflict between Navajo and LDS teachings. God made the earth, answers prayers, grants forgiveness, and cares for people. There has to be somebody that is greater than all of us. Some Navajo stories teach we are all the children of God, and that is what Dad taught. Culture was especially important to me and is how I show respect for my people.

When my mission ended, I really wanted to stay on for another couple of years but could only extend for a few months. Once released, I thought about going to work on the reservation; but before doing so, I went home to my foster dad. My foster mother had just passed away, and he was lonely. Early one morning we were sitting at the table when one of my missionary companions, Elder Burt Hamilton from Alberta, Canada, came in. It was a miracle because I had been thinking about going to college and all of a sudden he appeared wanting to go to college and asking me to go with him the next year. So we visited Utah State University and Weber State College and then Brigham Young University [BYU]. There I found a strong Indian program and met some Indian students who were good singers. There were a lot of Native American students attending. People in administration offered to put us in that very day if we were willing to start. Burt and I were both lucky; he felt he would not have gotten in if he had not been with me and I was anxious to begin.

These were tough classes that went from early in the morning to late in the evening, since we started in November on a block program. Long hours every day on this condensed schedule made us so busy that the next regular semester seemed a lot easier. I decided to go into wrestling while paying my way through school by working for the physical plant on campus and at Jolly's Chicken nearby. I had a lot of fun in school and decided that my main goal was to go back to the Navajo reservation and get a job with the tribe. Even though I received my associate degree I kept going, taking more classes until I graduated with a bachelor's degree in elementary education in 1974. Teaching was one thing that I really wanted to do, but I also wanted to coach in a physical education program. My first teaching job was in Blanding.

While I was at BYU, I had an experience with different students who were struggling with issues. One morning just before summer vacation, a professor approached me, saying: "Jim, we have been thinking of you. If you don't mind, we would like your help. We've heard a lot about the things you do and we have

Anglo, Spanish, and Indian students who are really having problems at school. They would like to go out on a survival trip." So I took a group of them to the National Forest on the other side of Kanab. Each student had his own bedroll and that was it. All I had was a blanket and a little tent. I really wanted to put my teaching across to them and show them how to live outdoors without much of anything—maybe find a sheep or goat and show them how to dry the skin then sleep on it with a blanket.

Many of these students were awfully picky. They would not eat or drink what was out there, which created concerns about dehydration. One girl became very dehydrated, so I showed her how to get water by cutting into a barrel cactus. At first she would not drink any of it. I squeezed some juice out into a small container and handed it to her, saying, "Do you want to drink it just like that or do you want me to put some sugar in?" "What do you mean, Jim? I don't want to drink that." "Hey. You're going to die if you don't drink this." "Die!" She got on her knees and started to cry. "Please, you need to drink this. You are dehydrating right now and that is why you are sick." She drank it and about an hour later she was better and willing to try other things. Her whole body changed.

Some of the students had their own jerky, but I had nothing. We spotted a cottontail rabbit going into a sandy hole. I got a long stick and pushed it in, stabbed a little bit, and twisted. The rabbit started screaming, but I kept pulling and pulling. One of the students waited close by with a stick, but I told him not to use it, just grab the rabbit by the ears, spin it around, and the head would come right off. Two of them together grabbed it and spun it around, then we had rabbit to eat. We laid it on a flat stone in an open fire just as if it was a heating plate and the rabbit cooked beautifully. Everyone had a piece of meat and learned that when people get hungry they can eat anything. I next showed them how to dry rabbit by cooking it on stones. When it was ready, I put a little bit in my mouth with some water, because when the mouth gets dry and tries to chew jerky it gets sore. I showed them how to hunt other things but told them that I did not want to see any lizards or snakes because that was against my religion. If the Anglo students wanted to eat those things then that was fine, but not me.

We went a little way when one of the girls started screaming: "Look at that thing. What is that up in the tree?" All the students ran to where she pointed and saw a porcupine high above them. Everybody had slingshots, and one Anglo who was really good hit the porcupine in the head two or three times. I warned every-

one to get out of the way and watch out for its tail, but some did not listen. The porcupine crashed through the branches, swinging its tail, catching one of the boys and a girl on the side of their arms. Luckily it did not hit their face, but they were in pain and started to run. As soon as the porcupine dropped, we hit it just as you would a pig, right between the eyes. Next I showed them how to remove the skin. I cautioned them not to touch it but just to build a fire and put the whole animal in. This burned all the quills and hair off so that they could be removed with a little stick. The body was damp and the skin peeled nicely, so we dug a little hole and cooked it for a while with everything in it.

When it was ready we opened the pit and took out the meat, just as with a chicken. Everybody loved that porcupine. There were two Chinese girls that were eating away, and I had to keep telling them not to eat too much or they would get sick. They all got their share. When I opened the stomach they looked at me. "Oh Jim." I took out all the intestines, which actually are a really good part to eat. After I cut them out, cleaned them, and started eating, everybody wanted to have some. The same was true with sheep, which we butchered two or three times during the field experience. Everyone learned how to dry and jerk the meat. It is sliced very thin and hung on a net in the shade. Later the meat can be cooked or eaten just as it is, dried. Some of the students liked it plain, but I preferred it being cooked. Sheep jerky is good and easy to carry; I kept mine in a small mesh sack that allowed the air to circulate and kept it fresh. Later, once it was totally dried, I put it in a container, sealed it, and took it out only when I was hungry. When pounded with a stone, it becomes softer and easier to chew. It tasted good, and the students loved it.

One time we planted some corn, squash, and melons in a canyon not too far away from where some Navajo people were living, but we never returned to see if any of it was growing. That is more or less the Navajo traditional way of planting, letting nature take care of things, but there were some children nearby who tended it in our absence. After we had returned to BYU, a man stopped by and brought what had grown. He commented on how big the squash and melons had become. The students also learned about herbs and how to use them. Whenever some were picked, they received an offering for what the plant gave. I taught them that because in Navajo culture that is how things are done. There were some lengthy conversations that I got into with some of the students, talking into the night about why this was so. Brigham tea and owl's claws were also used. Owl's claw grows in rocky areas, is hairy and gray, and looks like its name.[11] When picked and dried, it makes a good tea that is better than a lot of peppermint teas. If a person has stomach pains, this will settle it. The students really liked learning about herbs. I burned cedar leaves to make a white ash, which was separated from the dark ash. Both types are ground and used for upset stomachs caused by high acidity. I took this when I had an ulcer, and it cured me.

Another thing that we cooked was dried potatoes and wild onions. On the mesas there are two types of onions. One of them has a flat head and is called crow's onion.[12] You are not supposed to eat that one because it has a little bit of poison in it. The same is true with mushrooms, so you have to be careful which of those are eaten. Some of them cause blindness if they get in the eyes, but others are just fine to eat. Mushrooms are hard to find on the reservation, but onions were plentiful and used a lot in rabbit stew. The students made it by stirring some flour in cold water so that it did not get lumpy then pouring the mixture into boiling water. Add the onions and some rabbit—preferably jackrabbit, which is better than cottontail—and let it boil then put in some desert herbs. Tumbleweed, when it first starts to sprout and grow, has little leaves that can be eaten like spinach. Add to this some fry bread and you have a really good meal.

When the group returned to BYU, the students had a different attitude because they had learned what they could do. The group served on a panel discussion where other students questioned them about their experience. "What did you do and how did you overcome all of the pressure?" There was one woman who talked about how she had had a really hard time with her boyfriend who had left her. He thought that she was too picky, did not know how to cook, and he left her because he felt she was spoiled. She wished he could see her now. The experience had helped her overcome a lot of her problems. She felt now she could do anything she put her mind to. Before this, even her family did not pay much attention to her but just gave her money to solve her problems. Later, but before she got married, she left a message at my apartment. She wanted me to come to her wedding. So I did and was totally surprised to be called up to the stand with the bride and groom and asked that I tell everyone how I had helped her. She is now a councilor at BYU, working in the multicultural program. People were so amazed that she had overcome many of her personal issues.

There were also Indian students who had been on that trip. One of the Navajo women only spoke English because she had been raised by a white family. I was hard on her, speaking to her in Navajo all the time. She got really mad, telling me to speak English, but I did not. She still talks about that experience and how she is now glad that I used our language even though she thought I had used strong discipline to get her to understand. There were also two Ute men, one of whom works today as an Indian counselor at the University of Utah; the other is a singer. In all, it was a successful experience for many people, including me. I never did it again because I was so busy and trying to find some time to relax while going to school. The next year when they asked me to go, I said no.

Going to school was also a good time to think about marriage. Dad had earlier taught me about Navajo traditional weddings and how the parents paid for the young lady, making everybody feel good about the value of what was going to take place. Dad compared it to when a person finds a poor horse, which is then taken care of and valued and turns into a sharp and beautiful companion. The more money that is paid, the better the bride will feel about herself and her husband and the more her parents are going to feel the young lady is important to the man. The parents have already searched around with their eyes, observing the prospective family. If the family has a young lady who works hard, is always busy, and has a lot of sheep, she is the kind of person they want for their son. He is not the one to make the choice; it is the family. The parents also want to give more for the lady to show that the son is not coming from a poor family.

Another important consideration for marriage and life is respect for the Navajo clan system. My mother's clan and the one most important to me is the Deer Spring Bitter Water (Bįįh Bitoo'nii Tódich'íi'nii).[13] This line came through my great-grandmother, her mother, and so forth—all are of the Deer Spring clan. On my father's side his main clan is Red House (Kinłichíinii) clan, but he is also related to the Red Bottom (Tłáashchí'í) and Many Goats (Tłizíłáni) clans.[14] They are branches of the Red House clan. When you travel to Mexican Hat you see a lot of red stripes of sand and rock running across the mesas, which is part of the origin of the names of these clans. All of them become my clan, so anybody who belongs to them is my relative.

When I was growing up the clan was important to everyone. My grandmother always taught: "You are of the Deer Spring Bitter Water clan; do not forget about it because that is what you are. When you go out into the world you will find relatives—your cousins, sisters, or aunts on your mother's side, so you have to learn to respect them and their clan. You will never intermarry with a Bitter Water (Tódich'íi'nii)." For instance, if I was in Gallup and met a young lady who belonged to my clan, I would never intentionally date or attempt to marry her because she is considered a relative. On my father's side, it is the same within the immediate family. In either case there is no intermarriage unless on my father's side the person lived far away and was not closely related.[15] So if I were in Salt Lake and met a lady that is from my father's clan, I would date her to make sure she was not coming from the Red Lake area. If she comes from somewhere else, then it is all right to be with her. But my grandfather on my mother's side was an Edge Water (Tábąąhá), so they become my grandfather and my great-uncle.[16] My grandfather's father on my mother's side was Táchii'nii and my future wife, Betty, was from that clan, but I married her even though we are somewhat related.[17] I call her shinalli, so she becomes my mother-in-law. She always says not to make fun of her in-laws to our children. My mother was all right with our marriage because Betty was not from my immediate family. I would never date someone who is too close to my family.

A lot of people do not feel this way and will not marry if related to the father's clan. I would not date somebody who belongs to the Red House clan because they are my father's relatives. When I introduce myself, I refer to myself as Deer Spring Bitter Water and my father's side as Red Bottom or Red House clan. They will already have heard my mother's side, so I do not need to introduce my grand-mother, but I do my grandfather, who was Edge Water. I think it is so important to know your clan well because they are your relatives and you can draw those people to you. They come up and greet you saying, "I didn't know you were my cousin," or things like that. I have a lot of respect for those old ladies I meet in the store when they say, "Hello, son." I do not know who they are but I respect their way.

Members of your clan should be very good to help you. These relationships, the assistance and clan system, are sometimes compared to a stalk of corn. One side of the stalk will be your mother's side and your father's the other. My father said that Anglos and many other nationalities can only trace relatives back four generations, but the Navajo people have relatives that go back forever. It doesn't matter where you are, you will have relatives. I have a lot of support because I'm a Bitter Water and so when I meet someone who belongs to my clan, they call me "my brother," "my uncle."

These teachings about clans and marriage are important; however, there were other traditional practices that I did not agree with. My grandmother was very interested in a particular girl I was to wed and had made arrangements with the family. She had given the girl's family a lot of our family silver and turquoise, a very acceptable form of wealth, with the idea that the wedding would take place on a set date.[18] When the day arrived, I was nowhere to be found. I had fled to Flagstaff, where I stayed with some Mormon elders for five days. Once I returned home, I found an angry bees' nest of relatives; my grandmother had lost her turquoise, which would not be returned and she could not ask for it, and I was just as determined to select my own wife. As Charlie put it: "They got rich and we got poor."

My foster dad and mother also could not agree on what to counsel me. They "got on each other's case" because my father always wanted me to marry a Navajo and keep the ethnic lines pure, the culture intact, so that "your children are going to be proud to be Navajo." My foster mom, on the other hand, told me to follow my heart and did "not care what people said; I care that you have made the choice; if you love someone go for it and you'll never make a mistake. If she is a member of the church go for it." My foster dad just could not agree, and I was in the middle having a hard time knowing what to do. For three years, I dated an Anglo woman, and the relationship became progressively serious. One day I came to my father's home at Red Lake. He was not too happy with the direction I was heading, just like my foster dad, but my mom was pretty indifferent and did not seem to mind. It was at that point, as the two of us prepared for marriage, that I finally decided to give it up. It was really hard but seemed best.

I met my future wife, Betty, while I was on my mission, but I never knew her that well and we were not really close. Later I ran into her, and that changed my whole life.

Betty agrees but adds:

When he was on his mission my sisters and I used to give him a hard time. We teased him; he would tell us about an approaching event, and we would say that we would go with him but then hid when he showed up. Because he served in my part of the reservation, I would run into him when I returned in the summer from placement. The first time my grandmother saw him, he wore a big concho belt. "That man is rich," she thought, and probably would have married him, saying, "I want a man like that." Back then the missionary dress code was not as strict as it is now. Grandma really liked him; Grandpa didn't care.

The next time I saw him after he finished his mission was when some of the children on placement went to Lagoon, an amusement park, and I went with them.

After Jim and Betty's marriage in the Salt Lake Temple, 1968. Within a year and a half of this photo, the Dandys adopted ten of Betty's siblings, who would otherwise have been put in foster homes. Jim's response: "We are young enough to take them; their family will not be broken apart." After the experience: "Without Betty I never would have made it."

He was there and I talked to him, thanking him for getting me back to school so that I could finish. I was glad to have graduated. Later he asked if he could take me home and meet my foster parents. I agreed. We had a good visit with them, and then he started to see me every weekend. I was going to a cosmetology school and he was at BYU, and so we were both busy and available only on Saturdays and Sundays. One time he said, "I'm going to really surprise you when I come next time." I wondered what he was talking about; but when he came he handed me a little box, so I asked, "What's this?" He told me to look, but I had no idea it would be an engagement ring. We had dated all of four times, but I accepted. At the age of nineteen on August 13, 1968, right after I got out of school, I got married.

The first time I met my mother-in-law we got along very well, but his dad did not really like me until we started to have children. Then things changed. I think initially he wanted to have Jim marry someone from around his home area, not from some place he did not know. After our first grandson, he really liked me.

Jim also pleased his foster dad by marrying a Navajo:

He thought that was one of the greatest things that ever happened. He was so happy, and I feel to this day that the advice he and my father gave me was right. I was still a little bit on the traditional side, thinking like a Navajo, and that is one of the reasons why I wanted to have someone like Betty with me so that we could share things from our culture and not be ashamed. Now we can do anything together. When I took her home my whole family loved her. I have cousin brothers who are married to Anglos and they are doing well, but I am glad that my family's teachings have taught me how to be a successful person. I really respect my culture a lot more and my wife, children, relatives, and people support me in this. I can go anywhere with Betty because both of us have the same kind of background; and even though we have had a rough life, we are happy that we raised our children the way we have.

We lived in Provo for three years and had our first child, Jim Michael Dandy, before moving to Blanding. We were passing through the town on our way to see my family in Shonto. A cousin we met by chance lived in Blanding and mentioned that there was a job opening in the San Juan School District and that I should apply. I did, was hired, and have lived there ever since. After that we started having the rest of our children—Travis Eli, Raquel, Delwin, Shiloh, and Nate. All through this time, I tried to follow the advice given to me by Apostle LeGrand Richards, who married Betty and me in the Salt Lake Temple.[19] He said: "Brother Dandy, I hate to see you lying under a wagon, letting your wife herd sheep or haul wood. If you're going to do that you might as well baby sit. You are the one who should bring home the bread. Don't both of you work. One has to stay home with the children where the real responsibility is. Betty should be inside taking care of the house and the children. I hate to see you having your wife work." So Betty did not get a job until the children were old enough to be on their own. This plan worked out well, and I think the kids have had a good life and feel the love of their parents. This was along the same line that my father taught.

As with most parents, there were times when I had challenges with my boys. They were pretty good kids, but I worried about some of them in high school getting their hair cut and wearing earrings. At one point, I sat them down and told them that earrings were not acceptable. My mother was sitting there and said in a very soft voice, "Son, a long time ago your great-great-grandfathers all had pierced ears and wore turquoise. There is nothing wrong as long as a person has both ears pierced, not just one. With only one ear pierced, it means that a person is half and *half, half lady and half man. That is what one represents. I just want to say this to my grandchildren, but if they do not get out of hand, it's fine. If they start putting earrings, three or four in an ear, that's no, no. There must be one turquoise stone or silver in each ear." Mom was pretty clear about what they really were going to be representing. They got their ears pierced.*

Today my children are all employed and doing well. Jimmy is working at Monument Valley High School as a football coach and driver's education teacher, going out to Navajo Mountain and Whitehorse High School. Travis Eli works in the Grand Canyon as a hotel maintenance person and used to entertain tourists with traditional singing and a dance group. We went to the program one time and really enjoyed it. My daughter Raquel used to live in Connecticut, where she served as a nanny for ten years. Because Betty had some health problems, she returned to take care of her. Now she works with a physical therapist and interprets for the workers and patients. Delwin works at the White Mesa uranium mill and likes his job. Nate is a plumber in Blanding, and Shiloh is in Salt Lake City working for the Ford Motor Company. All our children speak Navajo and are LDS, but not all are active in the church. Most of them are doing well in church because we raised them in it ever since they were little. We all have struggles; that's life.

As Betty counsels her children, all of marrying age, she has stronger feelings about interethnic marriage.

When I was dating, my parents encouraged me to marry a Navajo. Now I see it is better. I felt more comfortable marrying a Navajo and encourage our children to marry within the race. One of my boys said it was hard because it seemed that whenever he met a girl, she was always related to him. Wherever Navajos go we are related to somebody. When they meet a girl, they are not supposed to marry her if she is from the primary clan. Mine is Táchii'nii, Red Running into the Water clan, my first clan. But they always seem to meet a girl whose first clan is their first clan. They say, "Mom, there is nobody that I can marry." "Well, you haven't looked around. There are a lot of Navajo girls." We encourage them to find a Navajo because we can tease, we can speak our language and do things together. They will know what is going on. It is hard for an Anglo spouse to go down on the reservation and talk and hear everything in Navajo and to joke around. In that situation a Navajo feels more comfortable.

Jim attributes much of his child-rearing experience to his father. He is proud of his culture and proud of his grandparents and family. Just like his father, he raised a lot of young children who were not officially his responsibility. In Red Lake, even though it was a small community, a lot of the neighbors' children spent time with Albert. They would go out to the cornfield, where he put them to work. When Jim was older, he wanted to follow suit, but his father grew concerned. Shortly after Jim and Betty married, a number of children on Betty's side of the family were in need of a home. In Navajo culture the family always lets the oldest brother or sister know that they could have these children if they did not want to see them adopted and wanted to care for them. Betty and Jim decided to take many of them in, all of whom were babies or little children. Eventually there were ten of them.

Jim remembers:

Raising them was a challenge, especially since we had not been married that long and yet had so many children and teenagers to care for. I'm glad I did it because I did not want to see them spread everywhere, so I wanted to keep them. We were raising these foster children when Dad came up to me and said, "Why don't you focus on your own kids, son? You've got too many children here already, how about your own?" I said, "Dad, you taught me to do this. You raised a lot who needed help, so I'm just like you." He smiled, walked away, and did not say any more.

CHAPTER SEVEN

EDUCATION AS A LIFE'S WORK

Serving the People

Armed with an education degree completed at Weber State College, now a family man, and with a clear understanding of important aspects of Navajo culture, Jim began his career in Utah working for the people of the Four Corners region. After being hired by the San Juan School District as a parent coordinator for the Head Start Program, he trained parents in education and child development classes, became a liaison counselor in the community, and coached wrestling at San Juan High School. For thirteen years he worked with a School Community Group (SCG) to foment change at a time when the roles of the county school district and federal Indian programs administered by the BIA were shifting. As these programs developed, Jim assumed a larger supervisory role, becoming the link between Navajo communities and the district, which in the 1970s were embroiled in a costly lawsuit to establish education facilities on the Utah portion of the reservation. Parent involvement, a buzzword of the 1970s and 1980s, became increasingly important if federal assistance for construction was to be obtained. Jim's school community group became strong partners by ensuring that administrators heard the Navajos' voice. He drew representatives from on and off the Utah reservation.

The lawsuit, known as *Sinajini* v. *Board of Education*, began in 1975 and resulted in the building of an elementary school and high school in Montezuma Creek (1978) and a high school in Monument Valley (1983) as well as the establishment of bilingual/bicultural programs at each institution.[1] Jim recalls:

The district hired me to work with the communities to build those high schools, Monument Valley, Montezuma Creek, and much later at Navajo Mountain, as well as helping with some of the elementary schools. Around 1975 I received training for a month in Portland, Oregon, along with other people from the school district. I had been hired to help solve the problem of so much busing—we were transporting students from the far side of Oljato and Montezuma Creek almost into Teec Nos Pos and Red Mesa to Blanding. The Navajo people from those areas felt they were being left out and their children were not receiving what they needed. That's why they decided to build schools down there. The training we received was in problem solving. I organized the SCG, composed of people from all different agencies to be representatives. There were also two members from the state board of education who came from Salt Lake City once or twice a month to our meetings. At first we gathered almost every week, which meant a lot of travel all over the Utah portion of the reservation as well as to Window Rock, Arizona, headquarters of the Navajo Nation.

The group was very successful. As we started working on the first high school, some of the people in the communities mistrusted the district to improve their education. The SCG started working on a needs assessment for each community's education plan. Anything would be better than busing all of those children to Blanding, but getting the work done was a tough job. We were not gods, and no miracles appeared. Some people kept telling us that there was no way a school would be built, suggesting that we would only get started then give up and go home. But the SCG members were strong people, and they continued through to completion. I spoke often with leaders in the San Juan School District and encouraged them to do all they could to avoid the lawsuit, but they did not listen, even though both the Navajo Tribe and the school district were on my side. Eventually the district said it had no money left to build an elementary school in Mexican Hat and that the SCG had better move on, but we kept working. We had started and would not stop.

The SCG was always on the road. One of the first tasks was to find a place to build the school. For example, in the Monument Valley area there were four possible sites. One was at the junction not too far from Train Rock, two places near Oljato, and one at Mexican Hat. The school board liked this last site because the electricity and water were already there. Navajo tribal representatives supported the school board, but we wanted to put it where the people desired, in a more central location in Monument Valley. The SCG battled for the site and won. Monument Valley was to be the place. The district took two busloads of people to visit schools at Richfield, Kanab, Window Rock, and elsewhere. At that time Page had

School Community Group in the Monument Valley area, 1975. Left to right: Tom Atene, Buck Navajo, Kee Yazzie Clitso, Robert Angle, Bud Haycock, Roy Atene (chairman), Sam Black, and Gregory Holiday. Jim trained the year before in Portland, Oregon, then worked with these men on educational and community issues.

a new school as did Tuba City, which we also toured. By the end, we had visited all of these facilities and the people had learned a number of things. First, they saw that the San Juan School District had better cultural awareness and Navajo language programs than these schools and wanted to see this continued and built upon. They also felt even more strongly that the high school needed to be constructed in Monument Valley.

The district still resisted the SCG because on one side there was the Sinajini lawsuit saying that schools needed to be built on the reservation while the other side stated there was no money. Members of the school board continued to support the high school being built at Mexican Hat. Federal officials conducted tests there and concluded that it was not the best place to build. Nearby there was a mill tailings site that had been active during the uranium industry days about twenty years before and problems with radiation persisted. Even though an elementary school had already been built there, people were saying now that a high school should not be. The study indicated that the radiation spread in about a two and a half mile radius, placing the school in the center of the concern. The federal government has since cleaned it up; but at the time, the site was dangerous. The school board and others did not listen. They would rather build a facility where it would be cheaper because the electricity and water were already there. They did not seem to care about the children.

Our committee grew with representation from many public agencies and private individuals. Social Services, hospitals, schools from other districts, the State Office of Education, and the Navajo and Ute Tribes all helped to organize and share ideas and ways to obtain funding. I thought it was good because it strengthened the people's voice and we listened. One time a representative from as far away as Washington, D.C., attended our meeting. But above all we listened to the people who lived in that area. The Monument Valley site received their votes during an election year because of its central location, and so that is where the school was built.

There were times when lawyers involved in the lawsuit came to our meetings, but we never said anything negative. We performed a second needs assessment to make sure there were enough students in the area to be served once the school was built. There were sufficient students eligible to attend; in fact, after the doors were opened, enrollments proved to be higher than anticipated. The schools in Kayenta were also concerned, afraid that a new school in Monument Valley would take some of their students away. If enrollment dropped, their funding could be jeopardized. So they joined the SCG by sending a representative to our meetings. This was particularly important because the federal boarding school in Kayenta enrolled a lot of students from Douglas Mesa, Mexican Hat, and Monument Valley. These surveys had to ensure that there would be enough children in the future to keep the schools busy.

When working with people, you really need to let them know what is happening if you want their help and support. A better education for the children in the area was the goal, but it would also provide jobs in the future. The Navajo people are always supportive of something like that. They are often suspicious about things until they fully understand the outcome. A problem arises when these goals interfere with others pursuing the same things. Kayenta schools did not like losing their students to the Utah school district and vice versa. This really became an issue when parents started choosing one school over another because of programs, educational opportunities, or family situations that made one more desirable. Both the BIA schools and the San Juan School District offered services in the Monument Valley area, providing a choice. Their budgets fluctuated with numbers, and so when students went to another school, in a sense, they took their financial support with them, creating chaos with planned finances. The school community group was concerned and wanted to keep all the Utah students in-state instead of having them go to an out-of-state facility. Some parents complained that there were not the programs they wanted for their children and transferred them, but generally the differences were worked out and both schools had enough students.

This was in the future. The main issue of having enough money to build the school in Monument Valley had to be answered. We received word that the seven million dollars needed to accomplish the task had already been spent in building an elementary school or invested elsewhere. We went on the warpath, which led us to the next school board meeting. The uninvited school community group walked in and protested. We told them that they had organized us so they should listen and all of us work together. Again we heard there was no more money. How could this be? So I talked to Lynn Lee, a local grant writer for the College of Eastern Utah, and he contacted Tom Sawyer, a member of the Utah Indian Affairs Commission, who used to work in Washington, D.C., had political connections, and knew of funds available from federal sources. Lynn Lee and Tom Sawyer did a lot of work for us. They obtained the money so that Monument Valley High School became a reality. The school district also found funds for an auditorium and football field. We worked hard to get that school.

Before construction actually started, there were some people who needed to be relocated away from the site. One incident that hurt me was when the daughter of an older lady who was ready to sign papers for her removal angrily approached us. The daughter insisted that her mother would not sign the tribal forms necessary for relocation. The Navajo Nation was going to help her with a home until the daughter grabbed all the papers and ripped them up. She hit her mother across the face and told her she was a crazy woman, asking why she was giving away family land. There were other things that happened after I left, but I was really angry and could not believe what I had seen. The daughter blamed me for these people having to move and taking away their land. The mother, however, was totally happy with where the school was to be built and with the arrangements that had been made for her. Most of the people in the community really supported the school, so eventually they signed the papers.

The SCG was a very good group to work with and never gave up on the difficult tasks it faced. There were a lot of very smart Navajos, although they did not have formal education, who worked well together, especially the elders. They were kind and careful about how they dealt with people, but we still had fun. A number

Jim as liaison counselor and San Juan School District's process facilitator for the School Community Group in his Monument Valley office, 1984. Jim proved an effective communicator who was able to combine leadership from various Navajo communities into an effective planning effort that represented the People.

of them came into the schools to counsel students and assisted in developing cur-riculum programs that taught Navajo language and culture. I was very hurt when the SCG program ended and felt it was a mistake. Recently there have been efforts to start a parent involvement program the way it used to be, but the school district is still having a hard time.

In 1983, when Monument Valley High School opened its doors for the first group of students, I accepted a position to help with the new school and serve as the athletic director. Although I joined the staff for one year, I ended up being there for eight. With me as the wrestling coach, we put together a team that won the regional championship and took second in state its first year. Betty served as a family liaison counselor for the school district, encouraging and advising students and their parents to do what was necessary to succeed in formal education. She kept track of students' progress, excessive absences, and gaining parental consent for various activities. All this time we still owned a house in Blanding, so Betty got to the point where she wanted to return. The school district offered a different assignment, and so we left Monument Valley.[2]

Betty really enjoyed her eight years on the reservation but welcomed returning to her former life:

I think Blanding is friendly. Everybody we've met is friendly, the Anglo and of course the Navajo. They are the same way to us. A lot of Navajos and Anglos think Jim is a real good man. We get along well. I never had anyone say anything to my face that was against us, but some people say that LDS Church members are really prejudiced. The Anglos can be really friendly, but they also can say things behind your back. But I have never heard anybody say bad things about me or my kids. It's not that way with me. I am now outspoken like my husband and get along with people.

Jim continues:

When I moved back to Blanding in 1990, I taught Navajo culture, worked as a liaison counselor traveling to different educational facilities on the reservation, and coached at the high school and middle school. That really kept me busy. As head wrestling coach in Blanding, I had a different experience than when coaching wrestling, football, baseball, or other sports on the reservation. The Navajos do not see sports as something important enough to be taught. "How are you going to make a living with that?" they would ask. Wrestling helps keep people in good physical shape, while skill in it is not based on size. But Navajos do not look at it that way, and parents do not support their children the way white people do. Anglos are there cheering for their children because they want them to go out into the world and be motivated.

Navajos view wrestling as just another game that will distract their children from going to work or finishing school. They see the child staying away from home and unavailable to herd sheep, get water, or haul wood. The student just plays basketball or wrestles all of the time. It is hard for them to support him, and they do not realize it is all part of being in school. Some of the kids I know actually remained in school because of a wrestling program. Students involved in this sport learn to work and be competitive, which spreads to other parts of their education such as reading and math. It takes a lot of work to really understand those subjects, and the same is true with success in an athletic program. You have to be alert and motivated. It took a lot for me to get Navajo parents to support their students until I had them come in to see what their child was learning. That really helped a lot. Once they got used to it, they really followed wrestling. For instance John Yazzie Holiday never missed his sons' matches after he saw what they were doing and how it was helping them. He was really dedicated to having them succeed once he caught on.

As an assistant in the Parent Involvement Program (1972), Jim wanted to integrate Indian children into an all-white football program. Facing explanations that the teams were filled and the children were too young or too light, he set about recruiting from the local Navajo and Ute population. Fifty children enrolled, causing concern about having too many Indian children. Eventually integration was no longer an issue: everyone was welcomed.

As the head wrestling coach in San Juan High School, the first question the administration had was how I felt about teaching white students. Their concern was discrimination. I assured them that I would treat everybody the same, whether they were white or Navajo, there would be no difference. I was actually a little bit stricter on the Navajo kids, but everyone worked hard for whatever position and weight class they held. Still, one time a white student wrestler whose father was in administration went home, telling his dad that he was not going to be able to compete. He had not stayed in shape or practiced and so was beaten twice. I let another wrestler take his position. I had given him two chances because he was a varsity wrestler, but he had lost both times. His dad talked to me, asking why one of his sons was not wrestling in a tournament, and so I explained how he had lost his spot and how the person who took it came to practice every day and worked hard. The administrator's son felt I was putting a Native American first, showing favoritism. I said that was not the case and followed through with the plan. The son learned his lesson and came back strong; he refused to be beaten for that spot again. Later the dad apologized, said that I was right, no longer had concern about my coaching, and thanked me for helping his son improve.

Still things did not go smoothly. There were two incidents that really bothered me. The first was when I had a wrestler who had won his regional matches and was about to go to state. Between the two matches he slacked off enough so that I would not let him go. I sat down with the staff and told the principal and the assistant principal that I did not like doing it but that the student had broken the rules. When we were ready to travel to the match, here was the boy sitting on the bus. I said no and asked the office what he was doing there. I explained that as the head coach that I had made a decision and that the principal had agreed to it. My assistant coach, however, had approved his going, and soon the boy's parents were in the office. I gave up. I felt I was not getting the necessary assistance from the principal or the assistant principal just because the parents were shedding tears. I did not say any more, but I had not been supported. The boy did well, taking second place in state.

Another incident of nonsupport happened during the same season. The high school administration had assigned an assistant coach not of my choosing—in fact I had no say at all. At first we worked well together, but as time progressed there was more friction. We did all right until the wrestling tournament in Wayne County. Two of our wrestlers—one an Anglo, the other a Navajo—got in trouble. At the end of the matches the two boys, as they packed their things, found a video game on the bleachers. Both of them saw it, decided to take it, and put it in the Anglo boy's bag. They were already on the bus when I came out of the gym and saw police officers climbing aboard and searching the bus. Because the white boy was on probation, the Navajo boy switched the video game to his bag, where it was found. The assistant coach grabbed the Navajo and pushed him against the bus, threatening: "We don't want you. You did a bad thing and we don't want you to be in our program." I told the coach he could not do that and asked what had happened. "These stupid guys stole a video game. They just barely took it out of so-and-so's bag and he was the one who put it in there." I said, "Even though he's done wrong, you shouldn't be handling him like that." He asked if I was going to let the young man get away with it and said he did not want him in the wrestling program. That was my decision not his.

The police were still on the bus but should not have been, and I told them so. There was more conflict as I commanded the coach to leave the boy alone. Angrily he tossed his notebook across the floor, and the quarrel continued. By now the police were dragging the Navajo boy to the squad car, pushing him inside. I told them not to treat this young man like that because he was not resisting in any way. "He's a thief." "Where's the other boy who was involved?" "That one is not involved. He's the one who put it in his bag. The other boy told us where it was." The Navajo boy knew at the time that the white boy had originally put it in his own pack. They both knew about it. I insisted they were both involved and to take only one person was not right. The officer told me to leave then threatened to put me in jail. I really got mad and told him to take me if he wanted, that I had done nothing wrong, and that I was concerned about the boy. He took the handcuffs off but promised that the boy would not get away with it. We climbed onto the bus and left, but it was a quiet ride home. The next day both boys were suspended from the team. I reported the incident to the principal, attempted to apologize and work things out with the assistant coach, and explained what had happened, but no one was happy.

After thinking about it a lot, I decided to resign and give the team a fresh start, even though I had three of my sons wrestling that year. Resigning from the program was my decision, but I felt that there was no support from the administration. I stayed calm and just walked away without making a big fuss about resigning. I am glad I did. They never said anything and just ignored me. I did, however, feel badly that I did not coach my boys. They wanted their dad to help them, but I told them to stay with it and do their best. I had a lot of people come to my house to ask what had happened and why I was not coaching. I just told them I retired.

Jim was not through with teaching. He spent time at the Blanding Elementary School for a year then moved to Kayenta and taught sixth grade for two years, but it was too far to travel. He next served as head wrestling coach at Whitehorse High School and taught at the elementary school in Montezuma Creek before working for the Bureau of Indian Affairs in Aneth for three years. This was a productive time that passed quickly. Concerning teaching, Jim said:

I really enjoyed being in the classroom, especially in the elementary schools. I did a lot of teaching in which I used Navajo curriculum that I helped develop for the San Juan School District. As a Navajo teacher, there are traditional elements within the culture that can cause problems. Some instructors are nervous about certain topics. For instance, the practice of dissecting a frog shows disrespect to that creature but needs to be done to teach certain principles in biology effectively.[3] There are ways you can work with parents to explain these kinds of things and why the students have to do it. Parents need to know that their children will never be exposed to something that is not good. A blessing may be given so they can participate, but a teacher still has to be careful. The reservation is very powerful, and the Navajos will work against you if you are not sensitive to these things.

My father always felt that each nationality is given its own beliefs. That is why he supported cultural awareness. He said: "Son, I want you to know all these sacred songs that I have taught you, but do not teach them in the classroom. They can harm somebody's child. Any ceremony can affect individuals and make them sick. When a child comes from a very traditional family, he may be viewed as superstitious, but remember that belief and faith affects a person. It is like a shock, even with a song, a child can go into shock." That is why a teacher must be able to communicate with the family to make sure that what is taught in the classroom is all right. There are a lot of medicine men who come into a school and start singing. My father was always careful about that and told me to avoid it. But there are social songs that have no curse on them. Those that do are very strong, very powerful, and could kill a person. Those are the ones Navajo people are careful about.

My parents and grandparents taught that they would not be there for the children all the time; but until they died, they should be the ones to teach the children. Today many of the elders are gone and those who are not do not have or take the opportunity to teach about their culture. When I was growing up, my situation was different because my mother and grandmother always said they would not live forever and so I should learn as much as I could. "You ask your grandfather, ask your dad, ask your uncle for more knowledge about these things. Learn what you can then you can pass it on to your children. If you don't you're going to be handicapped the rest of your life. Your children are not going to succeed. You are not going to be able to depend on your grandmother or grandfather. You need to learn for yourself as much as you can. You don't know what's going to happen to your grandparents. Be prepared." That is what they always taught. Now I believe what they said.

Members of every generation coming up depend on their parents to teach. But today mothers and fathers do not sit there and teach their children. In my case, my father suddenly got in a car accident and passed on. The grandchildren have lost him, and my brothers and sisters have a harder time. They woke up, but he

The San Juan School District sponsors the Ndahoo'aah ("Relearning the Culture") Program at Monument Valley High School. Jim has been instrumental in sharing his traditional background in curriculum development and programming to encourage Native American pride. He also has worked extensively with role models like football player Steve Young (not pictured), Nedra Roni (director of Nu Skin) in the center, Dale Tingey from BYU to her left, and curriculum specialist Don Mose Sr., to her right.

was gone. Now they are going to have to step into the place of their father and do the teaching; but many families cannot, and so it is left to the schools. I know this is very hard on families and hard on the children to adjust to their own parents' teaching culture and language because many of them do not know it. I have always taught my children, because even though I grew up a lot different from them, I held onto my culture. Today this is very important to me, and I will not just let it die and handicap them. I have told them that they need to teach their children how to speak Navajo. That is their responsibility. I think that is how it should be as far as teaching.

I got into curriculum development when I first came to Blanding to work as a Head Start parent coordinator. I assisted both the school district and the Head Start program. The district received a grant to develop Navajo Coyote stories and teachings about different animals. I helped with the music, the movies, and putting informational books together. When we were working on the traditional Coyote stories recorded on video, I was partly involved in acting out parts, in creating

Monument Valley Regional Championship Team, 1984, coached by Jim Dandy.

my own music, and using some of the stories that my grandparents and father had taught. I shared them with the people producing the curriculum. Sometimes we met in Monument Valley with the SCG group and worked on curriculum together after we held our own meeting. Someone would bring in a picture of a mountain lion, a bobcat, or some other animal. The elders and community members would talk about it, sharing a short story about these animals, how they were used, and beliefs surrounding them. When I was involved in the parent coordinator program, some of the old folks liked talking about herbs that they used, and a specialist recorded what they said.

From these and other sessions came curriculum about the Navajo shoe game, with its story, instructions, and music; the Coyote stories with music sung by children from Monument Valley; the stick game stories; and general Navajo culture. I have not heard anybody complain about it, and I feel it is good. I do have a concern, however, when I heard recently that the school district announced that it would put the Coyote stories and other materials on CD. I do not know what is going to happen, but when we put this information together we did not want it to get out of hand. These teachings were to be used only for education. We did not expect it to be given out freely without the appropriate understanding of how the stories are to be told and how to show them proper respect. I have heard now that they are being sold freely and in some cases without permission. When they were first made there was an agreement that they would not leave our office without a clear understanding. These stories should only be told during the appropriate times of the year. If this is not done, traditional people will start to complain about their use. I am concerned about all of this.

The Navajo Nation and the San Juan School District are also concerned about the loss of Navajo language. I have been involved in testing children to determine how familiar they are with it and how best to teach it. One Navajo instructor in Montezuma Creek became concerned when we did language testing because of how we asked questions. She was never taught enough Navajo language to become fluent, so she struggled to understand. The testing that we were doing was to determine how well the children comprehended Navajo. The problem arose when giving the test and limiting an object or thing to one word. When teaching Navajo children we found that a child living in a hogan, for example, may never have used a drinking glass but only coffee cups with a little handle or "ear." So the child might understand a drinking cup by its name that recognizes the "ear" as opposed to a tall slender glass. The two words are different. Maybe this person from the Western Agency would use another word or say it differently. So when I tested the children I tried to use a variety of words. A child may understand Navajo and what I am talking about but needs to be approached with the vocabulary she is familiar with. Then it is easy for the child to ask questions and discuss things. I was trying to determine how much Navajo they understood, but that woman wanted me to use just one word while I was using two or three to make sure that the child understood what I was saying. She eventually grasped the problem.

As I worked on Navajo language instruction and testing there were some employees who were a little concerned about teaching traditional culture. I had to explain clearly what it was and how it was being used. Many of them had never learned about it. There was one family in particular who opposed it. The mother wanted to meet with me when I was teaching in the Montezuma Creek Elementary School. She insisted that she did not want her child to learn about traditional Navajo culture because she was a Christian. She did not believe in anything traditional and did not want her daughter to learn it either, not even the songs. We sat there for quite a while, then I told her that you never know what's going to happen. Once her child graduated, she could go to college, maybe graduate as a teacher,

Utah Navajo Development Council Head Start Days in Bluff, 1981. Daughter Raquel Dandy, third from left, at a young age started performing Navajo songs and dance taught by her father. As an adult today, she continues this family tradition.

and return to the reservation. If she did not understand the culture she was work-ing in, it would be very difficult to respond to some things she encountered even if it was not in her subject area. Perhaps her daughter might choose to teach Navajo culture once she has grown up because she would have the freedom to decide. As parents we just do not know where a person will end up, and we cannot stop them once they have chosen. The mother left after our discussion but came back later and said that she had changed her mind and agreed with my point of view. Her child remained in my Navajo language and culture class.

Sometimes I would use my own children as an example, pointing out that I was really glad I had taught them Navajo language and culture. People in the com-munity recognized that they were fluent in both, and I believe it is because I taught them when they were young. By the time children reach the eighth, ninth, or tenth grade they will not listen to a parent on these kinds of things. They think it is non-sense to learn about their culture. But if you teach them when they are little, they carry that knowledge into high school and then to college and will never be embar-rassed about their culture. Also, because my children are fluent Navajo speakers, I believe it helps them in other areas of education and as a member of the work-

force. My daughter Raquel works at the nursing home. She never thought that she would be helping people in physical therapy, but there are many traditional Navajo elders there who depend on her to translate. They know that she really cares as she communicates and laughs with them.

I have done much of my teaching through music. Young people, especially if they are in kindergarten, first grade, or second grade, love it. They seem to learn faster than when trying to get them to just speak Navajo because they are involved and sometimes use hand gestures or other motions. Navajo children love singing. A little while ago there were a couple of Navajo ladies and an older man who came into my class to listen to me teach. They sat there with tears streaming from their eyes, happy to see how the children were grasping their traditional language. They were motivated to learn in this way, with their culture and language embedded in the music.

Although Jim loved teaching, the effects of old age began to take their toll on him and on Betty, who by this time had developed some serious health problems that limited her activity and qualified her for disability retirement. Jim decided to stay home and take care of her as he also began to slow down. Former students would see Jim and Betty and thank them for helping them through school and making sure that they did not quit. Many appreciated Jim's teaching Navajo culture. His own children kept saying: "Dad, you've done enough. You've had all these years of teaching and now you better take it easy." While working in Aneth in 2004, he began not to feel well. He had a slight heart attack and became very sick. It happened one evening, as he returned to Blanding with Betty's brother. He became worse, did not eat anything, and went straight to bed. After a difficult night, he told Betty to get him to help; he just did not feel well. Doctors at the Monticello hospital determined that he had just had a slight heart attack and sent him immediately to Salt Lake City, where he had eight by-pass surgery. Following the operation he improved and resumed a normal life, retired but busy with his family.

What of Zonnie and Charlie, holder of the family mountain soil bundle? What impact have the placement program and the LDS faith had on their subsequent lives? Zonnie picks up her life story following boarding school:

After boarding school I attended Northern Arizona University. Harold, my future husband, came from Dennehotso then attended school in Shalako. I met him in 1962 and thought he was very nice, so I told him I needed a ride home for the Christmas vacation. He drove to Flagstaff, hauled me and my luggage home, and met my father, who really liked him. Harold at this time managed a traditional singing group. Perhaps that is why my father, as a medicine man, got along so well with him. When I arrived home my father was involved in a Yé'ii Bicheii dance; but as soon as it ended, he drove to Dennehotso to visit Harold's mother. In no time he arranged the wedding, and before I returned to school for my second semester in 1963 I was married. There were two ceremonies—a traditional one held in Kayenta in a hogan and one in the LDS Church. The whole process was fast, but that is the way Dad was when he found something he thought was good. Father told me to stay with this man, so we moved to Mexican Hat.

Harold worked in the mill at Mexican Hat. I did not like it there and wanted to go back to school, but now I was married. Occasionally we visited his mother, who was fluent in English, at Dennehotso. Harold and I agreed that we did not want to live in a rural setting where there was no electricity or running water because by now we had become used to having them. During one visit in October 1964, two white ladies came to see my mother-in-law. One was small, the other tall, but both embraced her as an old friend. After shaking hands with me and my husband, they asked if I wanted a job working with children. I had never done that before, but they insisted I would be successful and they needed me that night from 10 P.M. to 6 A.M. All I had to do was go back and forth between buildings and check on the children as they slept in the dormitories of the BIA school. I agreed to try it.

That night Harold brought me to the dorms and I received instructions from the lady who was on the shift before me. I worked two nights and did not like either because it was so scary walking between buildings in the dark. I was just too young and did not want to be out after the sun went down. My supervisor gave me a schedule with some time off, offered a trailer for me and my baby to stay in, and told me to come back for the Wednesday night shift. I returned to Mexican Hat with one of Harold's cousins and told my husband that I did not want to work because I was scared at night. I did not dare tell my supervisor, so I asked Harold to call. He did, and they changed my hours to start at 1 P.M. and end at 9 P.M.; I began working with the boys, twelve to sixteen years old. Now I really enjoyed my job at Dennehotso because I just did the children's laundry, checked on them, and cleaned the dorm and restrooms. It was easy, but I learned a lot as I worked there

Jim with NFL football player Steve Young and his future wife, Barbara. Jim has a long-standing friendship with Steve, who "asked for his approval" to marry Barbara. Jim was delighted with both.

for the next seven years. My husband received a janitorial job three years after I started and joined the staff.

He moved to Dennehotso but he did not do well. He loved to sing and so went with his brothers and cousins to Enemy Way dances to have fun. One time he ended up in Cortez in jail with some of his relatives. I firmly told him that I did not want to be associated with any drunks and that I was moving back to Shonto to the boarding school where my mother worked. He changed his attitude, said he would behave, and moved with me. We did a lateral transfer within the BIA system and remained in Shonto for the next thirty-nine years. Harold worked there until he passed away from cancer at the age of fifty-six; I moved back to Red Lake after I retired in 2002 to help raise my grandchildren. Because this has been our family home for a long time, people around here think that the Dandys can handle anything. We take care of ourselves and do our best to raise our children to become what they want to be. My mother and father were just like that, too, and raised us to be that way. Mother loved learning and took pride in knowing how to do things. She always wanted to be doing something, and I am the same.

Charlie Dandy has a similar story in which his life and livelihood are linked to education. He recalls that when he was growing up there was a

girl whose family lived nearby who used to wink at him when he was branding cattle. He did not think much of it because he was busy cowboying, but
later he started to pay attention. During the winter of 1967–68 a powerful
snowstorm blanketed the reservation, stopping travel and stranding families.
This young woman, Virginia, a freshman in high school, lost her parents during this event. After their vehicle slid off the road, her parents remained
inside; carbon monoxide fumes asphyxiated them and one brother. Virginia
described herself at this point as "a lost dog gone astray. My uncle and aunt
took my younger brothers and sisters, but they did not want the older children around." She was adrift.

Charlie knew nothing of this when he returned from attending BYU and
met Virginia at the Shiprock Fair. "My father had met her before, knew her
situation, and saw us together. That was all it took. One day he approached
me when we were alone and said: 'Son, what I'm going to ask you I do not
want you to turn down. You have almost everything you need—a job and a
pickup and I think you're about ready to have a family.'" Charlie thought:
"Oh man. Who is the girl?" His father had already talked to the girl's grandparents, and they had agreed.

When my father told me who it was, I accepted the arrangement and he said,
"Good, the wedding will be in five days." He had already paid for everything as
part of the Navajo tradition where the groom's family provides goods to the bride's
family for the marriage of their daughter. My father really helped my wife a lot,
taking her in just like a daughter and trying to help her through the process of
mourning for her mother and father. He knew what she was like and helped fix her
feelings. We were married in 1972 in a five-day ceremony and have been together
for thirty-five years.

Right after we were married, we lived in Blanding, where I worked for the San
Juan School District. We took in Virginia's three younger brothers, who really had
nobody. I was working hard but did not make much money—something like $300
a month. We managed to feed everyone and made it through. Virginia and I moved
back to this area because my father became really sick with a nosebleed that would
not stop. He had chosen the place where we built our house, and I was used to the
area because this is where in the past we brought our hundred head of cattle for
their summer range every year. A lot of times I did it myself, thirty head at a time,
and that is how I first learned to work. My dad wanted a rodeo ground nearby,

so we built one; and for four or five years every summer we held events using our own bulls before moving them back to other pastures. I received a job in Tuba City working for the school district. Just before retiring I was the dean of students at the high school. Now I stay home and am doing well in the rodeo and cattle business.

We have had six children, with one son who was killed in a rodeo. Our family has always been involved in rodeos and has done a lot of bull riding. When I was going to BYU I rode on the college team and continued to ride bulls after I was married until a horse trampled me and broke my sternum and ribs. Virginia told me that I had better lay it down and stop riding. Then eleven years ago my son Albert, who belonged to the Rocky Mountain Rodeo Association, had a horse kick him in the head, paralyzing him before he passed away. But rodeoing has always been in the family. Now my granddaughter is riding bulls. We encouraged her to just ride the barrels and enter less dangerous events, but she wants to ride bulls. I could not say no. She enjoys it, so we support her; and she recently won a beautiful saddle in competition. That's how we've been in this family, and it has kept us together. Rodeos have been good to us. As for religion, because my mother entrusted me with the mountain soil bundle to hold the family close, I have to respect her and my father's wishes to carry on what they gave me. This is what helped them all the time as traditional Navajos. I feel like I have my religion and follow in their footsteps.

JIM DANDY'S TEACHINGS

CHAPTER EIGHT

HOLY PEOPLE,
THE CREATION, AND ITS END

The Navajo World

Note: This chapter and the next three chapters are entirely in Jim's voice. These are the teachings and experiences that he either has learned from his grandparents and parents or has obtained otherwise as he has lived a traditional life. Navajo ceremonial practices and the traditions from which they come are complex and rooted in a mythology that is far more lengthy than that of many Native American groups. While much of Jim's information is self-explanatory when accompanied by the endnotes, those who are unfamiliar with Navajo tradition should consult more basic texts referenced in the bibliography. (See Aileen O'Bryan, Navaho Indian Myths; *Paul G. Zolbrod,* Diné bahane'; *Washington Matthews,* Navaho Legends; *and Karl W. Luckert,* A Navajo Bringing-Home Ceremony *for renderings of the Creation story.)*

HOLY PEOPLE

In traditional Navajo thought, everything was created spiritually before it was created physically. Twelve holy Grandfathers called Ceremonial Yé'ii Bicheii were the ones who helped make the world and gave things their power.[1] Each of these men has a name, but the one who leads the other eleven and directs the singing is Talking God; he is dressed in white.[2] The last one is Tó Neinilii (Water Sprinkler God).[3] These performers are versed in ceremonial knowledge and work with stronger spiritual powers than women—their power is male.[4] Female Holy People also assisted during Creation, but today men are the ones who follow in the footsteps of the Grandfathers and control the more dangerous ceremonial practices.

All of these Grandfathers were extremely intelligent and spiritual, so that through prayers and songs they imbued the world with this male power. A group of twelve songs and another of twenty-four songs are still used to call upon these forces, especially during the Yé'ii Bicheii ceremony performed during the winter.[5] For a healing ritual, there might be twelve songs before the medicine man starts into a different series of chants. But these twelve are the main ones that must be sung. Another example is during the Enemy Way when six songs are performed in one area and a second six sung in another camp where participants are holding the candy rush at the beginning of the last day. Together there are twelve songs that lay the foundation for any others that might be sung. At least six of them must be performed.

All twelve holy Grandfathers established their individual elements and powers in the world, but they also complement each other.[6] This relationship is symbolized in the structure of a hogan, whose upright posts in the base not only support the form but also hold the spiritual powers that connect the beams that form the top. These holy beings shared their power with others, including First Man, First Woman, and the Twins, assisting them as they established a way of life upon the earth. In ceremonies all or some of these Holy People participate in a male hogan, since it was blessed and prepared for rituals from the beginning of time. Female hogans are also used, but stronger powers are evoked from ceremonies performed in the male hogan.

As these and other Holy People participated in the Creation, conflicts arose, one story telling of the separation of the sexes and the development of gender roles in the world beneath this one.[7] It seems that one of the women was cheating on her husband, so she pretended to be sick. She required him to carry her down to the river then leave her there for the entire day before returning to pick her up in the evening. He suspected that she had other motives, thinking, "I am going to see what's going on, what's happening," so he began to spy. As soon as he disappeared behind a hill, another man emerged from the water and slept with the wife. The husband was furious, went to the water, brought her home, and punished the wayward spouse. Other women became involved, and so all of them were separated and punished by the men who had them live on the far side of the river.

During this time of separation, the men fulfilled their own responsibilities. One person took care of farming, others hunting, others medicine and

healing, and each received his own name. Eventually the twelve holy Grandfathers met to decide if the women had suffered and were lonely enough to
take back. The men had survived better because they had with them a person
who was a man who chose to live as a woman (*nádleeh*) and was able to fill
both roles when performing chores.[8] He was very knowledgeable in cooking,
planting crops, and accomplishing other women's tasks. Today Navajo people
appreciate those who know how to do many things. The nádleeh is highly
respected for these qualities, while parents still emphasize having skills and
knowledge and teach their children to be self-sufficient: "You're going to die
in your sleep; you'll be helpless if you do not know how to take care of yourself. What will happen if sometime your wife puts your saddle outside the
door and tells you to leave?"[9] That teaching about being helpless is associated with this first separation and how important it is to be able to take care
of yourself. After the men and women joined back together, they worked in
harmony, fulfilling their roles. Each of these Holy People is still involved with
the earth in seeing that the plan started at Creation continues.

One aspect of this plan concerned the earth, sun, and moon. Mother
Earth sits here to provide for our needs. But the Holy People also realized
that there should be a night and day. The story of the shoe game teaches that
neither the night creatures nor the day creatures had their own way, so days
and nights are evenly divided for the welfare of the people. During the night,
the moon and stars become providers to lessen the cold and shed light so
that there is not total darkness. The moon takes care of the night people. In
the day the sun takes care of us, providing warmth and energy for plants to
grow. Its greater power connects with Mother Earth and together they control
the elements that bless the people. Every heavenly being provides for us. In
Navajo teachings the sun controls the things in the heavens. Since the earth
cannot grow plants alone, the sun assists and they work together. Because we
are born on the earth and everything that grows is helped by the heavens, we
are heavenly, spiritual beings. The rain, water, air, wind, and sun's heat come
from this power above.

All three of the heavenly bodies have a gender. Mother Earth (Nahas-
dzáán) is female; Sun Bearer (Jóhonaa'éí), who carries the sun across the sky,
is a powerful male; and Moon Bearer (Tł'éhonaa'éí) is his son. Sun Bearer
carries a male turquoise disk and Moon Bearer carries the moon disk (*oljéé'*),

which is female. In the songs and prayers we always address Moon Bearer and Sun Bearer as our fathers, but we do not pray to the moon disk. Sun is spiritually the most powerful of the three. It is very strong, like a bolt of lightning and other things found in the heavens, and so is not trifled or played with. A person can dry fruit different ways but should use the sun sparingly because it is so powerful. People also have to be careful as to how much exposure they have to it.

The moon, on the other hand, has a lot of teachings about its role in controlling temperature and the seasons. It maintains the right temperature on the earth so that it does not get too cold. With the help of the stars and other planets, it provides a little warmth and light when the sun is not available. The moon is a type of barometer for the weather and calendar for the seasons. The temperature and moisture that will be sent to earth are forecast in its crescent tips. When the crescent faces up or to the north, the moon is indicating cold with freezing weather ahead; when its tips point straight out (not up or down), temperatures will be moderate; when the points of the crescent face down or to the south, temperatures will be very hot. Some people say that when its tips point down there will be a lot of rain, as if a cup holding the moisture is upside down. So like the points on a dial, the more the crescent faces down the hotter or wetter it will be; the more they face up, the colder. Snow and rain are also forecast by how wide the rings around the moon are. The moisture lines surrounding it in a circle tell of its approach.

The moon is shown respect in many ways. For instance, you do not point at the moon, sun, stars, or rainbow with a finger. That is very rude; so your thumb, which has a lot of strength, is used. During the time of an eclipse, I remember my grandmother insisting that we show respect to the moon or sun by not talking. Both types of eclipses are described as the sun's or moon's death; they are treated as if it were a dying person. Respect for them is shown by stopping all activity, sitting still, not eating or drinking or looking at the eclipse as it occurs. Normal activity resumes after it is finished, thus maintaining harmony. Even under regular conditions, you do not stare at the moon. The only time this is polite is when learning about it, the stars in heaven, and what they represent. So Navajos can look at the moon as long as they are teaching or learning, but many do not even want to talk about what is in the sky.

There are teachings that address a child being born during the full moon.[10] The infant is a special person arriving at this time when the sun and moon work together. The old people used to say, "Where is a child being born?" meaning that somewhere a gifted one has come to the earth. Wealth and blessings belong to those who enter the world at this time of new beginnings. Ceremonies are the same way. If a person has a ceremony planned and a relative or someone close dies, then it is postponed until the next month and the next new moon. If it is someone in the immediate family then you have to wait for a whole year. The new moon gives the right of way to hold these ceremonies because respect has been shown by waiting for the proper time. For a young woman about to have her puberty ceremony it cannot start until the moon and stars are in the right place in the heavens. She does not sleep much the last night, and so the singing does not start until the moon or stars are in a certain position, sometime before early dawn. I think all the ceremonies are like that, going by rules in certain areas with the moon serving as a calendar.

WEATHER

Lightning is highly respected in Navajo culture and should be totally avoided unless a person is knowledgeable about how to handle its power and the objects that it has struck. There are two types: male lightning is long, jagged, noisy, destructive, and shakes the earth; female is soft heat lightning. If it appears in the wintertime, it is called white lightning and is female, but if it is really dark and charges strike all about, then it is male. When lightning hits a tree the wood is never used; if it strikes close to home, the house and surrounding places have been exposed to that power.[11] Prayers are said so that there will be no harm, such as cancer that does not heal, coming from that radiation. Powerful people can use lightning to strike their victims. When somebody is hit by lightning in the summer, there should never be an Enemy Way ceremony. It does not matter if the person is a relative or not; the ceremony should be canceled. With supernatural powers, water is the same way as lightning. If there was going to be an Enemy Way and somebody drowns, the ceremony cannot be held that year. You have to have it the following year. It used to be like that, but now they just go ahead and do it. This is

Jagged bolts of male lightning arc across southeastern Utah skies. Navajo people have a deep reverence for this force of nature, which both is a Holy Person and is controlled by other powers. Even the smell of lightning-struck wood is avoided; only those who understand how to control its effects should be involved with anything to do with this force. (Photo by Kay Shumway)

wrong and does not help an individual. Instead a lot of people go home very upset, and that is worse. If participants will not help with the healing, the ceremony will not work.

Canceling a ceremony can occur for a number of reasons, not just because of lightning or drowning. For instance, when my mother passed away, I canceled everything. I was going to have an Enemy Way about a year ago when all of a sudden one of my relatives was killed in front of the Red Lake general store. I was hesitant and postponed it for another month. During that time mother became ill with a bad case of pneumonia. She was old, and even though a lot of people told me that she had lived a full life and it was about time for her to leave, I held a family meeting. We decided to have the ceremony the next year. There was a real feeling of respect from older folks, who thought it was very appropriate to wait for my mother. On the other hand, I heard recently about a couple of people killed near Piñon, but the community still held the Enemy Way. That should not be.

When Navajos talk about winds, there are two types. Níyol is strong, the one felt blowing against your face. Níích'i is the Holy Wind or spirit guide that gives life to things and helps direct and protect against evil. In Christian thought, nítch'i is like the Holy Ghost that whispers, teaches, and brings help to people. Níyol is controlled through nítch'i and its supernatural power. For instance, a tornado can be stopped by leaving an offering and saying a prayer. It is through nítch'i that the destructive force is commanded. When the winds blow, some will be soft, while others, like tornadoes, are hard. Those winds that pick up objects are always male. Strong whirlwinds that turn and tip over trees have a power that must be respected, so if it breaks a pole or rips branches off a tree, just as with lightning, they are not used, for they belong to the wind. When a strong wind visits a home it is not by chance but may have been sent by a person involved in witchcraft who wishes to destroy something at that place. When destructive winds like tornadoes strike a community, scheduled ceremonies should be postponed. Wind can also cause cancer, swelling, and other illness.

Round objects belong to the wind. Round stones are called Wind's Rocks and when picked up cause it to blow; these should not be brought home, because they are the wind's babies, just as sticks that have been carried and piled up by a river belong to the water. In either case, proper respect must be shown or else wind or water becomes angry. Do not lie down where the wind has left a trail or build a home where a concave impression is found in a rock, because they are the wind's home. Do not place a finger in a sheep's eye socket when butchering, since its shape is that of the wind's home. Playing ball inside a house and whistling causes the wind to wake up and blow; leaving a window cracked causes it to whistle, creating hearing loss.

When a whirlwind approaches, everybody says "naa daaní, naa daaní, naa daaní," meaning "your son-in-law, your son-in-law, your son-in-law." This male wind heading in your direction will change its course and miss you.[12] If a small whirlwind passes over a person, he says a prayer that its effects will not bother him. These winds bring messages that are not good. For example, I know a man who learned from a whirlwind that he should move his camp from where he had established it. That night lightning hit the tree that he had been staying under. Because the whirlwind warned him, he was not hurt. Just like water, these winds have a lot of power. That is how I look at it when people talk about things like this.

Sometimes sons-in-law are not very well accepted because they are strangers to the family and might be a little trouble.[13] Anglos also joke about

Navajo classifications of snow reveal an observant relationship to this blessing that comes upon the land. The hogan pictured here is a warm shelter with lots of insulation, while the open structure to its left is used in the summer for cooking during ceremonies like the Enemy Way. (Photo by Kay Shumway)

their in-laws and how they are different. To Navajos, an in-law can be helpful by keeping the wind away and may protect a family. By saying "naa daaní" their power helps push the wind aside. An early winter snowstorm is called an "in-law chaser." When the first snow comes in as a blizzard with sleet and hail, it is the start of the winter season. Accompanying hail drives in hard and fast, encouraging a person to move quickly and get all of the chores done before it is too late. This storm is an in-law chaser, as the little hailstones encourage the in-law to carry the water, chop wood, and get livestock fed. A person might come into the house and say, "The in-law chaser storm chased me all over." When you talk about this everyone laughs at the situation it describes, bringing families together.

People don't usually use the first snow for water. I do not know why, but it is not melted for cooking, washing, and drinking like the snow from later storms, but instead is left alone.[14] Families do not let the snow from these later storms sit in the sun to melt but bring it inside to heat on the stove because the sunrays are so powerful with radiation. For this same reason, people should not lie in the sun or sunbathe. Snowballs are not thrown because, just like wind's rocks, they belong to the wind. When snow falls slowly and gently it is female, and when it comes with a strong wind it is male. Anything that is soft is female; clouds that are white and fluffy are female; dark, threatening storm clouds are male; hail that is driven and hurts or damages is male; little, light balls are female.

In the beginning First Man put four clouds in his medicine bundle—a white one (east), blue (south), yellow (west) and black (north)—one for each of the four directions. He carried all of them for their moisture and gave them names. The yellow and blue clouds were female, the white and black clouds male. These same colors in traditional beliefs are associated with male (white) corn pollen and female (yellow) ground corn used in blessing. Thus the colors in the heavens and those found on earth continue this pattern of male and female qualities.

Navajos classify snow in layers according to its type. When the frost lies even on the ground it looks like a very light blanket of snow. They call it *shóyiiba'*, and it is the beginning of winter. This frost is hairy and soft like cotton. Once it snows there is no doubt that winter is here, as winds get stronger and cold breezes freeze the rainfall into snow. Next there is a thin layer of snow called *yas nááná'*. Then there is *háách́ííl*, which means very little snow. When you say *yasyítsoh* there is a lot of snow, *yas nitsaago yidzaas* is a deep snow, and *yas bikáá yistin* means there is a hard layer of ice sitting on top of the snow. Once the frost is in the ground and snow upon the earth, it is appropriate to talk about all of the different animals that cannot be discussed during the rest of the year. By this time they are hibernating, back in the mountains, or have gone south. The snow is a signal, saying it is all right to tell their stories without offending them.[15]

Many of the teachings about rain involve Coyote. The beginning of the Enemy Way story starts with his worrying about the drought that had tired the land. One very hot day, he was trotting along, thirsty and dry, when he decided to get something to eat. He prayed, "I wish clouds would form," and soon they did. Then he asked for a little breeze and it happened, a little sprinkling rain, and it did. Everything went as he requested. Next he said, "I want to be able to float by water to where I can find food," and the rains began. The water took him to a place filled with prairie dogs and rabbits. He joined forces with Skunk and fulfilled his wishes. Coyote's ability to control the rain is very important to the Navajo people, who believe that these animals must exist in order to have rain come to the land.[16]

Another animal associated with rain is the mud puppy or mud dog, a salamander that is found where it is damp. The powers of this creature are appealed to during a ceremony that is part of the Enemy Way and serves as a request for rain and other blessings.[17] I participated in it a lot when I was young and really enjoyed it. Still, it is performed as a prayer that brings heavy rain showers. The teaching for this says that when it rains really hard, a person can go to places where water collects in streams and rock basins and find these water dogs, frogs, and tadpoles swimming like fish or resting in damp cool spots. They bring the rain, come with it, and are not to be killed but left alone.[18]

At one time these were people, just like the water monsters and water babies. They were Holy People, and so by acting like them they will bring rain and bless others with their power. They represent rain, wet earth, and fertility; these are the blessings that a mud dog shares with the people when they call upon these powers. Participants in the ceremony become what they are representing and obtain their blessing. Just as with Coyote, when he calls for rain it happens. The other day I found in my yard a big mud dog that had been in water for a long time. It was yellow and striped like a zebra. When one is found, you give it a prayer then leave it alone. Just like a frog, they should not be killed but put in a safe place. They are the water people and must be respected.

Once there had not been rain for some time, a real dry season. The people held an Enemy Way ceremony that I participated in then held a mud dog blessing. They said a short prayer before we went out and dug a large hole, perhaps ten feet in diameter, then added water so that it filled with mud. Stripped down to loincloths, a number of men went running after the people, brought them back to the mud hole, and threw them in. My sister was making fun of me while I was on horseback, feeling just so light, quick, and strong because of my involvement in this ritual. The ceremony also helps a person to think fast. With this added strength it was easy to grab someone and toss her in the pit. We took her, even though she was dressed in fine clothes and beautiful jewelry, and threw her into the mud and water. She

These "Mud People" participating in the Ch'ąąshzhinii portion of the Enemy Way ceremony bring rain and health to the land. The Holy People are pleased with this type of boisterous activity and do their part by blessing the people with moisture. (Courtesy Milton Snow Collection, Navajo Nation Museum)

became a mud dog like the rest of us, grabbing others and pushing them into the hole. Following the roundup, a prayer is said and people are placed on a rolled blanket, swung back and forth, then tossed into the mud as the participants sing. This is a blessing not only for rain but also for those who need to be healed from sickness or are under stress. We become the medicine, the Holy People, helping to get that person well. After obtaining as many as you can to assist, the people line up to receive their blessing by putting a little bit of mud on them with a prayer. People may line up for a long time to receive this. The ceremony is exciting and a lot of fun to watch. The last time I participated was about ten years ago at Cow Springs. I took my children over there, and they became mud dogs.

Water, whether it falls from the sky or rests on the land, is vital to life and treated with respect, just as grandparents should be. The reason water is referred to as a grandparent or parent is because it provides for the People. In a ceremony, it is used with yucca to cleanse before starting, during the ritual, and at the end. The residue of supernatural power that participants have been exposed to must be removed. This water is like food that has been used and is now returned to Mother Earth. Rain adds to other sources of water on the earth, and together they care for it and work together to help the People. Both earth and water are our grandparents and are addressed that way when we pray. Water is considered female in our prayers and so is treated as a living grandmother who holds lots of power.

This power is felt in rivers that have Holy People living within. Traditional Navajo people talk a lot about leaving an offering in or by a river and saying a prayer before crossing. The Holy Person wraps itself around and protects the individual as she leaves the safe boundaries of Navajo land and enters into that of the white man and Ute. There are four sacred rivers that surround this safe territory—the Colorado (female), San Juan (male), Rio Grande (female), and Little Colorado (male). Male rivers are generally characterized as crooked and female as straight. I still say a short prayer when traveling for protection. Corn pollen offerings are given to both male and female rivers, each of which has its own ceremonial name, but they may also be referred to as relatives. For instance, the Colorado River is called grandmother or young lady, while the San Juan is grandfather or young man. Their spirit listens to you, recognizing that you know them and are asking for help.

MOUNTAINS AND PLANTS

Each of the four directions has not only its colors but also a mountain with power associated with it. To the east is Blanca Peak (male) near Alamosa, Colorado; to the south, Mount Taylor (female) near Acoma, New Mexico; to the west, San Francisco Peaks (female) near Flagstaff, Arizona; and to the north, Mount Hesperus (male) near Durango, Colorado. The East (white) holds the powers of positive thinking, planning, new beginnings, and life; the South is turquoise, health, learning, summer, and leadership in daily activities; the West (yellow) is adult life, power, strength, adulthood, and autumn; the North (black) is self-protection, guidance, old age, and winter. The powers of these mountains are great and complex. Take the North, for instance. Black stone represents your weapons and arrowheads. Anything that is used in war or for protection in ceremonies and that a person "sits behind" for safety is associated with the North. In an Enemy Way ceremony, the sacred stick that is carried to different camps always goes to the North because it represents a weapon, like an arrow, against evil. Anything to do with protective black clubs fashioned from stone symbolizes the North.

Navajo Mountain on the Arizona-Utah border is considered by some to be a northern mountain and very strong. People say that it will never be harmed by earthquake or volcanic action and will never be destroyed. Weapons like arrowheads are built into Navajo Mountain and are there for war and protection.[19] In Navajo culture, mountains are not to be climbed without spiritual preparation. If someone does not say the prayers and give offerings before going up on it, he will not return, because the mountain gets bigger and he will lose his way back. You also do not climb rocks, because they too change, grow, hide the way down, and become very slick. Navajos also believe that no livestock, mountain lions, or coyotes will go on Navajo Mountain until the last days of this earth. That is when these things will happen to show that it is the end of the world.

This mountain is said to be the head of Earth Woman, a reclining female form. Black Mesa, the area down to Red Lake, and land all the way to Rough Rock compose part of her body. Look over this torso on top of Black Mesa all the way to Red Lake then to Indian Wells then back down to Kaibito. The whole body is amazing if you think about the story that comes from the woman's side of the teachings, that it is the head of Mother Earth. Of course everything on Navajo Mountain itself is more about men and weapons made of flint, the male side of the teachings. That stone is hard and perfect for battle. In some Enemy Way ceremonies, the weapons used are made at Navajo Mountain. I have heard medicine men say that it could have been the northernmost of the four sacred mountains. But the way the mountains are situated now, they are further to the east and south. A lot of people, like my father, were never satisfied with the explanation of where all these sacred mountains are located. Navajo Mountain could have been the northern mountain but is not because of where the main population of Navajos is located. The La Sal Mountains or Five Mountains outside of Moab also have not received proper recognition.[20] The only sacred mountains that surround us in the north and west are Navajo Mountain and the La Sals.

Plants found in both the mountains and deserts are very important to the Navajo People. There are many teachings about their creation, use, and how to show them proper respect. My father believed that as soon as a seed goes into the ground a plant is alive, just like a baby before it is born. Since herbs and plants are living, before picking them they must be prayed to and given an offering to thank them for their help. This is the way to have their power heal a person since all medications are made from herbs. The offering is given to both the plant and Mother Earth. The prayer is said to the type of plant that will be picked, but the one that receives the offering and prayer is left so that it can continue to remember the blessing. Others nearby are the ones that are actually taken. During the prayer the name of the person and illness is mentioned so that the plant's healing power will understand who it is to assist. That is why my grandfather said that it is best not to buy these herbs in a market place, because no name or prayer or offering may have been given. The plant may still help but is not as powerful. My mother told me: "Son, if you really want to heal the person who needs the herb, take him with you and find the herb yourself. If you go with another person to help you find it, let him give an offering, say his prayer, and use your name, stating so-and-so is going to use this herb. The sick person will be healed but needs the plant's power to help. A lot of people go looking for herbs with a medicine man who says a prayer and understands that with faith it is going to work." That is how Navajos do it; they don't just come and gather without giving a prayer, without giving Mother Earth something to help heal, and so they carry corn pollen as an offering to the ground and the medicine taken.

Plants also tell the story of life. A seed goes into the soil, just as our earthly father also planted a seed. When we are born we are a small green bud. By midsummer we are pretty and continue to grow, but eventually our leaves turn colors in the fall and we start to get old, becoming more and more helpless with age. Grandparents are old and dried out, their skin falls off, and they go to pieces. As soon as the wind blows the leaves are gone, ending life.

Life in ceremonies is prolonged by using cedar [juniper] leaves that do not wither like other kinds. Cedar trees stay green and last a long time, never appearing to die because they grow deep in the ground.[21] Unlike the pine that dries and dies as soon as the water is gone, cedars remain. Cedar ashes are used to bless Navajo people and serve as protection against evil, which fears this tree's soot. A young cedar is very much alive and will have a long life, so by leaving an offering with it a person is blessed to grow the same way as that tree. When blessing the cedar you start from the bottom, pray, and motion upward with the corn pollen, because that is the direction the tree grows.

Jim prepares yucca for the Navajo shoe game that he will conduct later. Yucca belongs to the lily family and is used for many things—food, soap, twine, games, and ceremonial practices.

Yucca, like cedar, is green all of the time and never dies. It takes a long time to dry, does not need a lot of water, and lasts once it gets moisture. They are just like a camel and never get thirsty. A person has to be very careful when taking its roots out of the ground because it is used like shampoo but also gives a blessing. Before digging the root a prayer is offered, the plant is called by its name, and its use is explained. The root should not be dropped; if it is, the person will start itching around the head and body; following a ceremony and washing with yucca soap, the root and residue are carefully disposed of. To make this soap or shampoo, the root is peeled then pounded to soften it. The pulp is swished in a bowl of clean water, preparing it for use, but there are not a lot of suds that come from the milky liquid. After washing with the solution a person feels as if she has never been that clean before, a feeling that remains all day.

During the Enemy Way ceremony, yucca is used for protection because it has sharp spines that keep evil spirits and dangerous things away. That is why a person, after the squaw dance and during the ceremony, has to wear a

yucca bracelet around the wrist. This band can be made from either the nar-
row leaf or broad leaf yucca, it is all one. These plants can also be fashioned
into horse bridles, hackamores, ropes, and ladders. Navajos still use it when
they do not have a manufactured rope or bridle. The plant is prepared by
taking the tip off the spine and tying or braiding the fiber together. It is also
used to make baskets, while its ripened fruit is delicious. The "banana" pod is
baked in an underground pit and tastes like cucumber.[22] The stick that grows
out of the center of the yucca and holds the fruit is made into the stem of the
pipe smoked in the Evil Way ceremony.

THE END OF THE WORLD

Eventually the world as we know it will end. The Navajos have a number
of teachings that explain what and how this will happen. Even at the time
of Creation there were patterns established that foretold of this event. I am
referring to the story of the time when Coyote was so concerned about all
the people who became corrupt and greedy, causing food to become scarce.
Everything turned dry because Mother Earth and Father Sky refused to work
together. Instead they battled each other, saying, "I'm the holy being; I'm the
one that rules." Consequently, there was no rain.[23] The same could happen
to us now, just as it did then or with the Anasazi later. They faced a similar
situation where the gods punished them because of bad behavior.[24] There are
a lot of things that are going to happen to us—some say we'll be destroyed
by fire, others say by wind, others by water. Now Wind is warning people,
especially those on the east coast, but also in other places where there have
never before been problems with winds like tornadoes. Even on the reservation there are strong male winds that have not been there before, bears and
other holy animals moving on Navajo lands, and destruction of livestock. A
final sign is when an Indian person travels to the moon. These are the types
of things that are supposed to happen at the end of the world.

The time for performing ceremonies affects changes in weather, another
indicator of approaching problems. For example, the Yé'ii Bicheii ceremony
that should be held no sooner than mid-October is now starting earlier and
earlier each year. The people are worried about it. "Why did they do that?
It's not time for winter yet. It will cause the frost to come early." They fear

that those who farm will lose their crops to freezing temperatures brought in prematurely. "You have caused the cold to come. Now it's going to be winter." Other people start telling Coyote stories too soon or sing Coyote story songs, which are other ways to cause frost. To tell these stories before there is frost is to risk offending the animals and insects that the stories are about. The Yé'ii Bicheii ceremony ushers in the cold and helps a lot of people at the same time.

Mid-October is the earliest that any of these activities should be held. If cold or snow comes at their normal time, then it is correct to hold these ceremonies. But now people are holding Enemy Way ceremonies, which are only performed in the summer, later and later in the year. This ceremony should never be held after the Yé'ii Bicheii ceremonies have started, but it is happening. That is why there is a mixing of the seasons with warm winters and cold summers. By mid to late October seasonal change has ended, freezing has taken place, the harvest is in, and people say, "Put all your medicine bundles away and start the Yé'ii Bicheii ceremony." They are afraid and complaining about what is going on now and feel that the climate has changed quite a bit. This is what has caused the changes, so now a lot of thundering takes place after the ceremonies and male lightning strikes in the winter.

What we should be doing is following our schedule of seasonal preparations, just as the animals do. People should be getting their corn out of the field and ready to dry then gather and prepare ingredients for kneel-down bread so that it is available for the year. Hunting takes place in the fall, and the meat is preserved. By doing this you are saving and preparing just like the coyote prepares for winter. But we are not willing to follow those patterns, so the seasons are getting confused; people are worrying about it, especially those who farm, because the frost is going to hit them all at once. That's what they're afraid of. I have heard Navajos say that Holy People are going to go to our medicine men and tell them what to do to correct the situation. Many feel that the time has come for this to happen, but it is going to be hard. I do not know if a lot of the younger medicine men really know what to do the same way the older ones did.

Another teaching about the end of the world is that the Navajos and Apaches in the south will come together to join the Athabaskan-speaking people in the north. My father and great-grandfathers always taught that

Jim with Hanti men and women in Siberia. This Athabascan-speaking group shared its teachings with their Navajo guests, which brought surprises to both. Similarities not only in language but also in cultural practices spoke of earlier ties between the two groups.

there were people like us who came from the same tribe but separated a long time ago. Navajos call those who live in Canada, Alaska, and Siberia the Diné Náhodlóinie (Those Who Exist Elsewhere). The people in those areas call themselves the Beday Diné, which translates as the Winter People.[25]

Once I visited these distant relatives who speak our language living in the Yukon and Siberia. In the community I went to in the Yukon, the people had four sacred mountains just like the Navajos. On the western side of their tribal lands they own yellow gold mines; to the north is a black gemstone mountain; to the east is a white shell mountain, a big white rock mountain where they gather stone; and they say there is a turquoise mountain. I do not know what kind of turquoise it has, but I have one that came from there. These people believe they are located in the center of their ancestral lands. One time all of these mountains erupted, covering the land with ash. A lot of these Indians did not survive but were buried by the debris, while others moved away because there was no food. They say these were the ones who came through the Rocky Mountains, while others escaped and went toward Siberia. Stories are told of quite a few groups traveling to Alberta, Canada, then heading east and south. That is how the separation occurred, with people going in different directions because there was no food, while others stayed, survived, and live in the Yukon.

When I was in Siberia those Athabascan-speakers said that there were about thirty different tribes living in their region and that theirs was called the Kets. There is another group similar to the Náhodlóinie in Canada living close to British Columbia and Alaska. These people really look like Navajos with their high cheekbones. During one of our meetings, an old man sang a song very similar to the music that I sing. Their language is similar; for instance they like the Navajo say *gah* for rabbit. Their word for dog is *łį́*, which in Navajo means horse, but for the people in Siberia a similar word is used for caribou because this animal helps with transportation. So the word for a dog or caribou is the same.

One of the Indians shared his traditional teachings concerning the thumb. They use it to show respect by pointing with it at things in the heavens like the stars and the moon or when pointing at a person. The same is true for the Navajos. If someone gives you a thumbs-up, it means you are good. You always use your thumb. I know they also have a ceremony similar to the Navajo puberty rite the kinaaldá, when a girl becomes a young woman. I do not know exactly how they perform that ceremony, but there was a woman who talked about it. Another shared practice is in an architectural feature found in the male hogan. The entryway that sticks out from the main room is similar to that in the skin tents of the people in Siberia. I saw one that is built like that; inside it is just the way Navajos used to live.

I think the older traditional people have a special ceremony at the beginning and end of a hunt, the same way the Navajos do. When it is a young person's first time, they perform a little ceremony for him before going out to hunt with a group of adults. Another practice we share is that when Navajos kill a deer or sheep, they eat everything. Nothing is left lying around, and we do not throw food away or waste it. There are only a few parts of the animal we do not eat, and it is the same way with these people in the Yukon. They do a lot of hunting of caribou, elk, deer, and moose. They are talented in tanning buckskin to make clothes. They also do a lot with fish. Those people in the north are hard workers when preparing fish for food in the winter. They dry and smoke enough to last through the cold season, turning the fish into jerky. I noticed that the way they clean their fish is different from the way Navajos clean theirs and they served a fish head stew with the eyes still in. It was nothing to them, they are not picky, but they still respect the animals and fish in what they do.

At the moose hunt gathering, a four-day celebration, there were all kinds of food to choose from. Many Anglos visited and participated; everyone had a really good time. There were lots of different activities and various drumming groups at a number of places. I made a very good friend who lives in a place called White Horse. He is quite an old man who gave me a very nice hand drum and taught me a lot about some of the things that his people do. He even invited me on a boat trip, but I did not go. Many of these people traveled to the moose hunt gathering by boat, a three-day trip, but my group drove around to a place called Top of the World to get to the celebration. The road took us through an old-time gold-rush town where we saw gravel pits in a row where miners had dug for gold. Going over the Top of the World was beautiful. There were all kinds of berries—blueberries, red berries, chokecherries. The Indians describe this area as a little mattress, soft with bushes and berries lying across the land where the bears come for food. They eat lots of berries and hibernate in this area during the winter, but if there are not a lot of berries they come out hungry. It can be dangerous, so you have to be very careful. Bears will eat anything they see. When I went there with these people, they seemed to be very spiritual.

I do not know if they have stories about eventually joining with other tribes like the Navajos. They were very happy to meet with my group and join together as relatives. A lot of the young people were not very aware of their own traditions, whereas in our education system we are teaching our youth their culture. They are concerned about losing theirs, and so we shared our teachings. That was a good thing for them because they never thought that there were people here who knew much about them. I learned some interesting things about their teachings and wanted to stay longer to learn more but had to leave. One of these days I might return.

Our ancestors always said that some day we would gather with all of our own people again, who speak the same language. I am not clear as to whether they will come here to the Southwest or we go to the North. There are some that are now moving onto the Navajo reservation, while some Navajos are living in the Yukon. At the same time, there are Navajos in Monument Valley who say we should never join with them. We will have to see what happens in the future.

Just as language ties Navajos to these different groups, another sign of the times is that we will lose our own language. Everyone will speak only one—not Navajo but English.[26] Almost everybody seems to speak it now. Most of the elders, who did not go to school, still just know Navajo. Once they pass away that could end fluent speakers, bringing us to the last days simply because younger people, for the most part, are not learning it. This is a huge loss in understanding.

The way we dress also challenges traditional values and is a concern. Teachings about the end of the world say that Navajo clothing will become immodest. My mother used to get so embarrassed at how girls began to dress, especially when wearing pants. She taught my sisters not to put them on, but this was quite a while ago. She would rather see them wear skirts down to their ankles, not showing their knees or any part of their legs. Mother believed that was best, but when the last days are here people are not going to care. They will go topless, and it will not bother them. Father always said: "We're going to go back. Television is not going to be good because what you see there is not what you're trying to teach." Today we teach our children not to get involved in drinking, but television advertises all kinds of things and that is what the children watch, saying it is okay to drink and how to do it. Dad always said: "They're going to put us, the Navajo people, in the pictures and advertisements one of these days and have us dressed in that way, teaching the wrong things."

Sexual promiscuity and abortion are other indicators of the end of the world. Life is given to a baby as soon as it is conceived. That child is alive and should not be harmed. Dad was very against abortion. A long time ago my grandfather said this was going to happen. "Grandson, I just want you to know that a sign of the end is when people do what they're not supposed to do." That happened way back at the time when abortions started. "You are killing that child; it's murder. You kill that child when it starts to grow, it's still murder." In traditional culture there is a ceremony called Ajiłee meaning Excess or Prostitution Way that can help when people overindulge in sexual passion, drinking, or other activities that are harmful.[27] The ceremony corrects the problem and returns the person to harmony. Deer smoke (*bįįh nát'oh*) is also used when a person needs to correct a problem, but the ceremony removes the curse that someone has put on a person and is stronger.[28] In either case, these ceremonies return an individual's thinking to harmony and put her back on the right path. There are too many problems like this now, and few people seek the ceremonial help they need to be in balance. These are all part of the teachings that the elders have given to warn about the end of the world. It is fast approaching.

CHAPTER NINE

ANIMALS, BIRDS, AND INSECTS

Their Place and Power

Animals are very important and hold powers that are explained in traditional teachings. Many of the animals were Holy People and involved during the Creation, providing a pattern for things as they are today. This includes their impact on land formations, ceremonial practices, medicinal cures, dietary rules, and situations to avoid. Many of these animals have powers that can protect or curse, depending on the respect shown and the offerings provided. Because the Navajos have lived close to the land for so long, it is important for these instructions to be preserved and passed on to future generations so that they can benefit from the wisdom and teachings of the past.

Parents try to teach their children about the power that each species holds. Some animals may have disease or some type of crippling force. For example, if you do not teach a child to avoid a snake, besides being bitten, there are other ways that it may harm. The same is true with red ants. If a boy urinates on them, he may have problems with his private area or have urinary tract infections.[1] So parents teach their children while they are young what dangers to avoid. The word *yííyà* means something to be avoided and warns of danger. A hot stove, an animal, a black spider, an Anasazi ruin may all be yííyà. This concept is one of the first things children should learn as they become familiar with their world. It prevents harm and makes them aware.

THE LOCUST

What was the first species to emerge from the underworld into this, the Glittering World? It was the locust when water still covered the earth. There was no land to live on, so only birds survived on the surface. The story starts in the three worlds beneath.[2] The first one was black and had only locusts, ants, and beetles. This First World turned to fire, and so these insects moved upward into the next world, which was wind, and joined other life forms. Eventually all of the insects and animals of different types lived in the Third World, which had a lot of water. Today's world, the Fourth or Glittering World, was above. While the animals and Holy People were living in the Third World, Coyote took two little babies that belonged to the Water Creature. Water became angry and sent floods to cover the land and force the inhabitants above. All of them started to climb upward inside of a hollow reed. The turkey has a little white on the tip of his feathers because he was the last to ascend through the reed; the foam from the rising water colored his tail.[3] The animals pled with Coyote to give the babies back as the water continued to rise. The animals kept moving, however, with Locust in front.[4] As he emerged into this world, he saw nothing but water and sea birds with long beaks (storks and cranes). They claimed the Fourth World and did not want the new arrivals to live there.

Locust challenged that. The birds dove and swooped in front of him, but he just sat unafraid and did not blink. The birds were impressed, stopping to ask what he was doing and why he had come there. When he told them he was looking for a place to live, they refused his request. Locust insisted, saying that he had people with him. "I'm not the only one that's coming up." The birds decided to test him. They pulled an arrow from their feathers, and one bird placed it in its mouth and pushed it down until it came out below. The bird next drew the arrow through in the opposite direction, reversing the process. "If you can do this you will come to live here," he said. Instead of Locust performing the act through his mouth, he pushed the arrow beneath his two elbows on his side. Today locusts still have a small hole on each side that is visible when they spread their wings. The arrow passed through with only a little blood on it; Locust dared them to do it. The bird replied that it could not because its heart was there. Locust had won.

Another bird was angry, challenging Locust to be hit in the forehead with a long club. Locust did not blink. He sat there and took the blow; that is why he has a little indentation on the top of his head today. The bird struck a second blow, this time in the stomach, rolling Locust over and causing a swelling that is still there, living proof that he had been hit. Still he had won and so brought the animals and Holy People to this world. The birds began to help, spreading their wings to create a wind that dried the land. Earth appeared, sacred plants found root that held the land together, and the ability to plant crops became possible. Eventually the animals and holy beings moved to the mountains, where they lived happily.

COYOTE

One of the most powerful and sometimes misunderstood animals is Coyote, who has been involved with the five-fingered beings [humans] since the beginning of the world. He is one of the greatest teachers of Navajo culture; little is said before someone tells a story about him that explains how a person should or should not act. Sometimes he does things wrong and so is seen as foolish or evil, but more often he is like a human, providing an example of what happens when a person acts in a particular fashion. There are three different ways to think about him. One is that he is very, very sacred.[5] Coyote helped put the stars in the heavens, controls the spinning of the world, provides rain, and holds powers that make him a holy being. Another way is to see him as evil. He brought death into the world, tricks and lies, and may be totally irresponsible to everybody and everything.[6] A third way to think of him is that he is really innocent, stumbling around so that through his mistakes things happen. He is neither good nor bad, just innocent and trying to understand how everything works.

Take the rabbit story, for instance. One day Rabbit spied Coyote, removed his coat, and stuffed it with rocks. Coyote, as usual, was traveling along when he suddenly saw what he supposed was a rabbit sitting in the open. Without thinking he grabbed the coat filled with rocks and greedily chomped on it, breaking his teeth. This story explains the origin of the toothache, something that everybody experiences. Another tale tells of when Talking God instructed Coyote not to open a bag of food packed by people he was deer hunting with. They had made it small for carrying, so they reminded him not to get into it because if he did everything would come out and be very hard to put back in. Eventually he entered a village of spiders playing games. They had lined up a series of strings then challenged each other to see who could weave fastest in and out of the obstacle course. Coyote sat there with his big bag, watching them play all of their games, then decided to look inside his container. He carefully opened the bag just a little bit and whoosh, the whole thing came apart. We have all had that same experience of learning that we must listen carefully and do what we are told.

Next he started picking at the spiders, who decided to teach him a lesson. They strung him up so that he could not get away then choked but did not kill him, because he is the ruler of the world. If they had killed him, they would be destroyed, even though it was not his game and he should not have gotten involved. You do not invite yourself or interfere with what others are doing, a lesson taken from this story.

Another time beavers were playing a game. Coyote teased them, saying that he was better at it than they were. They invited him to play; he did not follow instructions, so he lost his clothes in a bet that ended in further trouble. The story of the lizards sliding on rocks where Coyote invited himself, took the activity to excess, and was hurt again teaches not to invite yourself, to respect elders, follow instructions, and not overdo a good thing. This is the way we were taught. Our grandparents first told the story then repeated it, as we sat and asked questions. "Why is this here? Why is this happening?" At the end there was a discussion. Grandfather told me that if I did not listen I would become just like Coyote. "You have to be careful not to get involved with something you're not trained in or you are not meant for." Coyote, as he travels, often visits villages here and there and invites himself. Nobody else does that. We teach our children the same thing, not to get involved in something they do not understand or follow someone who will get them in trouble. When adults got after us, they said that we were acting like Coyote because we were not listening.

Coyote often chased after women. There is a way of describing a man who leaves a woman and pursues one after another, as did Coyote in some of the stories. He was always trying to start something, to find a young lady who he soon left. This is shown in the story about Badger, who is slow and methodical but tricked by Coyote, who wished to sleep with Badger's wife and cheat on his friend. Navajos say he was acting like a billy goat, a male donkey, or a bull. This refers to a womanizer who goes from one female to another without any commitment, often leaving a baby behind. There are many lessons for life that we learn from these kinds of teachings.

Coyote as a holy being has powers both to help and to curse the Navajo People. Sometimes the buffoon and trickster, he also controls rain, establishes patterns of life, forewarns of danger, and keeps the world and heavens in motion. Those coyotes now living on the earth are this Holy Person's representatives. (Photo by Kay Shumway)

Understanding Coyote is important, and all of the small coyotes on this earth are connected to him and hold certain powers. When a coyote runs across a person's path it is a warning, but it does not necessarily mean something bad will happen.[7] It is indicating that there is danger ahead and to be alert. You then have to do something like saying prayers and placing ntł'iz in his tracks as an offering.[8] If the coyote turns around and looks, that means he is carrying a message that someone in your family is dying. A lot of people do not like a coyote passing before them because they feel it is bad luck, but it is only a warning. Just like a policeman when you are driving too fast; you had better slow down. Often we do not listen and there are consequences. Coyotes are actually being protective of the Navajos. If a coyote does something wrong like kill sheep, then you have the right to kill him, but if he does not bother you, leave him alone.[9] A good coyote is like the ruler of the world and is protected by lightning. A lot of animals are like that.

One day the Holy People were trying to put the sun and moon in the sky and figure out how all the different stars and planets were supposed to work. Instead of having them go from east to west, they actually started with them rising from south to north. The sun went up in the sky then came down to rest. The moon did the same. The caves or alcoves on Comb Ridge are places where they temporarily settled.[10] Finally Coyote showed the Holy People how to have the sun and moon move from east to west and assisted in keeping them in the sky. All the Holy People were very, very intelligent, but they were still struggling with the problem and had disagreements about the order of things. There were some who got in the way and argued until Coyote arrived. "It's going to take you forever. This is going to take forever. Why don't you just do this instead of taking all that time," he said. Tossing upward the blanket that held all of the stars, he shook it into the air and scattered them in a random pattern. He was always hurrying and interrupting people. There was one star he threw up very high, saying, "This is going to be Coyote's Star. It is going to be brighter than all of the others."[11]

October is the first month or moon of the Navajo year. It is said to be Coyote's month because the seasons start to change.[12] Coyote begins to feel early winter approaching so prepares for the stories that are going to be told. This is when he changes his short-haired coat to one with long hairs ready for winter. He begins preparing because he knows how the weather is going to be. The middle of October is when storytelling starts and continues through the month of Slim Wind (November) to the time when baby eagles chirp in their shell (March). For these five or six months, people are very involved in playing the shoe game and storytelling.

Coyote controls rain. He does not do it through witchcraft but rather through prayers. He knows that he controls the rain and that by doing so the sky recognizes him. The two are connected. When coyotes are extinct there will be no more rain, because there has to be at least one somewhere on the earth in order for it to come. The teaching says that he has got natural power and will do something for you if you do not bother him. I remember when I was growing up a lot of people left home early in the morning. As we were eating breakfast suddenly the coyotes would start howling, meaning it was going to rain. The more howling there was, the more rain would fall. If there was a drought, you did not hear them; but once they began, the rains came. This is how communication went from Mother Earth to Father Sky, who recognizes this animal as a messenger.

Coyote's association with water in the heavens and earth goes back to the time of Creation when he took the two twin water babies that belonged to the Holy Person who controlled the water in the third world. This holy being, Big Water Creature (Tééhooɫtsòdii), got angry, so he used the water to force the people and animals to escape above. They did not know why the water was angry and that Coyote had stolen its two babies, hiding them in his armpit. Finally someone saw that he was carrying them and tried to get him to give the babies back, but he would not. One version of this story teaches that he returned them to the rising water, which then receded. Others say that he threw one baby into the sky and it became the clouds and that he threw the other on the land to become surface water. These two types of moisture are twins. When a cloud forms in the heavens, one stays on the earth with the big waters, such as the ocean or lakes. Thus when Coyote entered this world, he took one of the water babies and placed it in the sky for the clouds and gave the other to the earth, so the two remain connected.

Another story tells that as the water evaporated and the land appeared, many of the creatures living in the water remained with their powers, making it dangerous. Some elders do not like to talk about these powerful beings that inhabit rivers, lakes, and oceans. Although some Navajos fish, they are not supposed to eat them as well as crabs, crayfish, and ocean foods, since they come from water. Very traditional Navajos will never eat fish because it has a rainbow, like a snake, on its underside so is protected by the Holy People. Fish represent Father Sky because of this protective rainbow, a promise that exists for anything else that has these markings. They say the water is alive, very dangerous, inhabited by creatures that harm, and controlled by power that destroys, so leave it alone. When I was growing up, this is how I was taught, but now we eat fish.

My grandmother always said, "Do not play in the water, yíiyà." You should not be in the water when it looks like it is going to rain, and do not go near water while clouds are forming because lightning will strike. These teachings began when Coyote angered the power in water and stole its babies. You should not go swimming, even if it has just barely rained, but rather stay away because of what Coyote did. A lot of times when someone's reservoir gets really full, people say that there is a lot of power in the water and so you should not play or swim in it. Also, you should not throw or splash water on people as a joke; that is like spitting on a person, neither of which is polite. The only time you can play with water is when you think it is going to rain, but even then there needs to be a prayer said. Water is associated with heat. Boiling water cooks food, is used to drink after it cools, and gives life to things and so is respected. It also cleanses, and so people should not jump into it and start playing around. There has to be a reason to use it.

Water keeps humans alive and is a provider, so it is not treated lightly. When rain begins to fall, you should sit down, be quiet, and be respectful. There is no hunting in the rain because having a weapon that is sharp is offensive to lightning and does not show respect to the water, while killing opposes life that comes with rain. Mother Earth and Father Sky are in harmony at that time and blessing each other; to disturb their peace with death disrupts what is good. Children and adults should be mindful and settled.

SNAKES AND LIZARDS

Snakes, like coyotes, are messengers. When Navajos see a snake in their home they believe that something is going to happen, because it carries a very powerful message that may have been sent by an evil medicine man as a curse. All of the snakes that are found roaming about are related to the holy being Big Snake, who is very powerful.[13] A blow snake, for example, even though it is not poisonous, can still bring a curse, and so no one is to play with it. They have a fine hair, similar to that found on a cactus that serves as a long needle. If a person sits on a cactus this hair-like spine works its way into the skin and is very difficult to find and remove. Snakes have even littler hairs that also burrow into the skin when you are handling them. Picking up a snake is forbidden, but if a person does he may become crippled or swollen or have back problems. This sickness is associated with lightning because snakes are protected by it; their underside has all of the colors of a rainbow. If somebody is bitten by a snake, a healing ceremony is not performed until the next year and is the same one used to cure those exposed to lightning and lightning-struck objects. If you encounter a snake track, do not step over it but drag your feet across it, erasing any sign of the trail. A snake should not be killed if it is not bothering you; if you do, they will harm you later in life by crippling you.

A few years ago the San Juan School District got involved in a lawsuit. There was a teacher in Bluff who brought a snake into the classroom. Long before this occurred, a pregnant Navajo woman saw a snake eating its partly swallowed prey. She should have forced the snake to regurgitate its food and everything would have been all right, but she did not. The baby in her womb had now been exposed to this sight with no corrective action taken. When the child was born, its joints and hands began to swell. Everyone wondered what had caused it. They took the baby to the doctor, who found nothing wrong. Finally the parents went to a medicine man, who performed hand trembling and questioned the mother, asking if when she was pregnant she had had contact with a snake. She told him what had happened, and he explained why the boy was having all these problems. Another medicine man performed the cure, and the child immediately became better. Years later the boy was in school when a teacher, who did not understand Navajo culture, brought a snake into the classroom and exposed him again to its power. This created a big problem. The child went home and started having similar issues with swelling. The family found another medicine man and spent a lot of money to have a ceremony performed then sued the school district for its part in the problem. Encounters with snakes must be handled appropriately.[14]

Lizards are viewed in the same way and should not be allowed in a home.[15] They are messengers who announce that something bad is going to happen, just like a snake or a coyote. Lizards, like a snake, should not be touched or killed. Navajos say that they can draw a person's heart out and place a curse on it. The curse that all these animals carry is cancer known as the "Sore That Does Not Heal" and can only be cured by a ceremony. The medicine men performing the ritual use scrapings from dinosaur tracks as protection. Frogs are also not bothered and should not be killed for any reason. If you do hurt a frog you will be crippled and go hopping around. The best thing to do with all of these animals is to leave them alone.

HORNED TOAD

Horned toads are different. They are very special to the Navajo people and are referred to as Grandfather. There is a story that tells how one saved a young boy's life when threatened by a large giant who was eating the People. The boy lived with his grandparents, herding sheep. At this time there was a group of giants who did not like children because they did not want any more people around and so were killing them off. They went from home to home to make sure there were none; but if they found any, they would eat them. The little boy was herding sheep one day when his flock scattered at the noise of an approaching giant.

Frightened, the boy hid beneath a flat sheet of sandstone, but it was too late. The giant already knew where he was, stomped his feet, and said: "Come on, I'm hungry. Go gather some wood and build a fire." The little boy came out crying and began picking up pieces of wood, but there was not enough. "Go and get more," the giant commanded as the boy cried even harder. Suddenly he heard "Sssssshhhu." He looked around and looked around but was so scared he could not see what caused the noise. He picked up another piece of wood and heard "Sssshhhu" again. There sat a horny [horned] toad. "Grandson, what are you crying about? What's happening?" he said, lying there with his feet spread apart and wearing an arrowhead for a hat. The little boy cried louder, "Ahhhhhhhh." "Come on, Grandson, tell me what's wrong." The boy sobbed, "There's a big giant that is ready to eat me," then explained what had happened. "Oh don't be afraid, Grandson. We can get rid of that giant. Even though I'm small I can help. Here, take this hat of mine and put it on your head." The boy tried, but it was too small. The horny toad urged him to try again, and as he did the hat grew larger and eventually fit him just right. When you look at a horned toad's head you can see it is the shape of a completed arrowhead that is worn like a hat. Next the toad told him to return to the giant and when he asked the boy to take the hat off, not to do it until the boy had killed him. Just as the horny toad predicted, the giant said, "Awhhh, take that hat off. Please don't come near," but the little boy advanced closer and closer. By now the giant was scared, demanding: "That hat's dangerous. Take it off. I don't want you to wear that hat," but the boy kept following him. The giant backed up, not noticing the cliff behind until it was too late. He fell, shaking the earth when he hit the ground and died. The little boy was so happy that he returned to his new friend and gave back the hat. Horny Toad said, "Grandson, don't be afraid. I'll be there whenever you need help."

This story goes on and teaches how to relieve leg pain. All of the horned toad's clothing is protective, and his power is like a shield. When my boys were little, they would cry from aching legs at night. I sat them on my lap

The horned toad, small in size, is a being of power and protection. Maker and wearer of arrowheads, associated with lightning, this creature is highly respected by the Navajos, who understand his ability to cast off evil. (Photo by Kay Shumway)

and talked to them, massaging their legs. Soon they stopped crying and went to sleep. My grandmother used to do that for me, singing as she massaged my legs. It felt so good I just went to sleep. This creature's power, through song, removes pain in the body. I would sing "Horny toad's socks are my socks; horny toad's shoes are my shoes" as I rubbed my boys' limbs and called upon the protective force of his clothing to remove the pain. His shield is what I want to wear. So this story explains why horny toads are considered your grandfather and should not be bothered.

Horny toad is also an excellent corn grower, so there should always be one in every cornfield. His power protects the corn, ensuring a good harvest and that the corn is healthy because he is and anything he handles becomes that way too. When you find a horny toad, it is good to pick him up and hold him to your heart and say, "I am going to be as healthy and strong in beauty just as horny toad is," before putting him down. On both sides of a horny toad is a yellow stripe that shows his relationship to corn pollen, which is used to bless. He represents the pollen road—one of peace, blessing, and safety in travel. Just as a driver stays on the right side of a yellow line on a highway, there is protection.[16] Horny toads are placed in clean sand and sprinkled with corn pollen. These "shake-offs"—the sand and pollen—are then collected and used to bless babies in cradleboards by placing them under the infant's feet or sprinkling them on anyone who needs protection. His image is also used in many sandpaintings for protection.

In the story just told, the giant was very afraid, yíiyá, of horny toad because it is just like thinking about arrowheads, the weapon used during this time to kill monsters.[17] When the Twins journeyed to their father that was one of the things they brought back. Navajo people say that horny toads make arrowheads. This is very true. My sister and I were herding sheep near a sand dune where the wind blew out an area surrounded by rabbit brush. Not too far from the plants was a stone that was a half-chipped arrowhead. I had always been told that if you find something like that to leave it alone, do not move it. I believe this is true. About a year later I was in the same place where Brigham tea and rabbit brush grew and saw the arrowhead completed. It was about an inch and a half to two inches long and of a very nice tan or off-white color. I could not believe it; nobody had been there to finish this point. I don't think a human would do it like that, yet nobody believed me except my great-grandfather, who had always told me that this type of thing happens. I asked my mother, who had heard this teaching from her dad; she said that a horny toad looks like he is very sharp around his neck, lips, and tongue. Somehow he takes his time and chips with his tongue. A lot of people find these arrowheads, and I wonder why.

DEER

The deer is respected as a Holy Person with a very powerful spirit.[18] This is also true of elk, moose, and antelope, which come from the same family line. All of their meat is eaten and their hides used to make medicine bags, while deer hide is tough enough to fashion moccasins. Deerskin used in ceremonies has the face and ears still attached and tanned with the rest of the hide. You have to learn how to remove the skull and take off the whole skin together. People pay a lot of money for one of those hides when tanned by hand. Deer hoofs are used to make rattles for the Enemy Way ceremony. Three of them are attached to the end of the stick that is carried to the camps, representing the days of the ceremony and the three sheep that must be brought in to feed the gathering. Powwow people now use these hoofs like bells once they are dried. In traditional Navajo culture this is not done.

Deer meat is particularly powerful as a medicine. When a person is internally ill or has some form of cancer, she should not eat deer meat because of

Deer are seen as mountain animals whose eating of herbs makes their meat medicine, whose antlers protect from lightning, and whose role in nature demands proper behavior for those who hunt them. A complex series of beliefs and practices surrounds the killing, cleaning, and transport of deer. (Photo by Kay Shumway)

its power. My mother told Betty not to eat deer meat because she had kidney disease. The same thing is true with piñon nuts. You can eat them before becoming sick and deer meat, as a medicine, will prevent that kind of disease. This is because deer are in the mountains eating medicinal plants, which are usually bitter. This is good medicine, but once a person has an internal illness she should not eat deer meat because it is just too strong. Before getting sick it is fine to do this, after it is too late. With a sore already started inside, it is just too powerful.

When cooking deer meat it is not to be mixed with mutton; it must be kept separate, and deer fur is always kept from the sheep or else they will go wild. Men hunt deer and women herd sheep; one is associated with what is wild and hunting in the mountains while the other is with the home, the woman's place. If something from the deer comes in contact with the sheep, the animals get sick and skinny and become wild. If we have some part of a deer, a hide near the corral or even just loose hair in our yard, it serves as a curse. Nothing can be left lying around. The same is true of the livestock, because deer are such powerful supernatural animals. My clan is the Deer Spring People, and while I have not been taught this way, some of my clan members will not eat deer meat. I have decided that we are all right to do it.

People as well as animals must also be careful when exposed to deer hides, hair, and antlers. For example, if I had some hides or fur in my yard, I do not want my children urinating on them. Deer hair affects them with problems in urinating. Also it is a very powerful way to negatively affect thinking. Medicine men who do not have good intentions can use deer hair to attract women, getting them involved in excessive sexual relations, or can generally curse an individual. If there are antlers or a hide lying around the house, this person can pick it up and use it to work against someone. If the hair comes off when tanning a hide then it needs to be taken care of. The hide is okay, but the hair is the thing that can be used against a person to make him crazy. These are powerful things because of the deer's supernatural nature. The deer also has strong powers to positively affect the psychological well-being of a person. The hide is used in the Enemy Way ceremony for those who need to be cleansed of evil experiences. Sheep cannot be used to curse people, but they, too, can be affected by a spell placed on deer hair. The power, once it is opened, hurts the animals. They begin to have poor thoughts then become sick or wild.

While deer hair is very sacred, the antlers are especially dangerous and should never be brought into a home. If there was an antler in a house and my mother knew it, she would not visit. She felt it was a curse. Even looking at an antler can give an electric shock, because as part of a mountain animal they hold the power to control lightning. The shock, while looking at them, is part of their power and protection given by the Holy People. An antler will supernaturally disappear if it is put in your home; it will leave a curse behind. That is why Navajo people do not want it in their dwelling. It is associated with a power described as "unexpected shock from supernatural things" and is comparable to seeing the spirit of a departed soul who has been dead for a long time. It suddenly appears, moving about, terrifying those who see it, sending them into shock. It is hard to explain, this idea of being unexpectedly frightened, but that is why Navajos are so afraid of antlers and dealing with their power in the home.

Hunting deer must also be performed in a very sacred way. You do not go hunting just to kill. There has to be a reason, and people should hunt deer as if they were hungry.[19] Before going out, the hunter should smoke deer tobacco, because in some ways hunting will curse you if you do not follow traditional teachings.[20] Deer smoke takes care of you, removing the power of exposure to things that carry a curse. One way to show proper respect for the animal during the butchering is to ensure everything is used and nothing wasted or thrown away. The antlers are left behind, but everything else is carefully bundled with the head, hoofs, and bones in a particular method. Nothing is thrown around and scattered. Anything that is not saved is left where the animal is killed. When an unbutchered deer is brought home, which I have done at times, it is not showing respect. I have done this but was not supposed to because it is a supernatural being who should remain in the mountains.

When butchering a deer, things must be kept clean; the cutting follows a different procedure than when cleaning sheep. There is a certain pattern— another line for the incision—and the head is treated differently also. First we gather as a family, have a short prayer, and smoke deer tobacco.[21] This plant grows at higher elevations like Navajo Mountain, is the color of sagebrush, and its leaves look like hairy deer ears. Some people sell this tobacco at flea markets, but it is not good to purchase it this way because when a plant is picked, the name of the sick person and a prayer should be given before any of it is taken. If I do get sick from antlers or deer hair, I would hold a ceremony called the Deer Way, where deer tobacco is smoked and prayers offered.[22]

The process of cleaning a deer starts by making a cut while standing or kneeling behind or to the side of it. Even when taking off the hide, you avoid being in front of the head and antlers where its power is concentrated. Since antlers are left where the animal is killed, a problem with hunting laws arises. Wildlife rangers and hunters who butcher in the field say to tie the antlers to the deer tag. I do not know if they are aware of Navajo practices. If they are, they probably would not insist that Native American people do that.

Hunting is a very good way to provide for a family. Children must be taught these things. I take time to answer their questions because they always ask why. If I am going to go hunting, I do not sleep with my wife but stay in the front room. When I return I again do not sleep with her for a while. In the same respect, a woman is not supposed to hunt with her man, but she can hunt in a group of women.[23] That is what I heard, but others have told me they are not supposed to. A daughter cannot hunt with her father, especially when she is young. It is best to keep children on the safe side away from the deer's power. Because these animals are holy, you have to be very careful of what and how things are done. That is why I try not to butcher at home, but I often end up doing it because my children bring one to me instead of cleaning it where it was killed. They do not butcher it very well and put holes in the hide, so I end up doing it because I want to make a vest or moccasins from it. After skinning a deer but before going into the house, I take a clay pipe and blow deer smoke on the hide and my clothing to purify the power and prevent harm. I put my soiled clothes in a place away from children.

Finally, there is a metaphor in Navajo culture that says when the wife leaves, the deer doesn't sit still. What this means is that if a wife divorces a man, he is weak and will go hungry. He will not know where to turn, she will take everything, and he needs to change the situation. He must start looking for another wife; and if he is strong, he will do well and find a new, better life. In the Navajo way a person does not really choose his companion, because the parents are the ones who make that decision. They will find a young lady who already has been taught well, knows how to cook and herd sheep, and has a lot of wealth. But when there are problems sometimes the parents do not support their son in a divorce. If it is the woman who is interested in another man, then the situation is different. So in this metaphor, a deer or the husband is encouraged to find another mate and make his life better.

MOUNTAIN SHEEP

Both mountain sheep and desert bighorns are from the same family and more powerful than deer. Mountain sheep stand on top of high mountains or large rocks where lightning may strike but never get hurt because their power rests in their horns. Their hide, when hung in a dwelling, wards off lightning and forces sickness and harmful things away from the sheep. A person should not keep the horn in the home but at a distance. It is powerful and will move from place to place, so a stone is put on it so it will not move away. If this is not done, it will return to its original home. Some Navajos will not touch or eat mountain sheep. For others, the only part they use is the skin for medicine bags. Not only can the hides be tanned, but the hairs when burned are helpful for healing domestic sheep. They can also inhale smoke from a burning horn to get better. Now people buy expensive medication, but in the past they used to use these remedies to keep their livestock healthy. Mountain sheep horns are also used to hold ointments and medication; bighorn sheep fat is used in the Evil Way ceremony, and its skin is cut into strips to make a string for a bullroarer to chase evil away.[24] The thin strip of skin located between the two horns on the sheep's head is desired for its ability to get rid of aches by massaging.

BEARS

Bears are another powerful creature that must be treated with respect.[25] Traditional Navajo people do not even talk about them without either an appropriate reason or it being the correct time of year—winter, when they are in hibernation.[26] They are viewed as human because they stand upright and walk just like us.[27] Referred to as Grandfather, a bear should be treated kindly and left alone. Following the Creation, the Holy People sent bears to the mountains to live. They are not supposed to wander around on Navajo lands; but when they do, it is a sign that the end of the world is approaching. Bears on the reservation will not come down from the mountains unless the end is near. Until then, leave them alone.

There is a story of the bear acting as a human being. One time Black Bear was dressed in a ceremonial way for the Hóchx̨o'íjí [Evil Way] ceremony. He wanted to help and said, "I am going to a Hóchx̨o'íjí Hataal [Sing or Chant Way]," and waved his rattle. A medicine man at the ceremony was shaking his rattle in the same way when the bear entered the door. The singing stopped for a brief moment, then Bear came in and sat down. Suddenly the bear passed out. A man got up and looked him over, saying, "Now what has happened here?" In order to bring him back to his senses the Akéshgaan [Hoof or Claw Way] ceremony was performed.[28] This prevented these fainting spells from reoccurring. People bothered with fainting may have this same ceremony performed to rid them of the sickness.

Today when a ceremony takes place, a person should not look through the doorway, peeking in or out. Also, there are some rituals such as the sweat

Bear was one of the four Holy People to protect Changing Woman as she traveled about Navajo land. His power is also associated with those who now roam the mountains and so demands respect. Like many other animals, bears have a humanlike spirit and (when they remove their outer physical appearance) can think and communicate just like a person. (Photo by Calvin Black)

lodge and Blessing Way where people should not go in and out but remain seated as a participant. Because the bear did not understand this, he had the sickness transferred to him. When the medicine man cured him, the bear gave him his rattle, prayer, and bear song, which are now used in the ceremony.[29] The bear's claw is used to rip things, while his footprint is made as part of the healing process. My grandfather said that if a person is very, very sick with cancer or heart problems, he can use part of the bear to be healed. Bitter bear bile is given to the patient internally, but only when this medication is desperately needed. No part of the skin is used, and during this ceremony people avoid sitting or associating with things that are black, such as a black sheep skin, unless directed by the medicine man. When bear tracks are encountered, Navajos leave an offering then take some of the sand surrounding the footprint. This is used for blessings like my grandfather gave me when I was a little boy. He prayed that I would become strong like a bear and very competitive. Corn pollen sprinkled on a bear's body can be used to ward off evil.

BADGER

There are many uses for the badger, whose stories tell of what happened in the beginning. He was the first to wed, thus initiating the institution of marriage. Badger's bride wanted a man who was responsible and worked hard. Coyote, the trickster, on the other hand, was only looking for a woman to sleep with for a short time. He went to Badger's bride and asked what kind of a man she wanted. Coyote really interrogated her, hanging around, pestering to know what she desired, as Badger competed with him for her favor. He won her heart, so she rejected Coyote. However, a price had to be paid for the bride, and so Coyote suggested that the next day he and Badger go hunting. He thought, "I am the fastest; I can get more prey." In the early morning Coyote sang his songs, asking for snow high enough to cover curled grass and deep enough to slow his opponent. Badger sang for just enough to cover the ground, and his request was granted. It snowed and they were off, with Coyote ahead. Badger followed his tracks, seeing how Coyote turned corners too fast, while Badger went slowly, catching game animals along the way. Coyote could only catch rabbits by putting a stick down their hole, twisting, and pulling them out, while Badger climbed down the hole. Seeing Badger's success, Coyote suggested that he enter a hole but leave his sack behind. Badger was tired and his bag was full of rabbits, but he decided to get one more. He crawled into the burrow; but as soon as he did, Coyote rolled stones over the tunnel, took his sack, and left behind his almost empty one. People today are referring to this when they say, "You steal like Coyote."

He went straight back to the waiting bride, claiming he had brought in more food than his competitor would and that the agreement was that the one who did could claim her as his wife. The future bride argued that Badger had not yet returned, so how could judgment be made? It was a long time before Badger did arrive, exhausted from his day of hunting. He angrily accused: "You are really something, Coyote. You are not a good being; you rolled stones in front of my tunnel, left me with your load, and took mine." Soon the animals went to bed, but Coyote was still interested in Badger's bride. Before long he persuaded her to sleep with him then had his way in excess. Badger was so tired he slept through the night, not aware of what was happening until morning. He shouted at Coyote, who jumped up, poked at the fire, then left in disgrace. Before this time, there was no asking for a hand in marriage, no reason for a wedding. This was the start of marriage, adultery, and the teachings against a husband or wife cheating on each other.

There is also a song about Badger, who is in charge of rain and snow. His skin is used to make rattles as in the Beauty Way ceremony, where bits of badger skin are tied to rattles. In the song it says, "I am a shield, therefore I live," so Badger is a holy being. There are other stories about him that eventually interrelate, as do the songs in the shoe game. I have just heard parts of the ceremonies and that this creature is very sacred. When he travels, even though it might be far, the distance is never too far for the badger because he travels fast. He moves like an automobile in the twilight.

MOUNTAIN LIONS, BOBCATS, FOXES, AND BEAVERS

Mountain lions help with riches and protection, their hides being filled with gold and money.[30] Hanging their skin in your home will bring wealth and the kind of things your family wants. The home will be open to the good things of life; and like the arrows that hang above the door, a mountain lion's skin will protect the family from harm. Nothing evil will enter. A bobcat skin does the same thing and is used in making a quiver. Bobcat meat, especially the leg, is eaten, the skin brings wealth, and the animal has its own song in the Blessing Way Ceremony. The whole skin of the blue fox is used in the Yé'ii Bicheii dance as the tail of the Water Sprinkler holy being. If one of these skins is in a home, earthly goods will vanish and the owner will lose everything. Yé'iis wear beaver skins strapped over their shoulder to make the ceremonies of value to the Holy People. Beavers are believed to be strong medicine people, for we have all been healed by them in one way or another; parts of them are found on many ceremonial tools. Some of their hide is put on rattles as decorative tails or hung on flutes. Because they are doctors, beaver fur may be burned on hot coals and its smoke inhaled by a patient. It is used in many ceremonies in this manner.

SKUNK

Skunks are very good animals. Take the skin and let it hang in your home to keep out colds and disease. When sickness is going around, the smell of the skunk wards it off. There is a story about a male badger and a female skunk competing to see who could urinate the farthest. The one expected to win, Badger, lost the contest because he just pissed on the ground below him. The competition next turned to who was the most intellectual and again the woman, Skunk, won. She then vowed that her meat and urine would help the people in the future. Medicine men place a skunk's penis in smoke and have their patients sniff it if they are bothered by a dead person's spirit. If someone has a cold, inhaling this will also help. I remember my grandmother would skin a skunk, take off the penis, and let it hang in the corner of the room to keep disease and evil things away.

Skunk was here from the beginning and created the Enemy Way ceremony with Coyote's help. Coyote had been drifting in water one day before climbing onto the land, where he played dead. When Skunk came for water, he met Coyote, who called him cousin, meaning bosom friend, four times. As he lay there he said: "My cousin. You who came for water, we will have a feast." He then told Skunk to gather grass seeds and place them around his anus, arm pits, mouth, and eyes, which Skunk did. Next he told Skunk to return to where he was living and let the other animals know that old rotten Coyote was dead, thus attracting them so that the two could kill and eat them. Skunk went back with his story, but the other animals did not believe him. Instead they sent four fast runners—jackrabbit, antelope, gopher, and cottontail—to see if Skunk's story was true. They returned believing Coyote was dead.

Coyote had instructed Skunk to tell the animals once they were dancing around the body to look to the sky to see something then to spray upward, filling their eyes with mist. As the animals danced around Coyote, kicking him in the stomach, Skunk let loose, blinding them. Coyote jumped up, and the two clubbed and killed all the animals. They then baked their prey in the earth. This is the origin of the Enemy Way ceremony and why the round dance is part of it. Trickery and cheating also continues to this day as people act like Coyote and Skunk.

SMALL BUT POWERFUL ANIMALS

There is a difference between cottontail rabbits and jackrabbits. Both can be eaten and are considered to have clean meat because of the grass and plants they live on. It is good medicine. A jackrabbit can be kept as a pet, but not the cottontail. Cottontails, like mice, go underground, get into graves, and have contact with the dead. That is why they cannot be pets, but our ancestors survived on them as food, and, like the deer, they have medicine in their meat.

Chipmunks, however, are not eaten.[31] One story is told of a man who was asked to bring in a medicine bundle from outside. He looked for it four times but returned saying that all he could find was a dried chipmunk skin in the branches of a tree. When he brought it in, the skin grew into a large medicine bundle that healed people. This power of the chipmunk first became known during the time when Monster Slayer was killing different monsters on the earth. There is a song that goes with this story.

The monster Déélgééd was very hard to kill. Monster Slayer tried to approach him from the four directions but could not get close. Chipmunk said, "I can go up to the monster, get on top of it, and even give birth to my children in its body hair." Chipmunk went with the holy being to kill the monster, got next to its heart, and directed the Twin where to shoot. He remained near Déélgééd until it no longer moved then sang its song four times, saying that the creature was still.[32] Without his help, the monster would still roam the earth and humans would not exist. Now a chipmunk is viewed as a friend who foretells the future, warns of bad things approaching, and helps with hunting.

Porcupines were eaten when food was not plentiful, while their quills are used on rattles and other sacred objects. Quills decorate baby cradles to ward off evil, sickness, and bad thoughts. In the teaching stories, Porcupine was an ally of Coyote. One story tells of how a porcupine asked an elk for help crossing some water. Since the porcupine could not ride on the elk's back, he asked if he could go into its anus. The cow agreed and took the porcupine across; but once the splashing of water ceased and the elk was on dry land, the porcupine raised his quills and killed it. Next he looked for something to butcher it with. Coyote overheard the porcupine talking to himself about what he was going to do, so he convinced him that whoever jumped over the dead cow was the owner. Porcupine tried to get out of it; but after Coyote asked four times, he had to agree.[33] Coyote jumped high over the carcass, but Porcupine only covered half the distance. This is when winning took place. Next Coyote handed Porcupine a knife and told him to butcher the dead elk and take care of the meat while he went for his children. Porcupine agreed, carrying the meat high into a pine tree. When Coyote returned with his brood, he realized what had happened and begged for part of his prize. Only the skin lay on the ground, and so most of Coyote's children slept and lay on it while they waited. The youngest coyote was the only one alert enough to look through a hole in the skin at Porcupine. Porcupine dropped some of the large bones on the children below, killing all but the youngest, who had been watching. That was the end of it. This is where stealing originated, but Coyote lost in the end. Porcupine was the one who killed, Coyote the one who stole, only to have Porcupine steal from him; they were partners in this way. The loser turned back into a winner.

DOMESTIC ANIMALS

Sheep and horses are very sacred to the Navajo People, who protect them. They both have supernatural power. Sheep must be cared for with good grazing and water. Our grandparents taught that if someone sleeps late in the morning and does not get up before sunrise, he will never survive in this world. My mother said: "If you get up early in the morning make sure your sheep come first. You go out and take them to good feed. That is where you're going to be. If you herd them early in the morning, you're going to have good sheep. If you take care of them, they will be your income and you will have good clothes for your family."[34] Shearing, dyeing, and weaving wool were some of the skills passed on from great-grandparents. My mother and father learned how to shear sheep and would gather the family together twice a year so that everyone could help.

Goats were herded separately from sheep. They have a mind of their own, so that when you try to herd them one way and turn around, you will see them going in the wrong direction up some rocky mesa. Once in a while a half-sheep, half-goat may appear. Their hair is usually long and a bit harder to card. Goat hair is used to make the main strings for a rug because it is strong. When sheep are dipped to rid them of disease, they should not be butchered for about a month after. In the wintertime they get a little thin, so Grandmother would have about four of them she really took care of, giving them hay and grain once in a while to keep them fat. That way in the wintertime you still have some good mutton.

One year when the sheep became sick we had to gather and burn herbs with some deer hair to heal them. Inhaling the smoke of that medication helped. Herbal medicine is also used when a ewe is lambing and having a hard time. We would also use both sheep and goat's milk to drink and make cheese. One year when my mother and father were working on the railroad, my grandmother, the blind woman, raised my little baby sister, Marie. I remember they tied a goat inside the hogan behind the weaving loom. When the baby was hungry, Grandmother would take her to the goat to nurse. Since my grandmother could not see, she tied one of the baby's legs to the loom so that she would not crawl outside or go near the stove. When everybody was around, Grandmother untied her and let her run and do what she wanted.

Before a person killed a sheep, she would take some of its wool and place it in the mouth of another sheep, saying that its posterity will continue and not be lost. There will always be others to take its place. When killing a sheep there is a right and a wrong way to do it. The proper way is to cut its throat but not remove its head until the entire hide is off. By doing so, you will never lose your sheep. If you do not follow this practice, your sheep will never increase. By leaving the head attached, the sheep, although dead, is aware of its kind treatment.

Horsemeat is medicine. I think the difference between deer and horse meat is that the deer comes from the wild, has eaten medicine plants, and holds strong supernatural powers that can harm a person. The deer's curse is greater than that of a horse. The horse, on the other hand, is your animal, and its meat is good medicine because it eats very clean food like grass. They have some of the cleanest meat there is because of the herbs and medicines growing on the range, a lot of which Navajos use for teas or in cooking.

Animals kept around the home like dogs and cats are very powerful. If a person starves his dog, it can curse him, so it is better to feed him. My father always encouraged us to have a dog and cat around the home and never to live without them. He said the cat protects a person's home by not letting evil things enter. If a man kills one without justification, he will be crippled. The dog is a shield-type of animal who guards against things outside, keeping evil people and elements that harm away. Therefore both the dog and cat should be cared for and kept healthy.

The cat is a powerful animal, so the more you take care of it, the more it will take care of you. They are also very wise. If somebody is going to visit, the cat rubs its paws in its whiskers. It knows what is going to happen and communicates it so that a person can prepare. My grandmother told me that whenever a cat starts licking itself, she would put a coffeepot on the stove to warm water for whoever was coming to visit. She would be ready with a cup of coffee and either dry bread or fry bread.

The cat holds the image of the snake, can strike quickly, and is very flexible. A line drawn from its nose down the backbone to the tip of its tail represents this snake-like ability to move in a rapid, sinuous motion.[35] A cat is smarter than a snake and can kill it quickly before it can curse. Since the cat is a powerful species, it has the ability to protect the home against snakes, poisonous spiders, and mice. Mice must be kept out of a home because they get into the graves of the dead. There they either eat them or take things belonging to them, which brings a curse into the home. That is why elders say that if a mouse has chewed a person's clothing, it should not be worn but thrown away or burned. A cat will not allow mice into the home, so it protects those who live there.

CHAPTER TEN

OFFERINGS, SONGS, AND CEREMONIES

Interacting with the Holy People

An important part of Navajo spirituality is communicating with the Holy People through offerings, songs, and ceremonies. There are a number of things that can be used for offerings, but the two most important are corn pollen and sacred stones. Corn pollen (tádidíín) is whitish yellow, comes from the top of a stalk of corn, and is something a person should always carry. It is used in prayers as part of a blessing to thank Mother Nature for life.[1] Elders say they used spruce cone pollen and that there was a blue flower blossom employed a long time ago like pollen but that they changed to using corn pollen, which also represents life.[2] The cornstalk is straight like the reed that all of the animals and Holy People traveled through during the time of emergence. Now the stalk stands between Mother Earth and Father Sky in the land where the People live. The corn depends on both, connects the two, and communicates to each. The pollen offering is sprinkled to Father Sky and the heavenly beings and falls to Mother Earth.[3] The growing corn is life and represents the clan system; the offering is one of giving life that comes from the soil as it provides fluid for its branches and the sun feeds the corn through the little flowers within its seeds. Inside those seeds the leaf develops gold and white corn pollen, so that is what is used whenever a person needs help through prayers.[4]

A second type of offering is made of sacred stones (ntł'iz) made of four types of materials—white shell, turquoise, abalone, and jet.[5] These hold the powers of the four sacred mountains. For instance, blue is the color of the South, associated with Mount Taylor, and turquoise is the stone that stands for that direction and mountain. These colors also represent the seasons, the time of day, and the life that you live, all of which are part of a cycle. The seasons begin in the East with early spring when snow is melting and water running. To the south is summer when plants are green; to the west, fall with its red, orange, and yellow leaves. Winter season is dark and associated with black. These same colors are found in the four parts of the day with sunrise [white], morning to noon [blue], noon to sunset [yellow], and night [black]. Activity begins when you arise refreshed early in the morning for prayers and preparation for the day. Next is the work performed until late afternoon when you return home to the family to rest and pray, followed by night and sleep. Many Navajos do not do a lot during the night, so they go to bed early and get up early in the morning.

Ntł'iz represents other things. Take turquoise, for instance. A Navajo person should never be without it. When medicine men become very specialized in certain things, they are ordained and will have a little stone attached to their hat, signifying their high knowledge. This is why you are always told not to wear grandfather's or father's hat because there is a holy being that holds the power and recognizes the healer by that stone. A child should not wear his grandfather's hat or shoes because he might do things he is not supposed to and is not showing proper respect. You have to respect your grandfather's or father's hat to stay in harmony with whatever they represent and the authority given to them.

Turquoise is also found on a baby's cradleboard to bless and protect it. White shell, representing White Shell Woman, is very special for a young lady to have and may be attached to a woman's hair tie. Black stone is good to have and is used by men. Red coral is often worn by ladies on their sash belts or hair buns. You should always wear something to represent the People by which the Holy People will recognize you.

Accompanying the use of ntł'iz is blue pollen (*tádidíín dootł'izh*) that is picked between spring and midsummer close to the mountain. This plant does not grow large, about the size of rabbit brush, but its leaves were used like corn pollen in the old days. Both of these plant offerings can be used to bless a family, but this pollen is male, more powerful, and can protect the entire family. I think that plant was picked to represent moisture and growth, just as the sky and water are blue, and so it helps a family to grow like a blossom. The members become united and grow in a good way by the wealth that comes. Sometimes we say that everything we need is here in the family. People do not have to go running about earning lots of money. With the family you are always in the womb, you will not go hungry, and the necessary resources will be there.

Ntł'iz is also used to bless individual family members.[6] Every year when I was ready to leave for school, my grandfather blessed each of his grandchildren one by one with it. He would take out the offering and name each person then sprinkle some in a special place, saying: "For a lifetime you'll be safe, protected, and healthy. You will be strong from the prayers from each child in the household and from your mother and father." Every year when I used to go to school in Shalako, Oklahoma, my grandfather would bless me, giving the offering to Mother Earth and a young cedar. The cedar is just like a young person—has no odor and is pure, clean, and strong. The sapling has not had the trials of life and is innocent. After about the age of eight, a child begins to learn the ways of the world and loses this innocence.[7] My father also performed this for his own children as I do for my family. If members want to have somebody bless them but there is no one to do it, the family might ask an uncle or a medicine man who can. This produces family unity and harmony. If the children go away they will be safe, protected wherever they travel because they are surrounded by the power of the sacred mountains and these sacred stones.

Corn pollen and ntł'iz are used in different ways. Pollen is a female power associated with the Blessing Way ceremony. It is also used when a person wishes to travel safely, and so an offering is made in, say, a river that must be crossed. The power in the water ensures that the person will cross without problems, and upon returning another offering is given in thanksgiving. When something is bothering me or if I say a prayer for someone in need, I go to the mountains or find a real firm piñon or cedar tree in the desert to make my offering. You may use this form of blessing for someone who is away or in need of help. That is the way corn pollen with prayer is used. But ntł'iz is only used one time for a family or when something is to be given. If a person is sick, the healer goes into the mountains and obtains medication by making an offering with ntł'iz, which is a more powerful way.

Many Navajo ceremonies are another form of blessing, which may or may not use either corn pollen or ntł'iz. Take, for instance, the girl's puberty ceremony or kinaaldá. People come from all around to participate in blessing a young woman who has reached maturity. They sing songs all night to bring good fortune to her. Some may bring their own songs because they care about this young lady and wish to bless her even more. The more that is done for her, the greater is the power that enriches her life and increases her ability in the future. She also blesses herself when she runs early in the morning and on the last day when she cuts the earth cake and serves the first pieces to each of the participating singers; she is blessing them as did Changing Woman. This token from the young lady is her thanks so that all of these singers go home happy and in turn provide for their families with whatever they obtain.

That is how they used to perform ceremonies a long time ago, but now many people do it for the money instead of the blessing, saying: "I'm going to do it this way for this much. Two hundred dollars is not enough. Give me two thousand dollars and I'll do it for you." They tell you how much you are going to have to pay. Old traditional medicine men would never do that. My grandfather, my uncle Nate Shorty, and Buck Navajo were taught a long time ago never to ask and never to tell. They expected the people to know what to give if they were really going to be blessed by the Holy People. It is really up to the individual to show through payment how much the blessing means to her. The more someone pays, the greater the blessing, which is the same with tithing. It is the same thing—the more it is appreciated, the bigger the difference. People then feel good and blessed by the ceremony, and that is important.

Another way of blessing a person is through knowledge. During the puberty ceremony, the young woman is constantly being taught, while at the same time the women giving instruction are teaching each other. The kinaaldá teaches about the hogan and a woman's role. When putting the ingredients of the earth cake together, women gather and share this knowledge with the young lady who is participating while being taught by different people. Some of the old folks can really teach. I remember a lot as I look back at my older sisters, both of whom had puberty ceremonies. Now my oldest sister is very knowledgeable, having performed ceremonies for her own daughters and grandchildren. I also have an aunt who is often asked to lead a ceremony because she is a very good teacher. My wife and daughters have participated, and I am glad for their experience because now they can sit down and teach.

People who have been blessed with knowledge can turn around and bless others with it. Last year I was working in Aneth when some people learned that I knew a lot about songs, horses, and protection. A young lady and her mother were going to participate in barrel racing and roping during the Shiprock rodeo, so they wanted someone to do a prayer song for them. The mother asked, "Mr. Dandy, my daughter and I are going to participate in a horse race so we want a blessing. I heard you know a lot about horses and that you are a horse doctor. We want some winning, good luck songs to make sure we're protected and that nothing happens to our horses." I sang a couple of songs for them, but the day of the race it rained hard. Following the competition they complained about how the horses slowed on the slick turns and had not done well. Before this they had complained about the drought. I explained to her that the blessing was for protection and that they and their horses had not been hurt and that everybody had to participate in the rain. Their lack of winning did not mean that they had not been blessed; they could win in the future. I laughed and told them that when people pray to the Holy People, they may not be helped right away; it takes time to build stronger faith.

Later they went to a race in Chinle, and both the mother and daughter won. When I next saw them they were smiling and the mother said: "I misjudged you, Mr. Dandy. The horses did really well in Chinle because of your blessing." Then the mother asked if I could record the songs because she wanted to learn them. I hesitated, not wanting to share them. Often I have people asking to record a song, but I say no. They are something very special to me. I will pass them on to my children, because they are interested, but I am very careful who I share this knowledge with. A lot of times it gets out of control. For instance, when I helped develop Navajo curriculum for the San Juan School District, I sang songs recorded for the Coyote tales. These have been sold all over the Four Corners area and are now used by people who do not respect them. There is a teaching with this, and I was really disappointed when I heard that it was getting so out of hand. Some songs are more social

Jim's practiced voice in singing traditional Navajo music has been heard by thousands of people who have viewed curriculum developed by the San Juan School District. His preservation of elements of Navajo culture is a lasting legacy to be shared with future generations.

songs, but others are more serious and hold power. Another time a Navajo teacher obtained one of my songs, participated in a competition, and won. It was not a sacred song. She likes it and performs it well, so I do not mind. One night I was at the college where there was a performance and heard it. She sang it then said: "I want you to know that this is a song made by Jim Dandy. A few years ago I really wanted this song so badly that I had somebody record it for me."

But there are some songs that cannot be used because they are so sacred. For instance, the mountain song is a prayer song. All four of the sacred mountains have their own songs. They must be handled very carefully and not passed on to just anyone. When my father gave them to me it was all right because I am his son. But even so, he did it only after I promised to sing them often when needed. So I sing them when I go by myself and use them like an early morning prayer. When I travel to Salt Lake City or other distant places, I sing them because all of the mountains are very sacred to the Navajos. Not only the four sacred mountains but all mountains are sacred. When someone sings these prayer songs, he will be protected from the beginning of the trip to its end. So what I am saying about the blessings and the songs is that they protect an individual, a family, and their home.

Since the creation of this world Navajo interactions with other types of people have been expressed through ceremony. We have usually had good relations with our neighbors the Paiutes, who were excellent basket makers. We used to trade with them, and that is how we learned to make baskets that are used in our ceremonies. Many of the Utes living at White Mesa have married Paiutes and are also intermixed with Navajos. A lot of them are from the Tuba City area and journeyed into Cow Spring then Kayenta then Monument Valley. Many of them claim to be full-blooded Navajos, but they are not. Some of the people at Navajo Mountain are Paiutes, as are some of the folks at Douglas Mesa.

Another Indian group that I am familiar with is the Hopis. When I was growing up my family had a lot of association with them. I am part Hopi on my father's side, and that is why I'm short. We used to exchange with them in religious practices and trading food. Even during the summer we would go out and plant with them, since they were primarily farmers with not much livestock. They raised a lot of fruit, and so we took mutton to their villages and exchanged it for apples, peaches, and grapes.

One day Dad told me a little bit about the Hopis because I wanted to know why they claimed to be Anasazi, whose past provides religious teachings as to what Navajos should avoid.[8] Although Hopis say they are related to these ancient cliff dwellers, my father said this was not true. During the time of the Anasazi, those people died of a shock because they had angered the gods. This death came upon them suddenly, and that is why they are found sitting upright, unprepared for their fate. Others are found in caves holding babies, while some are fetching corn. All were taken by surprise. They did not know what to do when the lightning shocked them to death. Dad said that a lot of people think that it was the wind that blew in and killed them, but it was really lightning. They sat in their homes and suddenly died. That is his side of the story that he learned from his great-great-grandparents, who taught him.

There were only four cliff dwellers who survived as the rest went into shock. These four went far back into the mesa or cliffs and lived in a dwelling that looked like a beehive or cist high in the rocks. There are four plants called in Navajo *t'ósh chozhii*, which denotes the mud remains of a hive, and are associated with these four Anasazi ancestors. The only time that t'ósh chozhii is used is during an Evil Way ceremony for someone who has been exposed to a dead person by walking on a grave or coming in contact with something else from the dead that harms. This sickness is cured by using these plants, which are added as a medicine to a drink during the ceremony. It heals the sick person by purifying and cleaning her.

My father never believed the story the Hopis tried to tell. He thought they actually came out of the San Francisco Peaks near Flagstaff where there is a little mountain that descends into a big canyon. That is the place they came from. Today they are spread as far as the other side of Tuba City Mesa and all the way to Coal Mine, but they did not come into the Tuba City area until later. By the time they arrived, some Navajos were already homesteading at Tuba City. During that time some of these older people living at Tuba City received permission to settle in Moenkopi because they, like the Navajos, were involved in livestock and needed a place to range their herds. So the Navajos let them come in because there were not that many people at the time. In those early days, the Indians used to help each other. Because there were few, the Navajos protected them from the Spanish and others who tried to harm them during the time of the Indian wars. That is why my father has always been very supportive of both tribes and is himself part Hopi. He said they traded food with Hopi farmers who brought their fruit to the reservation. The Navajos traded mutton, rugs, whatever they had for this produce. Both groups were happy living there, rarely fighting with each other. Today the two tribes bicker over land. Father was taught that the Earth would never let her children fight, and so that is why he worried about what was going to happen.

White men are another group of people my father talked about, saying how they have the power to stare.[9] Although every human being is given this power, he thought that older white men had this power in a very strong way. My father felt they were very intelligent, could travel to the moon (which we are not supposed to do), and could perform many things that Navajos would not dare to do. If a Navajo woman married a white person, when the white man died his spirit could hunt her down. If the young woman is a Navajo, that evil spirit will remain with her until she has a ceremony to cure this problem.

A few years ago my mother and sister sponsored an Enemy Way ceremony for me when I was having a really hard time. Depression, stress, aches, and pains bothered me so much I could not sleep. For years I had been among the Anglo people, going to funerals, speaking in a funeral service, assisting with a burial in a graveyard, and touching a dead white man two or three times. All of these events pulled me down and overwhelmed me, especially because I had been around this dead white man and yet never had a ceremony. One time while traveling I came in contact with a man who had a heart attack by the side of the road. We took him out of his vehicle and gave mouth-to-mouth resuscitation, but later he died.

I had been exposed to all of these things, so my family, which was strong in traditional beliefs, insisted that I have an Enemy Way ceremony to remove the effect of those who had passed away.[10] At first I did not want to do it, but after praying, talking to both a church leader and a medicine man, and waiting two years to get better, I decided to have it performed. I felt that my mother had every right to direct me in this cultural belief, and so I followed her instructions. Following the ceremony I was much better and my wife, Betty, who had been going to the hospital frequently, no longer had to go. That is why our culture is very important. I think there are also psychological concerns that get into a person's thoughts that can then affect relatives. It is not that I attend a lot of funerals or do much speaking there. I just had a little ceremony to keep from being psychologically harmed and to be cleansed. When I had the ceremony I felt a lot better about my job, family, and things in general. I had been especially worried about my wife, who had been sick. She attended the ceremony to help her, too. Following it we both felt better.

There is a lot of misunderstanding as to what the Enemy Way is used for. It is most typically held for soldiers returning from war or people who in some way have come in contact with the dead. When soldiers are involved in combat, they are exposed to the spirits of the dead enemy as well as all kinds of disease, which can be brought back to their families. This acts like people who work in a uranium mine all day with radioactive materials. At night they return home and expose their family members to the radiation so that someday the wife and children may have cancer. The Enemy Way provides a cleansing of problems that are put back where they began. People suffering

This sandpainting image of Monster Slayer portrays the lightning and flint armor that protected this holy being as he cleansed the earth of monsters. Once this task was completed, the Hero Twin returned home for a purification ceremony (Enemy Way) to rid him of the ghosts of those he had killed. (Courtesy of Utah State Historical Society)

from these ills are no longer crazy or in shock after the ceremony. Medicine men cure this sickness by cleansing a person, making him free from death and destruction. The Enemy Way helps the individual culturally and physically by sending the disease back where it belongs. Even though it is expensive to have this ceremony, the person it is performed for returns with health and mind restored, ready to live a good life.

While the Enemy Way is best known for removing the spirits of the enemy bothering a person, it also can solve problems where intermarriage has occurred. Some white people believe it is performed to kill them off, but that is not true. My father laughed at this idea, because the ceremony is really to cleanse a person, in some cases from intermarriage. For instance, if my son married into a white family, there could be a problem. Anglos are not made like us so, there must be a blessing to smooth over the difference. The Enemy Way ceremony is the cure. The marriage and family is blessed by having it performed. Someday if the white person dies or leaves, the Navajo spouse can have this ceremony performed to avoid harm or evil dreams. You will still love each other, so the spirit will not return to haunt. The love will be strong within that family.

The Enemy Way can be compared to getting married in an LDS temple. The ceremony ensures that there is no conflict spiritually or physically. While white culture is different from Navajo culture, if a person has an Enemy Way blessing then things will be fine. It protects your entire family. That way you will avoid being cursed for having done something wrong like mixing the ethnic groups. Both of these ceremonies cleanse the couple, ensure they will be happy together and that things will be fine.

Just as Anglos have a blood test for compatibility before getting married so that their child will not be defective, Navajos do not want to have problems because of intermarriage with people who are different. They believe strongly in this practice, which extends even into our own clan system. My father said that white people are only strong enough to remember their relatives four generations back. Navajo relationships are remembered far into the past and go back to the origin of the clans. Therefore intermarriage with whites creates its own set of problems, because their spirits are different from ours. When a Navajo marries a person from another race, it is interesting to see what happens. I have a good friend who married a white woman but did not have a ceremony. Even though he is strong in the LDS Church, he has a hard time with arthritis in his leg and cannot walk straight. One of my cousins married an Anglo and also complains about arthritis in his legs. Even their wives are beginning to have health issues. I'm not too superstitious but what I am saying is that if you marry a white person there may be problems; and if she dies, her spirit is still there and will bother you. Someday it is going to be harmful because you have been exposed to another nationality.

A lot of our young folks walk around like blacks, dressed in baggy pants and other inner city clothes. We do not want that. The blacks are changing the world, and some Navajo elders think of them as cursed, having received the power to change a lot of things in the future. We are being turned to their ways. Already a lot of our young people follow that culture and are corrupting all of us. Dad always said "Yíiyaa" on that subject, but a lot of people do not understand why and so follow that path. Now you can see it happening.

Intermarriage with blacks is an even greater concern than marrying a white. If a Navajo woman marries a black man who then dies, nothing can be done. The reason for this is that they have not been given a ceremonial name like the Hopi or the white man to be used in the prayers of the curing ritual. This makes them a lot more dangerous. So if a Navajo marries a black man, when he dies he is going to harm her and there is nothing much that can be done to heal her. With a Hopi you can do something, with a white man you can do something, but with a black man you cannot do anything.[11]

My mother told my daughter who had a black boyfriend that she would be cursed, because that race had been cursed from the beginning in the First or Black World.[12] It seems that the Holy People had given instructions to the creatures there, which were mostly insects like ants, beetles, and locusts. The large black ant people would not follow instructions and wanted to have their own separate place.[13] They became corrupted and rebellious, and so the Holy People took away their sacred name, making it difficult to be cleansed from their influence. While other nationalities such as the Anglos, Mexicans, Germans, etc., still have their ceremonial names that can be used to correct spiritual problems, this is not so for the blacks. The belief is that blacks will still try to take over and rule the world, and some medicine men say that their power is difficult to go against.[14]

When a black man dies, his spirit will harm and take you down. For this reason Mother told my daughter: "Please, daughter, no. I don't want you to deal with the blacks, please. They're going to turn the world back to the point that it will be corrupted and destroyed. That is what is happening now. Yíiyá, that's what I'm saying."

Other spiritual concerns are addressed through events such as the shoe game [*késhjéé*], which combines songs, related activities, and group cooperation to bless individuals. This is held only in the winter when it is dark and may include families with young children as well as adults. The origin of the shoe game began as the world and its creatures were learning about different relationships during the time of creation. Father Sky was angry with Mother Earth, as each tried to control the other in order to be in charge. Father Sky would say, "This is mine; I'm the ruler," then Mother Earth would counter with: "I'm the ruler." They became so upset that they refused to cooperate, and the battle continued to the point that there was no rain, the earth became dry, and plants no longer grew. The people were also corrupted, greedy, and self-centered, gambling and doing some of the worst things. Coyote became aware of these actions and wondered what was going to happen. He grew suspicious as food disappeared, Mother Earth dried out, and the heat became intolerable. Coyote believed that everyone's actions were causing the drought. Hunger drove him to ask why the grass and berries had disappeared and what he could do to solve this problem.

Coyote set out to find the answer and met the very soft-spoken and lonely Gray Big God (Yé'ii Tso Łibáhí), who was just as concerned. "Hello, cousin," said Coyote. "Did you know that there's no food and I'm starving? I haven't had much to eat. Why is this happening? The whole Earth is getting dry." "I know that something is wrong with us. Everything is not as it should be. People are so greedy and proud that they do not think of others, only themselves, and they are constantly fighting. If you're concerned, why don't you go to one of the Holy People who live around here?" He visited Owl then Turkey, who both had the same concerns. Soon Talking God whispered in his ear: "You had better go back and talk to Gray Big God, who is a wise man and is the oldest of Sun Bearer's children. You need to have some kind of plan. I am worried about it, too." Talking God offered to visit some of his cousins who were also Holy People and ask them what they knew about the terrible situation. There was no question. They all understood the cause and knew what needed to be done to stop the drought. Talking God explained that the people had to gather for a meeting to discuss what they were willing to do. The deity insisted: "The only thing I'm going to tell you to solve this problem is that there must be a shoe game. You're going to have to set it up somewhere." There are a number of different places where the Navajos suggest the Holy People held this first game. Some say that it was played at Big Snake's home at Sugar Loaf Rock on Lime Ridge, while others claim it was at Chimney Rock, where Coyote is said to have run around that formation; still others suggest a spot on Black Mesa.

As the people arrived, some of the Holy People gathered around to watch. Finally they told the people to ask Big God to help them because he was the biggest, wisest, and oldest. Talking God assisted him, because he is the only one who can communicate with him and tell him what to do. Talking God had planted yucca in the east, so he sent the giant to collect the plants. There he gathered the yucca sticks, 102 of them, used in the game to represent the length of a person's life, from birth to death. A hundred sticks also stands for the children, each with its own name, while the two additional sticks represent the grandparents or mother and father. At the base of a yucca where these sticks or spines come together there is a little ball-shaped root material that represents life. It never dies and always stays cool and moist. This is the token used in the game to represent life.

Next Big God went to the south, where he found two young twin boys, said by some to have been cared for by a wolf. One of the boys raised the deer, so Big God received moccasins from him for the game. One pair of shoes was for daily activities, for walking about every day, the other pair for ceremonial purposes, but both were to be used in the game. He put the shoes in the sand to hide the token. Big God went to the San Francisco Peaks (west) where he received the token, the round yucca ball that represents life. Before leaving, Big Snake gave him instructions, warning that the game was very dangerous and that everyone must be careful. Cheating takes place, so you must always be aware. He then taught the players how to know where the token was hidden by being enlightened. "Remember that lightning and the rainbow will go to the shoe the opposing team puts it in." Finally Big God went to the north and received the weapon that was to be used in the game— a cedar stick about twelve to sixteen inches long to hit the shoe. The stick helps to know every time someone guesses where the token is hidden. Each group must work together to decide, so the stick is your weapon to help make the right choice.

Talking God, the one who planted the yucca in the east, was always there, whispering through the Holy Wind (Niɫ'chi) to the players. He explained that the yucca plant is similar to ntɫ'iz that medicine men carry. He told them the green yucca spines represent turquoise stones; when a yucca pod is opened there are black seeds inside that are the color of jet stones, while the yellowish color on the bottom of the pod represents abalone. The stalk that holds the fruit represents the white stone. The yucca plant is sacred and holds power to heal, bless, and protect, as does ntɫ'iz.

Before the animals began playing, they determined there were four issues that needed to be decided and that this was the only way to do it. One was the question of night and day, so the first game would determine that. All of

Jim performing traditional songs
at the Blanding Elementary School
Cultural Appreciation Day. The drum
was a gift from an elder from the
Yukon who came to southeastern
Utah as part of a cultural exchange.

the animals had strong feelings about what was best for them. The night animals who see and hunt in the dark favored having more darkness, while the
day animals argued that light was what was needed. Both were concerned,
arguing that there should be one or the other all of the time. Another question was how animals should look: their shape, face, colors, everything. The
third was if there should be hardship, and the fourth was death—how long
people should live.[15] These were difficult decisions that affected everyone.

Before they started to play, these Holy People in animal form chose
sides; the night people such as bear, lion, owl, bobcat, and snake were on the
north side and the daytime people such as jackrabbit, porcupine, sheep, and
gopher on the south. They all received instructions as to how to play. There
were four shoes, and each had to be used. The shoes remained on the ground
aligned from east to west. All the day people sat behind one pair of shoes and
the night people behind the other set so that the game could be played from
south to north. A blanket served as a veil so that opposing teams could not
see what the other side was doing. The white team on the south represented
day and the black team to the north night. Bat, who was always flying about,

decided which would be the first team to hide the token. He took a corn husk with its gray outer side and white inside and dropped it from the top of the hogan. White it was, so the day people started. But the night animals and birds like Owl were accustomed to moving about in the dark, and so the day leader always had to be watchful to make sure that the night people were not outside peeking in the smoke hole to see where the ball was hidden. Coyote, who enjoyed being the leader, decided that he wanted to be on whichever side was winning and so went back and forth between teams.

This is a game of concentration, and so songs are sung to distract the other players, hindering their ability to determine under which moccasin the token is hidden. If I had the token and put it under a shoe, they would sing against me to block my attention. All of the people on one side chant "łiba" or "łigai" (gray or white), and on the other side "łizhin" (black). Everyone is sitting, concentrating, trying to defeat the other side.

The first game began, and the token went back and forth without a final winner, making it so there would be an equal amount of day and night. This first game lasted all night; they all got so tired that they just went to sleep. The next day, when playing for how each should look, the same thing happened—nobody won and many fell asleep. The same with hardship and death—nobody won. This last game was the most difficult of all because no one wanted death. They sat across from each other, singing and playing to the best of their abilities, but again no one won, so there is both death and life. At one point, Talking God urged Gopher to burrow under the ground the moccasins rested on to find where the ball was located; he found nothing, but that is why there are holes worn in shoes today.

Owl actually had the ball, grasped within his claws, because he wanted more night; this is where cheating first occurred. Big God, the master of ceremonies, wept bitterly because he did not want death, but Owl was having a wonderful time singing and making fun of Big God. "Oh he's a cry baby because he did not want death." But once the animals discovered the cheating and restored order, the other team began to earn points, which made Big God happy because he wanted only life. Dawn approached. By the end of the fourth game the sun had not come up as usual that morning, so there was no daylight. Finally, the morning began to break, so the animals sang the last song, which almost brought the sun up. As the token changed hands for the last time, it fell into some water, so Coyote got involved, declaring that if something dropped, it meant it was either going to be death or daytime. What he said happened, so the sun arose and later there was death.

The animals scurried about, rolling in different colors of clay and sand as part of their winnings and new appearance that they had earned by playing the game. They then wandered into the mountains. But Crow and Bear had just awakened and were the last to choose colors. Crow found that they were all gone, so he rolled in the dead ashes from the fire then flew away. Bear awoke from his snooze with a start and in his hurry to leave put his shoes on the wrong feet, rolled in the ashes, the only remaining color, then traveled toward Black Mesa to disappear into the mountains. His paws have remained on the wrong feet to this day.

The purpose of the shoe game is for healing and not really gambling. Just as with most games, this one removes stress and depression by taking a person's mind from problems and by motivating. Even though it is only played in the winter when the animals are asleep so they will not be listening and curse people for talking about them, this game can solve issues that have arisen throughout the year. Any stories that go with the shoe game like those about Coyote or Big God are not told until there is frost or snow on the ground. A lot of Navajos today do not practice that anymore. Even the songs that accompany the game cannot be sung during the summer. Now in the spring when there's no snow we still talk about Big God and Coyote even though we are not supposed to. Also, the game is not to be played during the day or else the participants will lose weight or go blind. A lot of schoolchildren therefore hesitate to get involved, but teachers who do not understand expect them to play. If a child has had a short ceremony performed, the time of year is appropriate, and their parents agree to their playing, then it is all right.

There are a lot of rules associated with this game.[16] Briefly, depending on the position of the four moccasins there are four, six, and ten points associated with them. Addition and subtraction of 102 possible points keep the players trying to win all of the yucca spines. Players are to concentrate as to the location of the yucca ball; and when it is found, points are awarded according to which shoe it is in. The moccasin to the east, referred to as the door, and the moccasin to the west are worth ten. If I think the ball is in a particular shoe, I "kill it" with the stick and if right gain ten points and if wrong lose the same amount. Once the token is placed in a shoe, each group, either day or night people, starts collecting points taken from the bundle of one hundred yucca sticks. The two additional "grandparents" sit alone and are the last two to be taken, each being worth ten points. Once the bundle of sticks is gone, a team starts collecting from its opponents until their supply is exhausted.

Team members can assist the person with the stick but cannot touch the moccasin believed to contain the yucca ball. The one with the stick makes the choice and eliminates the other moccasins, which are put aside. She often looks at the opposing team's eyes to see if they will give any hint as to the ball's location and questions them as to which shoe it is in. In the meantime, the other side is doing all it can to distract and mislead. As long as the shoe is not touched, there is no commitment to a particular one. All of the team-mates are behind helping; but if someone knows exactly where it is, he may help but cannot choose. If the choice is wrong, the other team gets points, the amount depending upon which shoe was guessed.

When playing this game there must be more than just the entertainment and gambling. It relieves stress and depression as an individual puts so much in for stakes and finds a person on the opposing team who will match the amount. If someone puts two dollars into the kitty, someone else from the other side must do the same. The winner will take the amount that the pair put in. But if on the losing side, you should not feel badly, because that money was paid to heal a person in need. It is an offering of assistance to both the patient and you to feel better. Someone playing the game might be really sick. Every time a person hits ten points with the cedar stick, he takes that amount and starts massaging the ill person, praying, and singing for her. That is why the game is held and why you are there. When it is over, a person walks away feeling good. Everything that was killing her has left. The individual believes she can be healed and is. That is the purpose for playing.

There are new forms of religious beliefs on the Navajo Reservation, the Native American Church becoming one of the most widespread.[17] This religious practice came to us from the Plains Indians to the east. When I was growing up around the Tuba City, Red Lake, and Navajo Mountain areas I never had heard of it. When I returned from my mission around 1966 it had suddenly popped up, with many people excited about the practice. My father

Albert Dandy, medicine
man and community leader
in the Red Lake–Tuba City
area, provided protection
ceremonies for men going in
the service, performed the
Enemy Way, and doctored
livestock. He encouraged his
children to strive for his same
type of perfection.

had learned of it during his World War II experience. He said that a lot of
the "Aztecs" or Mexicans, known to Navajos as the "South People," took this
medicine to relax and not be afraid. They eventually shared it with some of
the Plains tribes during the time of the old Indian wars. These Native Americans began holding ceremonies that were passed to the Navajos on the eastern side of the reservation by Canyoncito, then moved on to Shiprock, and
then the Western Agency.

My father said that while he was growing up he never heard of people taking peyote. When our family members first became aware of it, they opposed
the Native American Church and worried about it. All of my brothers and sisters were really against it; and when one of them broke ranks and joined, the
others were shocked because this sister had been very traditional. People at
Red Lake began holding Native American Church ceremonies, while others
in the community were angry and refused to participate. Many did not know
where the beliefs came from, while my father took the position that it had not
been given to the Navajos at the time of Creation and so was not for us.

There is an herb called datura or jimson weed that is found on the reservation, which, like peyote, is a hallucinogen.[18] It is a powerful drug, far more

powerful than peyote, and is dangerous enough to kill a person. It should be taken only when an individual is really sick and the medicine man knows what he is doing. There is a song that goes with it; but if it is not known, the plant should not be used. My father had an experience when he was having a very hard time in life. He used this medication to cure cancer, but a lot of the time he did not know what he was doing. He was trying to cure a lady who lived near Red Lake, but in order to do so he needed to eat some of the medicine with her during the ceremony. At the same time he was depressed and going through a lot, so that the combination was very hard on him. That is what he said. He was a person who was not against any other religion, but he would not use peyote in his ceremonies.

Some older relatives thought the same way as other medicine men, who believed that traditional Navajo practices should not be mixed with the new beliefs of the Native American Church. They do not even want peyote mentioned around them. "That is not our religion. We don't deal with it; peyote is part of the snake's curse, it is snake food." Some Navajos associate the hallucinations produced by peyote with the effects of Big Snake, a powerful deity during the time of Creation. One medicine man felt that the Holy People never gave this medicine to Navajos as part of their healing powers, that traditional medicine men do not use it, and that to try to heal with it is dangerous. He said: "I'm not against it. If the people want it, I have no problem with that. Sometimes they ask me if I use peyote in my ceremonies and I say no, never. It's not part of our culture and it is not our medicine. It is very dangerous." I know that he does not want to be injured by something that he is not familiar with. I will not deal with it either. Some people are very touchy about this topic, especially Native American Church members. Whenever you mention something about peyote, some of them get a bit nasty and rebel.

One reason it is called snake food is because peyote turns a person's dreams to thinking about snakes. When someone hallucinates, everything is snake in the dream. Big Snake is there, and you dream of snakes.[19] So snake food is something that people should not deal with. It is during the hallucination that these snakes appear to the individual. I guess in peyote meetings there is always somebody trying to curse other people by using Big Snake through their dreams. They feel like they act like a snake, moving around quickly. I know a young lady whose family participated in the Native American Church. She went to a peyote meeting with her sister in Kayenta and was invited to get some medicine just to see what it would do for her. She felt uncomfortable, saying: "All of these fancy lights came into my mind and I got so weak. The day after the ceremony I slept all day. All I could see were these snakes crawling over me." She said she almost died while participating. I heard that a lot of people who take peyote get in arguments during that ceremony.

All I did with peyote was when I was in Monument Valley. I searched school children for possession, going into their lockers and cleaning them out. I often found pop bottles and so tasted their contents, only to find a bitter taste waiting for me. It is not only kept in small bottles but also as a powder that is mixed with tobacco and smoked. It is worse than taking snuff and has a unique smell. The students use it just to hallucinate and feel like they are walking in air. Now a lot of the young people are abusing it. When a road man [person conducting the ceremony] uses that medicine in a ceremony, he is very careful about how it is taken, but kids take advantage of peyote for its effect. They say that when you take peyote alcohol should not be consumed. This is why a lot of Plains Indians are very concerned, saying the Navajo People are getting out of hand and not using it correctly. It should be taken only when needed.

CHAPTER ELEVEN

THE LIGHT AND DARK SIDES

Avoiding and Curing Evil

Holy People hold certain powers that they share with humans who are worthy and follow the correct teachings. Those who receive these powers are recognized by the gods as having the right to use them and have assistance. Medicine men with the knowledge of different ways of healing hold these powers internally, while others understand psychological ways of healing. Some medicine men may not want to be involved in a lot of curing rituals but may find only one that they specialize in. Each person can hold only so much power.

Diagnosing what is wrong with an individual is the first step in healing.[1] Hand trembling is used for this and is viewed as a gift that an individual has in partnership with a holy being. The person who is to receive that power must receive it from one who already holds it, but it is through the spirits that divination operates. Usually the one bestowing this power knows a lot about it, is able to explain how to use it, and has the right to do so. The Holy Person who controls it, however, is the one who chooses the new recipient and gives that person the power to pass it on to others. But somebody has to have the key to give to a person who is about to start practicing.

I am not really sure how hand trembling works. I have seen people place clean sand in either a box or a sheet so that the person who hand trembles can tell what is happening. The patient draws or writes in the sand, and the hand trembler looks at it to discern what is bothering him. The sand represents Mother Earth, who tells the truth. The hand trembler may run her hand along the patient without touching him, and by doing so the hand will shake while the mind receives an impression that tells who invoked a curse. At the same time the patient's faith works to provide an answer, assuming he

227

believes in the power. If he does not have faith in it, the power of the holy being will not reveal information. A long time ago I had hand trembling performed for me, but I did not really believe in it. The medicine man performing the ritual said: "I can't get it to work. Maybe you're not really in with me. Maybe you don't really want to know." I think both people have to work together to have any results.

Hand trembling can be a good thing, but evil people can hand tremble too. They are probably the worst ones. As with everything spiritual there are some bad and some good people, which is also true of medicine men. Some of them are just like quack doctors who do things only to make money, but a good one can be very helpful. For example one year my father's cousin brother camped by the Bears Ears. Two of his young children wandered off, and no one could find them. After four days of looking, a family member went all the way back to Page to find my uncle named Many Mules, who joined them and performed a chant. Singing and praying can do much good; so by doing that and hand trembling at the same time, he knew that the two boys were still alive because he saw them and learned of the direction to search in. Many Mules told the family members to walk abreast in a straight line in a certain direction and that they would find the boys not too far away. While the searchers looked, he remained in camp singing. Sure enough they found the children, one sitting up a little higher on a slope with the other sitting below. They had survived on prickly pear cactus and piñon nuts, which the older boy crushed and fed to his little brother. Both were very thirsty, dry around the mouth, and physically dehydrated since sucking on cactus had not provided much moisture, but they were alive and happy to be back with their family. This is an example of how singing and hand trembling is used for good. Someone should hire a good strong medicine man, take him to Iraq, and let him find Osama Bin Laden hiding in some mountain cave.[2]

Crystal gazing, like hand trembling, is used to learn of things that happened in the past, present, or future. This is done with special crystals that show the image of a person causing a problem or creating a situation. The stone works only if the Holy Person allows its power to be used. Sometimes a person or two can be seen clearly and other times the image may be faint. If the people using the crystal really believe, I heard that they will see what they are looking for. During the time when Navajos were searching for uranium, one person mentioned that a man used crystal gazing to see where it was located. He could look in the stone and see a glow in the place where it was found. Others say crystal gazing cannot be used to find riches, but it can identify skinwalkers [witches], how they come to a home, and who is placing a curse on an individual.

The ability to use supernatural, superhuman powers for both good and evil is called álílee k'hego. This is the power that a skinwalker uses to get into her canine skin, but it is also the way that a medicine man heals people. Just as Moses used his staff to outperform the evil magicians of pharaoh in the Old Testament, a good person can use this power to stop harmful things, but it can also be used to harm others if someone wishes to do wrong. The power allows an object, such as a deer antler, to disappear miraculously. That is why traditional Navajos are afraid of antlers and will not touch them. They are very powerful. In the Mountain Way ceremony feathers in a basket are used as part of the ritual, and at one point these feathers start moving around and pretty soon are dancing upright. The medicine man who performs the ceremony holds a lot of power that lifts an object and can do a number of supernatural things. This and other ceremonies use álílee k'hego as a means of healing based in faith. My father said a long time ago that medicine men using this power would sing their songs and heal a person quickly. Now, when somebody is sick, she is taken to a doctor to be cured. Powerful medicine men in the past had the ability, through faith and training, to heal the sick as long as the patient also had faith. Faith in things that are good is very powerful; but witchcraft works on the same principle, so that if a person believes in it, he can be harmed just as surely as being healed.

This power can also be turned around and used to curse someone; through hand trembling, the person being attacked can find out who and what is being done and can have that power reversed and sent back to the individual causing the problem. The evildoer will be revealed. This is why an individual cursing someone does not talk about what is being done. I have a lot of respect for what my father taught. He warned never to tell anybody your songs or teachings that hold power because that gives a person working against an individual the power to harm. If the one performing evil starts to get the victim to believe what he is saying and understands the teachings, then he can curse that person because he believes what he is told. But if someone does not believe, it is not going to work. There is, however, a blessing that can turn the evil power around that heals and protects an individual.

The power of álílee k'hego can be used to shoot foreign objects such as stone, bone, hair, porcupine quills, and other small sharp objects into people. My grandfather, for example, had a very small hard lump sitting in the back of his shoulder, one in his arm, and another just below his neck. These had been shot into him when somebody cursed him. These lumps were probably made from a dead person's bone fashioned into a dart then injected through supernatural power and prayer. Grandfather was well known for being a good medicine man, but exactly how much he knew he never divulged, protecting himself that way. Whoever cursed him did not really hurt him, but for some reason Grandfather never removed those lumps.

These objects used to curse people are called *bi k'aa* (arrow). The person cursing someone puts poison corpse powder (*áńt'įįh*) on the darts, a practice developed in the past when Navajos fought enemies from another tribe and later the white man. It was not initially made for our own people, but now we use it on them, too. We have always been taught to carry medicine or yucca needles because evil is afraid of them and they combat the effects of a curse.[3] Those involved in witchcraft make these darts, cover them with corpse poison, then sing and pray, using the power of álílee to transport the dart into the victim. I heard that skinwalkers chant all the time; the songs cannot stop or their power ceases. Somebody has got to be singing while they are using their supernatural power.

An evil medicine man can also hypnotize a patient by staring or by singing to himself. This attracts a young lady to go with him or, if she does not cooperate, can harm her through álílee. One time at an Enemy Way ceremony in Kaibito, I arrived early in the morning to help with butchering a couple of sheep. After I finished, I went into the shade hut where a lot of people were cooking. They roasted some really good ribs, which were ready to eat. An old medicine man came in, hoping to have some, but a beautiful young lady dressed in fine jewelry refused to let him have any. She was very educated and intelligent, but she should have known better. I was eye to eye with her and this man when she told him: "That's not for you. It's for the people who have been working here. They are the ones who will eat, not you. You will have to wait." Suddenly the woman passed out and fell to the ground as people started running for help. I do not know if he said something or just looked at her. One of her great-grandmothers placed herbs in some water, washed the woman's face, and made her comfortable until she regained consciousness. In the meantime, others had gone looking for the man, but he had disappeared. I was nervous, wondering if he put something in the food. Once revived, she was all right but weak, so her relatives took her home. They did not want the old medicine man coming back to bother her again. With some of these very powerful medicine men things like that happen.

I had a similar experience when returning from work in Kayenta. I used to go home to Red Lake on the weekends to spend time with my father; but one night I heard about an Enemy Way ceremony at Cow Springs, which was in the direction I would be traveling. When I arrived at the dance I found some relatives, but my father had stayed at his home near Wildcat Peak. I remained at the gathering with my grandmother, aunt, and cousin sister. They invited me to a feast for those who helped with the ceremony. My grandmother had brought some food as part of her contribution, so we were all welcomed and started to eat. Everybody mingled and talked, but I was a stranger. At first I felt fine just sitting there but soon became very sick. As I ate I began perspiring then had chills until suddenly I felt like somebody had his hands around my neck choking me. I almost passed out. Grandmother and my relatives wondered what was happening, so she took me back to the truck, stirred some herbs in a cup of water, handed it to me, told me to wash my face and rub some of the liquid on parts of my body. I drank what was left and lay in the truck until the feeling faded. She recognized that someone had cursed me, but we did not know who and how. That night I recovered, decided to leave, and gathered my things together, and we all headed back home. This incident was similar to what happened to the woman in Kaibito. Now I am always careful and carry my herbs all the time.

I have watched other people in similar situations, and they usually pull out of it once they use that medicine. When medicine people gather plants, they give an offering and prayer for protection of the person who receives it. The herb is very bitter and is sometimes mixed with bile. You carry it when attending a large meeting or where there will be a lot of people. You take a little bit and put it on so that whoever is trying to curse you will not have any effect. In my situation, I never found out who was working against me, but

The healing art of the Navajo medicine man depends partly on the materials he has
to work with in his medicine bundle (*jish*). Here are some items used in the Evil Way,
including a bullroarer made of lightning-struck wood covered with pitch and secured by
a leather thong. The noise from this object warns evil to stay away. (Photo by author)

my family was suspicious about some of the people attending. Later I had a
hand trembling ceremony performed that told me that this incident was not
accidental and that somebody was trying to curse me. My family did not get
along with some of the people because we were living successful lives. This
kind of cursing can also happen if a person has more wealth and things that
others do not have. A curse can be on both an individual and a whole family.
I do not know what I did wrong, but I am careful about these kinds of things.

There are other teachings about simple ways that you can protect yourself from supernatural harm. For instance, Navajos have a number of rules
about spitting. If I got some of your spit on me, you will need to pay me
a small token to show proper respect. You do not spit on people. If you do
not pay, a problem will bounce back at you, so that if you are rich, you
may become poor. By paying a small amount you are saying you are sorry,
wish them well, and that no offense was intended. You may then become
wealthy yourself. On the other hand, if a person is angry and spits at someone, the one spitting may develop a sore because she is cursed. The gesture

comes back to the person, who will grow a sore that does not heal [cancer]. They have cursed themselves, creating a sore on their body or making them impoverished.

A dinosaur track can be used to turn a curse away from an individual. There is power in these tracks that medicine men use either to bless or to harm. A bear track can be used for the same thing. Dinosaurs were powerful creatures that at one time ruled the other animals. Powder or a scraping taken from a dinosaur's track can be used as a weapon to turn around and curse someone or as a protection for an individual who may be cursed. This power is used to harm the man who is working against that person.

Sometimes witchcraft causes drinking problems. If a person does not like someone, he might hire an individual to curse the intended victim with excessive drinking. This happens a lot when a child is having problems with alcohol; the parents and family suggest this as the underlying reason. Some parents say that so-and-so may have cursed their son and hired a medicine man to perform hand trembling to determine who is doing it. The diviner identifies the guilty person behind the drinking or behavior change, saying: "They made your child think like this and made your whole family go this way."

For example, when a family is trying to improve itself, there may be a lot of jealousy from other people. If a child is smart in class and doing well, she may suddenly have behavioral changes and the parents want to find out why. There has to be a reason, which is often found to be someone cursing the family. A medicine man is hired to cure the problem and sometimes does well. I remember one family that was very prosperous and popular when suddenly, for no reason, they started having issues. They declined quickly; many medicine men they hired did everything they could, trying to determine what was wrong. They finally found that one of the family members had offended a person who cursed them. So excessive drinking often has a reason behind it. When a person is encouraged to get involved, she may become hooked before too long. There has got to be a reason behind an individual's problems.

Sometimes a medicine man returns a person to normal. Family gatherings are also important. But even with this kind of support, there are always people out there trying to discourage you. One young man I know got in a fight with another student in school and really got hurt. His family believed this was also connected to his not passing his classes. During all of this there was a person behind it; and even though the parents tried to cure their son, he struggled. When you believe in something like this it becomes true. This is an important explanation about what is happening with our young men today and why they do not get good grades in school. Somebody may have cursed their whole family.

I have had my own struggle with these kinds of issues, making my life very difficult at times. The problem of the two murdered policemen in Monument Valley in 1987 is a good example of how people can be affected by evil.[4] I first learned about the incident when I returned from a wrestling tournament in Cedar City. At the time I was working as a community liaison for the school district, athletic director, as well as head wrestling coach for Monument Valley High School. The deaths took place on Saturday night, I returned on Sunday, and by Monday morning students were coming to me to explain what they knew of the occurrence. It did not take long for the parents to put a stop to any discussion, closing the community to any leak of information. I had some students who even a year later could not get anywhere in their studies because of their concerns. The FBI had investigated the death of these two local policemen; but before long there was a community meeting, and shortly thereafter the investigation appeared to stop. No one came forth with information.

Months passed, and still the murders were unsolved. A young high school student finally came forth after she became involved in religious practices that were evil and scared her. She came to me with a changed attitude, telling me how things were and what she knew of the killings. The night that they occurred she had been present, tied in the back of a pickup truck and threatened with extreme harm if she did anything to reveal who was involved and what had happened. She was very scared, so she dutifully covered everything up but now had changed her mind and wanted to tell me. Monument Valley is a very difficult place to have this type of thing happen, because family relations are so widespread and gossip is a powerful force. While I was really disappointed in that young girl for holding back information, I totally understood the pressure she felt to remain silent.

The principal became aware of what was happening and asked that I become involved because the students trusted me and would share information. So I brought this girl into my office to learn more of what had occurred. She just cried and cried. I asked: "Why are you crying? Why were you involved? Is it because you knew what happened then covered it up because your parents asked you to? All of this has turned around and is working on you." She admitted that she had been there when the killings took place and had been threatened with further assault. She again started crying hard and pleading, "Jim, if I tell you, will you send me away?" I agreed to assist, ensuring that she could safely leave the community with the help of law enforcement. She confessed that everything she had previously said was true: she knew who the killers were and had seen it happen. I calmed her then called the Navajo police in Kayenta. Before long the FBI arrived at the school; later the Navajo police appeared. They interviewed her in Kayenta, where she explained everything.

Soon the community became aware that a break in the silence had given new life to the investigation. I knew that with some people I was going to really be in trouble, but I just thought it was my job, I was hired as a counselor and community liaison, and so it was my responsibility that went with these positions. I could not hide or cover up for those involved. I went to Kayenta, where I sat most of the night with this girl, who was so frightened she wanted me to stay. I finally returned home, and she eventually went to Salt Lake City for her own protection. Soon others came forward and told their side of the story, how liquor had clouded judgment, who was involved, why the police officers were tied up in a van, and how the rest of the night unfolded. As a clear picture of events surfaced, an aunt of one of the participants really chewed me out. She said, "You're the one, Jim Dandy, who sent my nephew away." I was angry and told her: "You sit right there and let me tell you something. Those people who lost their sons are parents, too. How many children did they leave behind? I'm at this school protecting these kids and I have every right to help them. I am not hiding anything; I can tell you right now that I'm not the one who sent your nephew away. He sent himself away. What would you do if something like this happened to one of your family members?" She started crying and left. About a week later she apologized, admitting that I was right.

Still, my problems continued. Even though the families of the guilty parties knew they had been involved in something wrong, they worked against me with whatever they had. I was walking around with this burden, thinking about all of the things that had happened while trying to do my job. I was not happy with the position I found myself in. Some of the parents had put a curse on me, which slowed my work and made things difficult, even though I had taken the right action. Depressed, stressed, I did not know what I was doing and one day just left Monument Valley. I went to see my stake president to seek his counsel.[5] He told me he had a very strong impression that these problems were coming from Monument Valley and that I needed to get out of there as soon as possible. I told him I was not going to crawl away from the trouble but would stay.

This came at a time when I had been doing so well. I had beautiful horses in my corral, two brand new Suburbans, a nice pickup truck, and a lot of other property like horse trailers and regular trailers. Suddenly I went into depression for no apparent reason. Without thinking, I gave everything away and matters worsened. I lost everything then got into financial problems that became really scary. I grew increasingly concerned, went to church, and prayed a lot. One day while sitting in my room praying, I heard a voice tell me to go back to Monument Valley to find what was causing all of these problems. So I went to a very traditional medicine man who performed hand trembling for me. He saw [through an impression] the people working against me and told me I had been cursed a few years ago and that the only thing keeping me safe at this point was the LDS priesthood that I held.

I did not want to work against those cursing me. Those people had used a medicine man I knew who was actually related to me on my father's side of the family as well as one of their own relatives. They used deer hair and deer bone to work against my mind and bother me psychologically. The curse eventually went back to them, so they ended up struggling with it. My father learned about what was happening and came to Monument Valley. We sat and talked for a long time, my father agreeing that I had done the right thing. He never asked me to leave my job or said that I should not be involved. My mother laughed when I told her, "I'm going to be driving that old car, but they are not going to defeat me with their curses." I was going from riches to rags. Finally my brother did a short prayer to get me back to normal and show why it was happening. This helped quite a bit. My children were not affected by these problems because they know what is right and they are powerful. You have to be strong to be involved in this type of incident on the reservation; it is the hardest part and there are forces that are very powerful, especially if you are Navajo. Those who are weak go under. If you are strong and stay on top, pretty soon the people will leave you alone and start thinking you are alive because of what you know.

I think Navajos really hurt themselves because they work against each other instead of helping. People start to think that if they accumulate a lot of wealth that they will be cursed and so should not make an effort to improve their situation. They are afraid that if their children become successful in school or some other place they could also be cursed. If a child begins to participate, is a top student or athlete, the same will happen. No child is going to knowingly put herself in that kind of a situation. There is always danger. These forces are very powerful, and there is nothing a person can do if he is not as strong as the one opposing him. Parents teach their children about these things and encourage them not to get too involved or be outgoing. They are afraid of one another. These things still go on today; Navajos use a lot of supernatural power.

Another thing that Navajo people fear is death and the dead. There are teachings about what happens when a person dies and how her funeral should be conducted. If a person dies in old age and has lived a good life, her spirit will not affect a living soul the same way as that of a young person, whose spirit is considered dangerous.[6] Both spirits are a concern, but the younger one has unfulfilled needs and wants to stay with the living. I went to a funeral the other day, and the two sons of the deceased did not attend because their wives were going to be having their babies. The men and women did not want to be exposed to the spirit of the dead man. Even when a good person dies, they would not show up because of the power present that affects the living. They believe the spirit is going to harm the child in some way. So the sons did not go to the funeral because they feared their father's spirit would come back with them and hurt the unborn babies. Since the husband created the child, he supports his wife by not endangering the baby with attendance at the funeral.

Today the younger generation does not practice these types of teachings as much. Many think that if somebody dies and has lived a good life, it does not matter. Others are still traditional and would not go. As a general rule

Anasazi ruins are homes of the dead traditionally avoided by Navajo people. Betatakin ruin on the northern end of the reservation is one of many sites that teach of the destruction of its occupants because of their descent into evil practices. (Photo by author)

of thumb, if a child dies there is no problem with its spirit; if an older person dies and has lived a full life and has been good, there is no problem with that spirit; an older person who has been bad may create a problem with his spirit. For a person who is middle-aged or younger—say between the ages of twenty and fifty—you have to be careful with his spirit.[7] When anybody dies his spirit still exists, and so a lot of very traditional people will not attend a funeral no matter what.

At Navajo funerals you usually find a special type of cedar that grows in the mountains.[8] Its needles are flat and soft like those of a blue spruce or pine. The cedar is placed in water so that after the funeral people can wash themselves with it to keep personal harm associated with death away. Evil does not like the pungent smell of the plant. What you are exposed to during the ceremony will stay away. A similar concern exists for people who go into Anasazi ruins. These are places of the dead and so should be avoided. Navajos are not supposed to go to these ruins because they are a place where people are buried, who will be disturbed and haunt the intruder. Going there is like destroying their burial place; the dead will bother the person who does. They may have aching joints and soreness or contract some disease that sickens or weakens. This can be a real problem if the person is not protected by a blessing or prayers.

In the old days, following a funeral, the family moved away from their home, especially if the person died in it.[9] Even if the individual died outside, the traditional practice was to move in the direction of the south because the spirit was now journeying to the north. The south represents the blue world and life, while the deceased is going to the Black World in the north. The living avoid contact with the dangerous things of the Black World; they move in the opposite direction to the south, a very sacred place for the family. This is also why when a person takes a sweat bath, the rocks used to heat the lodge are placed to the north both in the hut and outside after the ceremony. Everything that is used up or finished goes to the north. Now many people do not practice this.

I remember a long time ago when my Aunt Mary passed away. She was so kind and sweet and very special to me because she taught me as I was growing up and herding sheep with her. She was also a very hard worker, talented in rug weaving, and did things that amazed me. When she passed away I was just a little boy, but I remember my family moving over the south side of a nearby hill and building a fire that we kept burning all of the time. My grandfather and grandmother's brother were the only two who took care of her body. When they left, we said our prayers as a family. In those days, the funeral consisted of burying the body in a small shade house and covering it with dirt.[10] There was no law saying how deep the corpse should be buried, so a wooden casket fashioned out of materials found around the camp was put in a shallow grave. While the two men buried the body, we were told not to go near. When they returned, they had a little ceremony and cleansed themselves with herbs. Later we had a small lunch of corn mush then did not do much except remain quiet, humble, and at home for four days. There was no showering, no changing clothes, or fixing hair, which meant letting it hang down. My grandfather and great-uncle came home the way they were, with ashes mixed with fat upon their faces, which was not washed off for four days.[11] We all drank herbs and waited for the mourning period to end.

Now at a funeral there are a lot of people, so it becomes a family gathering. In the past only specially trained or older people who knew what to do

The spirits of elders who have lived a full life and then die are not as powerfully antagonistic toward the living as the spirit of a younger person, who may have regrets about leaving life "early." Navajo teachings prescribe the proper behavior for treatment of the dead and protection of the living. (Courtesy Milton Snow Collection, Navajo Nation Museum)

were supposed to perform the graveside service. Elders could do this because the evil spirit was not as anxious to follow them. These old people were very spiritual and knowledgeable about caring for the body after death. They did not want to expose the family to harmful things and were highly respectful—something that we have to learn to do, too. But these traditional folks were also superstitious, fearing the spirit of the dead to the point of not keeping pictures of the deceased. Members of the younger generation are very different and display their dead grandmothers' and grandfathers' pictures.

Burial places are left alone; so if a body remains in a hogan, the structure is avoided. When a person goes near, he has to be very cautious. If in the vicinity of a burial you must be careful to spit in a cactus, yucca plant, or ashes. Ashes are also placed on a gun before shooting at a skinwalker because it overpowers evil, ensuring that the weapon will fire against the supernatural. Evil is afraid of things like this and objects that are sharp, so it avoids being harmed. The spirit in a grave will not come out and pick up a person's spit if it is protected by things the spirit fears or dislikes. Otherwise, that spirit will take a person's spit with it back into the ground and curse the individual by shortening her life. "You will end up in the land of the dead before your time is through." Elders also warned not to look at a burial place but to glance away. A person may see the spirit of the one buried there, which turns into a curse. I used to walk away from a burial with my head turned to the side, never looking over at the gravesite.

One time I had a supernatural experience with a graveyard, where I saw a fire that did not burn. It was late at night when I was riding my horse. I spotted a campfire in the distance and decided to see who was there. I turned in that direction, but suddenly the fire disappeared. When I reached the spot there was only a graveyard, no fire, and nobody present. This is why we are taught not to travel or look around at night. When you see a fire or light like that, it brings bad luck and can be dangerous. People talk about places around Monument Valley where lights appear, such as on Eagle Mesa, but nobody knows what causes them.

I have been told of another incident that is quite similar to what I experienced. A man had been out all day looking for his stray horses. Now it was late at night and he was traveling home, leading one of his animals through territory he was not familiar with. In the distance he saw a person sitting by the light of a fire. The individual was clearly outlined, and so the traveler decided to visit his camp by riding straight toward him. He was thirsty, not having had a drink of water for most of the day. A good cup of coffee would be welcome. When he reached the spot, nothing was there but an old hogan. The traveler decided to go on. About a mile later there was another hogan where he stopped. The people invited him in and gave him water, coffee, and bread. As he ate he told of his strange experience, explaining about the light and the person he had seen sitting there. His hosts told him there was a burial in that old home; now he understood what he had really seen. This is why we were always told never to look around at night, especially when traveling. This can all be part of a message or something that is not good.

A final type of evil connected with álílee k'ehgo, curses, and death is skinwalkers (*inaadlooshii*: "walks around like an animal").[12] These are men or women who change their form into a supernatural canine creature with powers to run extremely fast, curse people, and use evil to reverse things that are good. They carry poison herbs mixed with human flesh from dead bodies. A lot of Navajos are involved with witchcraft and are very powerful in their ways. On the reservation, if a person wants to get rid of someone, she is cursed with corpse poison powder.[13] It is very powerful, just as the white man makes a powerful powder out of radioactive dust for bombs. Navajos think of this radioactive material just like corpse poison, but it is the kind of power that only the white man controls. That is why things like bullets are used by white men while Navajos have supernatural power to harm people. In the old days we used this power against our enemies, but now our own people who turn into skinwalkers employ it against us. We have that power but are not supposed to be cursing our own with it. Now it is out of hand. This is also true with the use of very sacred songs that are turned around to do harm.

I had an experience with a skinwalker when I was working at Red Lake. During the time that the chapter house hired me, I used to buy a little hay for my horses, take their bridles off, and let them eat in the corral so that they would be well rested. After work I would catch one and be on my way home. One night after finishing my duties, I started for my sister's place with a big canvas sack filled with coffee, sugar, and flour she had purchased that day at the trading post. The evening turned dark, with the wind making a lot of noise. As I approached her house, the horse suddenly jumped high, bucking and twirling about. The only place I had to hold onto was the saddle horn and reins, but they were not much help because the horse was so scared. He landed in a rocky area then jumped with me off a little mesa. I thought I was going to fall and was barely hanging on as the animal snorted and bucked; I just sat there, held on, and let him run.

My sister heard the commotion; the dogs started barking, ran out to meet me, then ran past. At the same time I saw coming down the old road a vehicle with its headlights on; but as my horse crossed in front of it, I just clung to it and went all the way to my sister's house. By now the dogs had flown past and were barking in the distance. Dismounting, I noticed my hand was badly rope-burned and felt like it was bleeding. My sister and brother-in-law were scared and wondering what had happened. The horse was almost dead, covered with lather, and ready to keel over. My father arrived at this time, screeching to a halt in a cloud of dust. He climbed out of his car, saw what had taken place, put his hand on top of the horse's head, and said a short prayer. The horse stood straight and stopped staggering. Dad told me

Navajo Mountain, like every community on the reservation, has its stories of good and evil, positive protection as well as witchcraft. For Jim this area holds good memories, family members, and resources that help him live a balanced life of hózhǫ́. (Photo by author)

to walk the animal around, let him breathe a little more to relax, so I did. It was amazing to see my father putting his hand on the horse and the effect it had—that was powerful.

The man passing in the car stopped and told us that he had seen a strange type of dog not too far from where I was riding. Early the next morning a group of us saddled our horses and went to investigate. We traced where the dogs met the skinwalker, whose foot was strange looking like a wolf paw with real funny lines running across it. We followed its trail for about a half-mile, where a similar one joined in, then traveled almost to Red Lake, where there was another one. Toward Black Mesa there were two more, and when we reached the top of the mesa we found a couple more sets of tracks. There were a lot of them, probably assigned to go in different directions. We almost rode to an abandoned trading post called Kin Nitiel [Wide Building] near Piñon before losing their trail to a wind that covered the prints. We could not see too well, so we turned back.

My relatives have their own stories. An aunt tells of when her uncle came home one time and put his sheep in the corral. He then announced that he was going to so-and-so's house, where they were playing cards and gambling.

His sister was very sick, close to dying, so medicine men were at their home chanting, trying to heal her. There were no hospitals. The uncle told the children that he was going out to gamble then rode over a nearby hill. The children became suspicious, so two of them—my aunt and her little brother— followed their uncle's horse's tracks for about two miles before arriving at a little mesa where six other horses were tied with his to a tree. There were no tracks around the animals, which made the children even more suspicious. The two started walking and found tracks throughout the surrounding area on the hill. My great-aunt said when she looked beneath a large rock there was a hole, outside of which people had tried to erase their tracks with brush. Under the rock was a flat sandstone covering, which she removed.[14] There she saw a bigger hole, just large enough to crawl through into a little cave-like opening. The two children entered, only to find a buckskin hide about the size of a window curtain hanging in the doorway. Pushing it aside, they crept past a rock decorated with skeletons, skulls, and all kinds of turquoise and silver jewelry hanging on the rock. They went through another opening covered with buckskin, crawling through another hole. By this time the children were down to the bottom, where they saw seven people teaching and holding a meeting. They were deciding whose homes they were going to visit in pairs. My aunt's uncle was sitting there receiving instructions that this was to be the night that these skinwalkers would do away with his sister. He and his partner were going to her hogan while two medicine men remained behind to sing. There has to be singing in order to get the skinwalker pairs moving and to keep them in tune with their plan. Those traveling decorate themselves with different colors like white clay, black clay, red clay, and human blood before putting on their wolf skin. One of those who stay behind plays a drum to accompany the singing while the pairs are out. As one of the witches prepared, he could not get into the skin and realized that it was not working because someone was watching him. The one leading the ceremony knew they had been discovered; the children sensed they were in trouble, so they fled.

A shortcut to their aunt's hogan was the best way to safety. Behind them, the children heard the skinwalkers in pursuit. They drew closer; the girl realized that she could not outdistance them, so she climbed high into the top of a cedar tree with her brother and waited. Below she saw the men running about searching for tracks then heading down the trail. As soon as the skinwalkers disappeared over the hill, the children descended, traveling in a different direction. Somehow the witches sensed their mistake and soon were right behind the fleeing pair. As they neared the hogan where the ceremony was underway, a dog came out to greet the children. This saved them, because a dog has powers to work against skinwalkers.

The boy and girl breathlessly told what they had seen to the medicine men chanting in the hogan. They stopped what they were doing and immediately went to the place described by the children, caught the witches in the act, sang their songs, and destroyed some of the witches' evil objects. Within four days all seven of the skinwalkers were dead. Once they were caught performing their evil magic, there was no way they could survive. The sick aunt grew better and eventually returned to normal. Skinwalkers, once assigned to go to a certain location, travel long distances, just like the ones we tracked from Red Lake to Piñon. That is what I experienced myself; my aunt told this second story and said it was true.

My grandfather, Eli Shorty, also had an encounter while he was building a new hogan near Black Mesa. He had a good friend who lived close by and offered to help with the construction. They finished the home, and Grandfather moved in. He did not have a wooden door, so he used a blanket to cover the entranceway. One evening after putting the sheep in the corral and letting the horses out to graze, he went into his hogan for supper and to get some rest. His sheep dog remained outside on guard. The family sat around the fire; Grandfather dozed on his sheepskins, Grandmother spun wool, the little cedar fire crackled while smoke drifted through the smoke hole above. All was peaceful. The dog came in and lay by the fire, facing the doorway on full alert, intent on a strange noise outside. It gave a throaty growl and stared straightforward; Grandmother watched the blanket while giving Grandfather a poke with her wool twiner. She whispered to him about the dog, that something was not right. Suddenly the pet leaped up, almost tearing the blanket from the doorway in its haste to get outside. Grandfather followed fast on its heels with stick in hand. In the dark he heard human noises as the dog chased a skinwalker toward a steep canyon wall. Following the sounds, Grandfather found pieces of fur and skin that the dog had torn from the witch, slowing it down. He quickened his pace and caught up to the fleeing figure. As the skinwalker ascended the cliff, Eli reached out and caught hold of its tail, ripping part of the skin on its hind end off; the creature was too fast and disappeared into the night.

Grandfather returned home and built fires all around his hogan, burned the tail and skin, then sang songs and said prayers through the night that the evil would not return. In the morning he saddled his horse and followed the tracks, traveling a couple of miles before ending up at his friend's home. The man's wife was in the yard heating water, and so Grandfather asked if her husband was there. She replied that a ceremony was underway and that he was busy. Grandfather went in the hogan anyway and found his friend lying by the stove dying from dog bites. Grandfather asked why he had come to his house to bother him and received the answer that the man had been jealous over decisions that had been made concerning land use in a grazing dispute. Even though Eli had said that he could graze his flock there with no interference, the friend was still angry that the decision had not gone in his direction. Four days later he was dead.

EPILOGUE

J im's red-roofed, tan house sits on the corner of a busy residential street in Blanding. On any given day, when Jim and Betty are home, three or four cars line their side of the street, marking the comings and goings of brothers, sisters, children, grandchildren, and friends. Sociability is an important Navajo trait. Betty and Jim welcome all who arrive to visit in their modest living room, heated in the winter with a wood-burning stove that radiates warmth matched only by the array of family pictures on shelves and walls recording five generations of ancestors. Couches, comfy chairs, a large-screen television, and jostling children underfoot cram into a small front-room space about the size of a hogan. There is always one more place for another person to squeeze in.

Jim presides there, sometimes feeling the effects of old age but still active. Tanning deer and elk hides is a continuous effort that brings him joy as he fashions the skins into a vest, sells them to Ute friends for beadwork, or turns the pliable hide into some craft object. In addition, schools and individuals approach him to see if he will work as a consultant to teach children traditional Navajo ways. The Aneth Community School invited him recently to be a guest speaker for its heritage week, where he entertained with songs and stories. His grandchildren also benefit from this knowledge as he teaches

Jim and Betty today. Their
home is in constant activity,
visited by children and
grandchildren, friends,
and relatives who enjoy the
hospitality, k'é, and hózhǫ́.

them to sing and dance. When asked what fills his days, without hesitation
he announced that he sings his grandchildren to sleep at night with Navajo
songs: "That's what we do as grandparents."

Jim also muses that he wishes to coach again. Family members recall
the days when he spent hours on the mats, teaching and encouraging young
wrestlers to compete. One of his sons stops by to take him for a ride and
reminds his dad that he really ought to be using his talents to direct those
aspiring for the arena. But as he and Betty settle into retirement, it is apparent that those days are gone.

Gone also are the traditional times when Jim was growing up. The
changes that he has seen in his life—from horse and wagon to computers
and iPhones—are hard to comprehend. From his blind grandmother herding sheep and identifying medicine plants by touch, to the rough-and-tumble
years of boarding school, to an LDS mission, to a career of service in the San
Juan School District—Jim's life has been one of transition. Between the traditional teachings of yesteryear and the anglicized, homogenized world of
today, he spans a generation of change. Conversant in both worlds, he has
shared his teachings from the past to help people in the future. Wisely, his
grandfather and father steered him on a course that allowed him to be successful in both, as the changing world spun through the events of the last
half of the twentieth century and into the twenty-first. Now it is Jim's turn
to point the way for future generations of young Navajos interested in traditional teachings. That is why he had this book written.

NOTES

Introduction

1. Dale L. Shumway and Margene Shumway, *The Blossoming: Dramatic Accounts of the Lives of Native Americans in the Foster Care Program of the Church of Jesus Christ of Latter-day Saints.*
2. Ibid., 74.
3. Emily Benedek, *Beyond the Four Corners: A Navajo Woman's Journey.*
4. Ibid.; Louise Lamphere, Eva Price, Carole Cadman, and Valencia Darwin, *Weaving Women's Lives: Three Generations in a Navajo Family*; Joanne McCloskey, *Living through the Generations: Continuity and Change in Navajo Women's Lives*; and Walking Thunder, *Walking Thunder: Diné Medicine Woman*, ed. Bradford Keeney.

Chapter 1

1. Peter Iverson, *Diné: A History of the Navajos*, 1, 320.
2. For Jacob Hamblin's experience with the Hopis and Navajos, see Juanita Brooks, *Jacob Hamblin: Mormon Apostle to the Indians*; and Pearson H. Corbett, *Jacob Hamblin: The Peacemaker.*
3. Two excellent sources on Mormon settlement along the Little Colorado River are James H. McClintock, *Mormon Settlement in Arizona*; and Charles S. Peterson, *Take Up Your Mission: Mormon Colonizing along the Little Colorado River, 1870–1900.*
4. For settlements in Utah, see Robert S. McPherson, *The Northern Navajo Frontier, 1860–1900: Expansion through Adversity,* and *A History of San Juan County: In the Palm of Time.* For Colorado and New Mexico, see John Franklin Palmer, "Mormon Settlements in the San Juan Basin of Colorado and New Mexico";

for Ramah, New Mexico, see Evon Z. Vogt and Ethel M. Albert, eds., *People of Rimrock: A Study in Values in Five Cultures*.

5. Clyde Kluckhohn and Dorothea Leighton, *The Navaho*, 129.

6. LaVerne Powell Tate, "A Family of Traders."

7. For the Navajo perspective on the role of the trading post, see Robert S. McPherson, "Naalyéhé Bá Hooghan, 'House of Merchandise': Navajo Trading Posts as an Institution of Cultural Change, 1900–1930."

8. For the Navajo perspective on livestock reduction and its impact on their culture, see Robert S. McPherson, *Navajo Land, Navajo Culture: The Utah Experience in the Twentieth Century*, 102–20.

9. See Richard White, *The Roots of Dependency: Subsistence, Environment, and Social Change among the Choctaws, Pawnees, and Navajos*, 212–314.

10. David Kay Flake, "A History of Mormon Missionary Work with the Hopi, Navajo, and Zuni Indians," 110–21.

11. Evon Z. Vogt, "Intercultural Relations," in Evon Z. Vogt and Ethel M. Albert, eds., *People of Rimrock: A Study in Values in Five Cultures*, 71.

12. Ibid., 70.

13. Ibid., 69.

14. Arnold K. Garr, Donald Q. Cannon, Richard O. Cowan, and Richard N. Holzapfel, *Encyclopedia of Latter-day Saint History*, 539. Robert Gottlieb and Peter Wiley, *America's Saints: The Rise of Mormon Power*, 163, suggest that 70,000 were enrolled in the program.

15. James B. Allen, "The Rise and Decline of the LDS Indian Student Placement Program, 1947–1996," 96.

16. Steve Pavlik, "Of Saints and Lamanites: An Analysis of Navajo Mormonism," 21.

17. Allen, "The Rise and Decline of the LDS Indian Student Placement Program, 1947–1996," 91.

18. Ibid., 89.

19. Ibid., 93.

20. Ibid., 94.

21. Ibid., 93.

22. Brandon Morgan, "Educating the Lamanites: A Brief History of the LDS Indian Student Placement Program," 201.

23. *Foster Parent Guide*, 15.

24. Don Mose Sr. and Clayton Long interview with authors, June 22, 2009.

25. "Indian Student Placement Services Fact Sheet." Roger G. Christensen, assistant commissioner in the LDS Church Education System, provided the following statement concerning the end of the Indian Placement Program. Although he did not find any specific reference to its official termination, "There were passing references in Board minutes and other histories, but nothing definitive." Citing a recent doctoral dissertation suggesting that the program went from 1947 to 1996, he surmised: "The effectual termination of the program appears to have occurred beginning in the early 1990s as a result of a lawsuit." Christensen to author, August 24, 2011.

26. "Indian Student Placement Services Fact Sheet."

27. Ibid.

28. Ella Sakizzie interview with author, May 14, 1991.

29. Martin D. Topper, "'Mormon Placement': The Effects of Missionary Foster Families on Navajo Adolescents," 145.
30. Elouise T. Goatson interview with Farina King, November 10, 2007, 4.
31. Betty Dandy interview with authors, April 26, 2008.
32. Branch President materials for Indian Student Placement Program of the Church of Jesus Christ of Latter-day Saints "Leadership Program."
33. Geraldine Taylor Lindquist, "The Indian Student Placement Program as a Means of Increasing the Education of Children of Selected Indian Families," 23.
34. Topper, "'Mormon Placement,'" 149.
35. Tonia Halona interview with Jim M. Dandy Jr., April 10, 1991, 4.
36. Jerrald Hogue interview with Ernesteen Lynch, August 21, 1990, 4.
37. Bruce A. Chadwick, Stan L. Albrecht, and Howard M. Bahr, "Evaluation of an Indian Student Placement Program," 521.
38. Ibid.
39. Anna Begay Birtcher and Normand Birtcher, "Blending Cultures—Medicine Man/Temple President," 248.
40. Ibid., 519.
41. Ibid., 523.
42. Chadwick, Albrecht, and Bahr, "Evaluation of an Indian Student Placement Program," 524.
43. Allen, "The Rise and Decline of the LDS Indian Student Placement Program, 1947–1996," 110.
44. Chadwick, Albrecht, and Bahr, "Evaluation of an Indian Student Placement Program," 524.
45. Ibid.
46. Beth Wood, "LDS Indian Placement Program: To Whose Advantage," 18.
47. Ibid.
48. Lacee A. Harris, "To Be Native American—and Mormon," 146–47.
49. Ibid., 147.
50. Ibid., 152.
51. Goatson interview, 15.
52. Elise Boxer, "'To Become White and Delightsome': American Indians and Mormon Identity" (abstract).
53. Florence Billy interview with Ernesteen Lynch, August 12, 1990, 16.
54. Clayton Long interview with authors, June 22, 2009.
55. Ibid.
56. Don Mose Sr. interview with authors, June 22, 2009.
57. Ibid.
58. Lucille Hunt interview with authors, June 11, 2009.
59. Ibid.
60. Kendall A. Blanchard, *The Economics of Sainthood: Religious Change among the Rimrock Navajos*, 20, 22.
61. Ibid., 109.
62. Ibid., 117.
63. "Mormon Church in Navajoland," A-2.
64. "The LDS Placement Service: 'It's Not a Form of Kidnapping,'" *Navajo Times*, July 27, 1978, A-4.

65. Blanchard, *The Economics of Sainthood: Religious Change among the Rimrock Navajos,* 188–92.
66. "Agreement of Parties," 2, 7.
67. Genevieve De Hoyos, "Indian Student Placement Services," 280.
68. Brian L. Smith, "Indian Placement Program," 539; Matthew Garrett, "Mormons, Indians, and Lamanites: The Indian Student Placement Program, 1947–2000" (abstract).
69. Charlotte J. Frisbie, "Temporal Change in Navajo Religion 1868–1990," 481.
70. Ibid., 467–69, 496.
71. Ibid., 471.
72. Eric Henderson, "Kaibito Plateau Ceremonialists: 1860–1980," 167.
73. Ibid., 172.
74. Ibid., 174.

Chapter 2

1. *The American Heritage Dictionary,* 1233.
2. See Dan Vogel, *Indian Origins and the Book of Mormon: Religious Solutions from Columbus to Joseph Smith.*
3. "Introduction," in The Book of Mormon.
4. Carrie A. Moore, "Debate Renewed with Change in Book of Mormon Introduction."
5. William Stolzman, *The Pipe and Christ: A Christian-Sioux Dialogue,* 14.
6. See H. Baxter Liebler, *Boil My Heart for Me*; and Robert S. McPherson, "He Stood for Us Strongly: Father H. Baxter Liebler's Mission to the Navajo."
7. See Liebler, *Boil My Heart for Me.*
8. See David F. Aberle, *The Peyote Religion among the Navajo.*
9. D. Michael Quinn, *Early Mormonism and the Magic World View,* v.
10. Anthon S. Cannon, ed., *Popular Beliefs and Superstitions from Utah.*
11. See Howard M. Bahr, ed., *The Navajo as Seen by the Franciscans, 1898–1921: A Sourcebook.*
12. For examples, see Berard M. Haile, *Upward Moving and Emergence Way, The Gishin Biye' Version,* 189–91; Paul G. Zolbrod, *Diné bahane': The Navajo Creation Story,* 215–21; and Aileen O'Bryan, *Navaho Indian Myths,* 83–84.
13. Laurance D. Linford, *Navajo Places: History, Legend, Landscape,* 180.
14. Haile, *Upward Moving and Emergence Way,* 191–92.
15. Charlotte J. Frisbie, "Temporal Change in Navajo Religion: 1868–1990," 459–60.
16. Bruce R. McConkie, *Mormon Doctrine,* 317, 359, 577 (quotation).
17. Clayton Long interview with authors, June 22, 2009.
18. Marilyn Holiday discussion with author, September 23, 2007; Jim Dandy discussion with author, September 24, 2007.
19. For examples of white testimony to the reality of this power, see Franc Johnson Newcomb, *Navajo Neighbors*; Hilda Faunce, *Desert Wife*; and Gladwell Richardson, *Navajo Trader*; for this same phenomenon among the Hopis, see Frank Waters, *Pumpkin Seed Point: Being within the Hopi.* A friend gave a more personal example. He is devoutly LDS, raised by his family on the Navajo Reservation, and lived on a number of trading posts. While he is strongly entrenched in his own beliefs, he told of an experience when his father had some things stolen

from the store. His father sought help from a hand trembler, who identified the exact location where the stolen goods were hidden and then sent the trader to retrieve them. They were exactly where he had been told.

20. Lucille Hunt interview with authors, June 11, 2009.
21. Don Mose Sr. and Clayton Long interview with authors, June 22, 2009.
22. For examples, see Haile, *Upward Moving and Emergence Way*; Zolbrod, *Diné bahane'*; and O'Bryan, *Navaho Indian Myths*.
23. Don Mose Sr. interview.
24. For a very detailed discussion of the creation and nature of the soul, see Berard M. Haile, "Soul Concepts of the Navaho."
25. Maureen Trudelle Schwarz, *Molded in the Image of Changing Woman: Navajo Views on the Human Body and Personhood*, 83, 86.
26. James Kale McNeley, *Holy Wind in Navajo Philosophy*, xviii.
27. See note 12 for different versions of the Twins' journey to the Father.
28. Other versions of this story suggest that the four monsters that remained were Old Age, because it brought wisdom; Hunger, so that nothing would be wasted; Thinness, because the people led an active life; and body lice to encourage cleanliness.
29. O'Bryan, *Navaho Indian Myths*, 99.
30. See Haile, "Soul Concepts of the Navaho," 87–92.
31. Gary Witherspoon, *Navajo Kinship and Marriage*, 37.
32. Vincent Denetdeal, "K'é in Marriage and Family: Live What You Teach," *Leading the Way* 3, no. 7 (July 2005): 16.
33. John E. Salabye Jr. and Kathleen Manolescu, "Where There's Fire, There's Prayer," *Leading the Way* 5, no. 9 (September 2007): 9–10.
34. John E. Salabye Jr. and Kathleen Manolescu, "Keeping Things Holy," *Leading the Way* 7, no. 1 (January 2009): 14.
35. Eugene Yazzie, "Living with K'é," *Leading the Way* 4, no. 3 (March 2006): 2.
36. Gary Witherspoon, *Language and Art in the Navajo Universe*, 84, 88–89.
37. Ibid., 126.
38. Witherspoon, *Language and Art in the Navajo Universe*, 18.
39. Ibid., 25.
40. Ibid., 25–26.
41. Farella, *The Main Stalk*, 102.
42. Long interview.
43. Kendall A. Blanchard, *The Economics of Sainthood: Religious Change among the Rimrock Navajos*, 225.

Chapter 3

1. The life of a Navajo baby begins with conception when the father's moisture joins the mother's moisture to create the child. Once the heart starts to beat, four sacred winds enter the body, creating the whorls on the baby's fingers, toes, and top of the head. The Black Wind and the White Wind enter at the toes and leave through the hair on the head. That is why a Navajo person has black hair when young and white hair when old. The Yellow Wind and Turquoise Wind enter at the top and exit through the toes, explaining why toenails are yellow with a bluish color around their edges. The Holy Wind is another wind that stays inside and helps to communicate about what is right and wrong as the person matures.

When the individual dies, it departs. John E. Salabye Jr. and Kathleen Manolescu, "The Creation of an Individual," *Leading the Way* 6, no. 4 (April 2008): 3.

2. Jim Dandy was born on September 9, 1940, at Tonalea (Red Lake), Arizona, the third child in a family of three boys and six girls.

3. Arrowheads are used in Protection Way ceremonies to ward off evil. Both a male and a female arrowhead exist, the male type having two barbs above the base. Women are not supposed to see arrowheads being chipped because this is connected to hunting and killing, which are part of the man's domain. Women can use a point to cut an umbilical cord, however, as a means of providing future protection. Milton Jordan, "Making Arrowheads," *Leading the Way* 6, no. 2 (February 2008): 22.

4. Songs from the Evil Way and Blessing Way ceremonies can be sung by a man during labor. "Unraveling songs" from the Evil Way ease the pain and coax the baby into this world. An herbal mix called *azee'bee ná ooltáadii* is given during labor and a month following birth to stop bleeding and assist in healing. Bahe A. Begay, "Chasing the Baby Out," *Leading the Way* 6, no. 4 (April 2008): 4.

5. Wildcat Peak is a conical volcanic neck located north of Tuba City and is one of a number of local land formations created by the deity Changing Woman to confine restless animals the night she stayed at Red Mesa (near Tuba City) on her westward journey. As the Holy People traveled about the land naming places, they noticed that Wildcat was exhausted, his feet worn, and that he had lain down to rest. Only his head stuck above a ridge, as he pronounced that he could go no further. The place he lay down is known as Wildcat Peak. Stephen Jett, "Wildcat Peak," personal communication with author (1987).

6. By rolling in the snow and running in the winter people learn endurance, gain mental and spiritual strength, and receive good health for their future life. Snow from the sky is considered male; the water from the earth is female. Rolling in snow provides a stronger male power and was often done four times with short warmups in the hogan between repetitions. The Holy People see a person doing this and provide additional blessings. Deana O'Daniel and Kathleen Manolescu, "Áłtsé yidzasgo," *Leading the Way* 1, no. 1 (November 2003): 9.

7. The Fearing Time hearkens back to the early 1860s and the time when the United States military forced many Navajo families from their homes and sent them on the Long Walk to Fort Sumner. Navajo accounts make it clear that only those who were vigilant survived and remained free. Albert's concern about being "attacked" was part of his training, long after the Navajos returned to their homeland (1868) and assumed a peaceful life.

8. The Red Ant Way belongs to the general Navajo classification of an Evil Way ceremony. It is used to cure people who have come in contact with an object struck by lightning; patients who have injuries inflicted by horned toads, ants, and bears; people affected by the influence of ghosts and animals that travel in darkness; and those suffering from urinary tract or intestinal problems as well as skin rashes. The ceremony lasts up to nine nights and includes ritual bathing, extensive chanting, sandpaintings, and sweat emetics. See Leland C. Wyman, *The Red Antway of the Navaho*.

9. The ideal situation is to graze sheep within walking distance of a camp so that the animals can be corralled at night. In many instances this was not possible.

10. Long before the Fearing Time as well as during the Fort Sumner period, many Navajos were cast into slavery by Hispanic (Spanish and Mexican) people. A

general practice throughout the Southwest, the slave trade immersed hundreds of Navajos into this foreign culture. See David M. Brugge, *Navajos in the Catholic Church Records of New Mexico, 1694–1875.*

11. When a person dies in a dwelling, it is abandoned so that the deceased will not affect the living. The grandmother, sensing that the end was near, asked to be taken outside so that the hogan could continue to be used.

12. Navajo teachings tell of how the North is associated with the dead, so a family moves south as a means of avoiding continuing contact. The distance of this move varies, in some cases less than a mile and in others ten to twenty miles.

13. Ashes are cleansing and protective agents that have power to help people through daily life. They are often used in ceremonies for the same purpose: repelling evil.

14. The livestock reduction of the 1930s, associated with the Great Depression and conducted by the Soil Conservation Service, removed wealth on the hoof, forcing the Navajos from financial independence to dependence upon the government and the wage economy. The trauma caused by this act is still bitterly remembered by elders who lived through it. Following the reduction, the land was managed through a system that measured its carrying capacity (how many sheep, goats, horses or cows could be supported by a certain amount of acreage).

15. See Robert S. McPherson, "Navajo Livestock Reduction in Southeastern Utah, 1933–1946: History Repeats Itself."

16. The mountain soil bundle contains earth from the peaks of the four sacred mountains, which brings the blessings of wealth, prosperity, health, and protection to the home where it is kept. As part of the Blessing Way teachings, this bundle is a powerful positive force in the daily life of a family.

17. The Renewal Ceremony starts by placing a Navajo wedding basket on top of a sacred buckskin then putting the mountain soil bundle inside the basket before unwrapping it. A song for opening the bundle and another to look inside are performed before removing the objects inside, which are then placed in the four cardinal directions. John Holiday, a medicine man from Monument Valley, explains: "The bundle and its contents represent our mountains. We need to look at our mountains every year. To show respect for the mountains, we put pollen inside and tie the bundle back up. Pollen is the essence of a long and happy life for the bundle and its owner. Once the bundle is put back together, I conclude the ceremony with a Mountain Prayer. Now the bundle and its owner have become one. The bundle is now part of the owner. . . . The basket represents Mother Earth. The red coils represent water and the inner black figures represent clouds extending into the water (towards the center of the basket) and the outer figures represent clouds extending out of the water. The Navajo people were created on top of a buckskin. All medicine bundles are created and rededicated in a basket on top of a buckskin." John Holiday, "Renewing the Mountain Soil Bundle," *Leading the Way* 4, no. 11 (November 2006): 26.

Chapter 4

1. Corn pollen (tádidíín) is used for personal and ceremonial prayers. White ground corn, which is considered male, is used in prayers to start the day, while yellow ground corn, which is female, is used as an offering to the Holy People at the end of the day. Corn pollen can be used anytime. When placed on the tongue it

feeds the body and speech; when placed on the head it blesses the person's spirit and beliefs; and when sprinkled in front it provides the pollen path that the individual walks through life. Many Navajos carry a small sack of pollen for daily use; but it should never be mishandled, such as bringing it to a funeral or blessing something that is dead. Pollen represents life, growth, and well-being, not harmful things and death. Kathleen Manolescu, "Pollen Is Life," *Leading the Way* 1, no. 1 (November 2003): 1–15.

2. Bears are powerful creatures assigned by the gods to live in the mountains. The origin of different species is found in mythological stories that speak of their qualities. They serve both as protectors and as a danger. One of the four guardians of Changing Woman was Bear; yet in another teaching Coyote helped a beautiful, benevolent woman turn into an evil bear that killed its loved ones. In one story Bear protects Navajo travelers, while in another he and Big Snake use witchcraft to marry two beautiful sisters. Usually bears are feared for their power and strength.

3. The Navajo cosmos is divided so that everything comes in pairs and is either male or female. From the four sacred mountains (Hesperus and Blanca are male, while Taylor and the San Francisco Peaks are female) to the four sacred rivers (San Juan and Little Colorado are male, while the Rio Grande and Colorado are female) to clouds and trees and hogans, this dichotomy pervades Navajo thought. Even the human body is divided into these categories regardless of sex, the left side being male and the right female. So it is not surprising that a male form and a female form of the hogan exist.

4. Fire is a fundamental element of life, as are water, air, and Mother Earth. "All living species have fire within them. Even a flea, lice, a dog, birds, chickens have a fire within them. A puppy's fire is at the tip of its tail. This is his spirit. If you cut off your dog's tail, you shorten your life. . . . The horse's fire is behind its ears. . . . In humans the fire is inside, close to the heart." The hogan is viewed as a living entity and so must also have a fire to keep it well as a home of warmth. Francis T. Nez Sr., "Fire: The Heart of Life," *Leading the Way* 2, no. 10 (October 2004): 1, 16.

5. See chapter 11 for an explanation of skinwalkers.

6. Ceremonial participants are not supposed to lean against the wall but rather to sit forward: when the Holy People come to visit, they walk behind them and view what is taking place to make sure that all is being done correctly. Don Mose Sr. interview with author, June 7, 2011.

7. The fire poker is both a practical instrument used to stir the coals and bank a fire and a tool that holds many sacred teachings and powers. It is a protector of the home and is associated with prayers concerning the hogan's well-being. To hit a person with it turns its sacred protective powers against the individual and home.

8. The roof of the first hogan built by the Holy People was made, in its spiritual form, with a rainbow.

9. "Weavers leave an opening in their weaving as a means of escape. In any situation, there is the potential to trap oneself. With an opening, you will never be cornered by sweet talk or appearances. All of Navajo art is this way. It is intentionally left imperfect. This represents a way out of life's difficult situations."

Maggie Yellowhair, "Why Weavers Leave an Opening," *Leading the Way* 6, no. 5 (May 2008): 21.

10. All snakes are related to Big Snake, a very powerful mythological creature who can both protect and curse an individual. Often associated with evil, snakes can either be messengers or bring a curse with their presence.

11. This woman's power is kept separate from the power of a man and thus cannot be associated with hunting and certain ceremonies, or infect men with the blood's presence on napkins, and so forth. Male power can be diminished or spoiled if it comes in contact with this blood. Following the start of the first menses, a young woman is still safe to visit a ceremony; but after the second menses, she must be ceremonially treated, as must the medicine man who treats her and his paraphernalia. Elsie Kahn, "The First Kinaaldá," *Leading the Way* 3, no. 4 (April 2005): 2.

12. Begochídí (One Who Grabs Breasts) is a god connected with sexuality, fertility, and trickery. In sandpaintings he is pictured with a humped back. The god is characterized in various ways, suggesting that he was the youngest son of the Sun, could assume a wide variety of forms, was responsible for using this power to play tricks on others (often sexual in nature), and controlled a wide variety of wild and domesticated animals. The humpback that Jim mentions ties Begochídí to fertility through menstruation and his own physical appearance. Gladys A. Reichard, *Navaho Religion: A Study of Symbolism*, 386–90.

13. Sheep dipping was an annual practice in which the animals were forced to swim through a narrowly constructed trough in which a chemical solution covered the entire animal to prevent skin diseases (scabies) and infestation by ticks and other vermin.

14. The Enemy Way ('Anaa'jí) is directed against the influence of ghosts or evils that are bothering a patient. Belonging to the general Evil Way category of ceremonies, the performance can last up to five nights, while events are held in a number of Navajo camps spread over a long distance. One aspect of the ceremony is the creation of a decorated juniper staff called the rattle stick, which is approximately a yard long. It bears symbols of Monster Slayer—an important Navajo deity associated with war and protection, sacred buckskin, feathers, plant materials, and yarn. The stick is carried by a young virgin woman as she travels to various camps. Other activities associated with this ceremony are dances in the evening (giving the ritual its popular name of "squaw dance"), a giveaway of food and presents, blackening of the patient, and exorcising of the evil influence. Franciscan Fathers, *An Ethnologic Dictionary of the Navaho Language*, 366–67.

15. "Cousin sister" is an English rendering of a kinship term in Navajo terminology: a person's biological mother's sister (aunt) is also referred to as a mother, so her daughter would be a cousin sister.

16. Evil Way is a general classification of a type of ceremony as well as a specific ceremony called Evil Way (Hóchxǫ'íjí) within that classification. Like the Enemy Way, this rite lasts either three or five days and removes the influence of ghosts of nonforeign enemies, while Enemy Way removes ghosts that are foreign. The most prominent ceremonial characteristics include blackening the patient's body with ashes, brushing evil away from the patient with an eagle feather fan, and cutting yucca fiber tied around parts of the patient's body. All of this is accom-

panied by songs and prayers. See Leland C. Wyman, "Navajo Ceremonial System," 536–57.

17. Mountain tobacco (*Nicotiana trigonophylla* [Torr.]) may be used to say prayers at night, remove health problems, and calm people who are upset, dealing with grief, or acting undisciplined. It is one of the four sacred plants (along with corn, beans, and squash) pictured in sandpaintings. The plant is harvested from mid-June to mid-July. The flowers and leaves are dried over a two-week period, crushed, then either rolled in a cigarette paper or smoked in a pipe. Mountain tobacco is an herbal medicine and does not contain any harmful chemicals. Thomas Yellowhair, "Collecting Mountain Tobacco," *Leading the Way* 5, no. 8 (August 2007): 1, 12–14.

Chapter 5

1. The chapter is a local political unit that provides governance for Navajo residents living in a specific area. There are 110 on-reservation chapters and a number of off-reservation chapters. The Red Lake Chapter (Be'ak'id Halchíí'), certified in 1958, has a population of approximately 2,500 people. Every four years a president, vice president, and secretary are elected to preside over monthly meetings in which local issues are discussed and information is disseminated. See David E. Wilkins, *The Navajo Political Experience*.

2. The Evil Eye (Naayéé' Anáá'í) monsters had many eyes that could kill by staring at a person. Monster Slayer took a bag of salt, threw it in a fire, blinded these evil beings, then killed them. The origin of sore eyes and the admonition not to stare at people come from this teaching. Aileen O'Bryan, *Navaho Indian Myths*, 98–99.

3. Navajos believe in total avoidance of the dead. Contact with the deceased leads to fainting spells, physical illness, and being haunted by the spirits. Depending on the type of dead, either the Enemy Way or Evil Way ceremony is required to correct the situation. The foster mother's insistence on Zonnie's involvement in this accident scene shows total ignorance of traditional Navajo practices and insensitivity to the young girl's desires.

4. Jacobus Franciscus "Jim" Thorpe (1888–1953) was of mixed Sac and Fox Indian and white parentage and was raised in Oklahoma. Renowned for his athletic skills, he competed and won gold medals in the 1912 Olympics and then played professional football, baseball, and basketball. In his later years he struggled with poverty and alcoholism, but not before he had earned a reputation for excellence in sports.

5. Kneel-down bread (*nitsidigo'í*) is made from fresh green corn cut from the cob with milk and a pinch of salt added. The batter is then wrapped in green husks and tied with two strands of the husk into a small envelope packet that is baked in an underground pit that has been heated and the ashes removed. The pit is lined with a damp burlap cloth. The kneel-down bread is placed on top and covered with wet paper or sand then dirt, with a fire built on top. In an hour and a half the bread is ready to eat. Kathleen Manolescu, "Nitsidigo'í: Kneeldown Bread," *Leading the Way* 2, no. 9 (September 2004): 1, 4–5.

6. The kinaaldá is a four-day ceremony held for a young woman after she has her second menses. During this time she is immersed in traditional Navajo teachings

that center around the role of Changing Woman, one of the most beneficent Navajo deities, learning how to incorporate this Holy Person's qualities and experience into the young girl's life in preparation for womanhood. Activities include running in the morning, grinding corn, learning about personal care, baking a large cornmeal cake, and being "molded" or blessed according to traditional values. See Charlotte J. Frisbie, *Kinaaldá: A Study of the Navaho Girl's Puberty Ceremony.*

Chapter 6

1. The LDS Church encourages all worthy young men who turn nineteen to serve a two-year mission for their church. They must be ordained to the Melchizedek priesthood, be morally clean, and pay for their two years of service from their own finances. Young women at the age of twenty-one may serve a mission for eighteen months, while other church members (including senior married couples) can also participate in various types of service and proselyting missions for differing lengths of time. For all, it is a voluntary opportunity pursued through personal choice.

2. An elder is a position in the Melchizedek priesthood in the Mormon faith. The Aaronic priesthood is a preparatory priesthood held by young men starting at the age of twelve. The three offices in the Aaronic priesthood are deacon (twelve–thirteen years of age), teacher (fourteen–fifteen), and priest (sixteen–seventeen), after which a young man moves forward to elder then high priest in the Melchizedek priesthood. All of these advancements are dependent on appropriate righteous behavior and being ordained to the office. Missionaries are elders and can start a two-year mission teaching the Gospel as early as nineteen years of age.

3. Ezekiel 37 in the Old Testament tells of taking two sticks—one for the tribe of Judah and one for the tribe of Joseph—and putting them together to be one in message. The sticks are interpreted as scrolls or the writings of the Bible (House of Judah) and the Book of Mormon (House of Joseph), through which both are complementary in their teachings.

4. George Patrick Lee (March 23, 1943–July 28, 2010) was the first Native American general authority (1975–89) in the Church of Jesus Christ of Latter-day Saints. He served faithfully as a missionary and later in the First Quorum of Seventy until the church excommunicated him in 1989 for molesting a child. Lee eventually divorced his wife, with whom he had seven children, and died, having never returned to the LDS Church. His autobiographical account is found in *Silent Courage: An Indian Story—The Autobiography of George P. Lee, a Navajo.* Jim considered Lee a very good friend and was disappointed that he left the church.

5. Garments are symbolic undergarments that a person can wear after receiving his or her endowment in an LDS temple ceremony. In order to have this privilege, covenants are made between the individual and God that have accompanying blessings. As long as the wearers are true to these covenants, LDS people believe that they will have spiritual protection from harm.

6. Hand trembling, a form of divination, is used to determine the origin of illness through supernatural communication with the spirits. The hand and mental impressions direct the hand trembler to understand what is causing the sick-

ness or problem of the individual. Once the reason for the sickness is revealed, an appropriate cure and ceremony is prescribed. While personal revelation is an integral part of LDS beliefs, divination as practiced here is not.

7. The Twins, Monster Slayer (Naayéé Neizghání) and Born for Water (Tóbájíshchíní), are Holy People whose experiences recounted in many stories are fundamental to many traditional Navajo practices. Born of a virgin birth and anxious to know who their supernatural father was, the two boys left their mother Changing Woman (Asdzą́ą́n Nádleehí) and journeyed forth, enduring many trials until they reached the home of their father, Sun Bearer (Jóhonaa'éí), in the sky where they were again tested. Eventually they returned to the earth and killed a group of powerful monsters who were bothering the Navajos.

8. Navajo beliefs explain that at the time of Creation people inhabiting the four worlds (Black, Blue, Red, and Yellow) before reaching this world, the Glittering World. In each of the worlds beneath this one, the inhabitants endured trials and tests; in each instance, things went wrong and the world was destroyed, but not before its inhabitants moved upward to the next world. LDS beliefs teach that three kingdoms will exist at the time of final judgment by God—starting with the highest, the Celestial, Terrestrial, and Telestial kingdoms—as well as Outer Darkness, where Satan will live with the most rebellious spirits. Jim is comparing these two beliefs, finding compatibility between them.

9. Here Jim is referring to the twelve Yé'ii Bicheii and comparing them to the apostles of Jesus.

10. Each person has a spirit referred to in Navajo as níłch'i hwii'siziinii, which is glossed as the "Inner Form That Stands Within." Everything has this inner spiritual essence. "This inner being gives life. Without an inner being, there is no life. Each inner being has its own unique characteristics that establish a relationship with the outer form that life takes. Your inner being defines you just like your fingerprints define your physical body." John E. Salabye Jr. and Kathleen Manolescu, "Hogan Teachings Series, Part III. Biiyi'dzistiin: The Inner Beings of the Sacred Mountains," Leading the Way 2, no. 2 (February 2004): 15.

11. Owl's claw or foot (ná'áshjaa' bikee: Psilostrophe sparsiflora) is used as a Life Medicine to treat wounds, as a poultice, as a postpartum blood purifier, and for a person who dreams of an owl (ghost). Leland C. Wyman and Stuart K. Harris, The Ethnobotany of the Kayenta Navaho, 49.

12. Crow's onion (gáagiiłchin: Zigadenus paniculatus) is given when sheep bloat and according to some people can be cooked with meat and corn, while others agree with Jim that it is poisonous. Ibid., 17.

13. This clan name comes from a group of traveling Navajos stopping at a place called Deer Springs, where they met other people. This group had a pet deer, an unusual practice, so the place and the people took the name of Deer Spring clan. It is one of eleven clans related through the Bitter Water clan (Tódich'íi'nii), one of the first four original clans created by Changing Woman. The Bitter Water people received their name as they traveled and became thirsty. Taking a sacred cane given to them by Changing Woman, they dug a hole for water, but the water that came from the ground was bitter, so they became known for this. Don Mose Jr., "Tódich'íi'nii Group Stories," Part III, Leading the Way 2, no. 6 (June 2004): 2.

14. These three clans are part of a larger group called Black Streak Wood People (Tsi'naajinii) who originally lived near Blanca Peak, Colorado (Sisnaajiní). The mountain had a black belt of pine trees at its base and another row of trees

running from top to bottom: hence the name "Belt with Black Streak Coming Down." Red House clan (Kinłichínii) began when "young Navajo warriors raided a Pueblo tribe at a place called Kinłichínii, which means 'red houses.' They returned with captives. Among the captives was a young girl who married and had many children. This girl's descendants continued to live in red houses similar to their ancestral ones. This girl was very respected among the Navajo and in her honor, her descendents became known as Kinłichínii." Don Mose Jr., "Tsi'naajinii Group Stories," Part IX, *Leading the Way* 3, no. 3 (March 2005): 2–3.

The Red Bottom People (Tłááshchí'í) were not named for having red buttocks, as some people have suggested. "Tlaa means bottom, beneath, or under. This clan name refers to people who once lived near the bottom of the red cliffs in canyons. It is said that they were descendents of the Apaches that came south. . . . They were adopted by the Diné." Ibid.

"The Many Goats Clan (Tłízíłáni) is a breakaway clan of the Kinłichínii. They were once enslaved by the Navajo people. As they increased in numbers, they herded goats and became very wealthy. They used goats for such things as clothing, food, and weaving, and they became famous for their expertise with goats." Ibid.

15. An individual belongs to both her maternal and paternal clans as well as those of the maternal grandfather (*chei*) and paternal grandfather's (*nalii*) clan. But it is the mother's clan side that is most prominent in relationships. While an individual generally should not marry into either the mother or father's clan, there are exceptions. "If your paternal clan is the same as your suitor's maternal clan, then the suitor is your cousin. You can marry a cousin if the cousin is not a member of your mother's or father's extended family. When marriage occurs between these cousins, we tease them saying, 'You've reclaimed your father's clan.' If your chei or nalii is the same as your suitor's maternal clan, the marriage is acceptable as long as your suitor is not directly related to your mother and father and the two families are not from the same region." Howard Black Sr., "Can I Marry into My Clan?" *Leading the Way* 3, no. 9 (September 2005): 4.

16. The Edge Water People joined the Mountain Cove clan on the edge of the Rio Grande. Through intermarriage the Navajo clan grew, and the strangers became an adopted part of the original band. Don Mose Jr., "Tábąąhá Group Stories," Part VI, *Leading the Way* 2, no. 9 (September 2004): 2.

17. The Red Running into the Water People (Táchii'nii) were from an area west of the San Juan River with that place-name. They joined another group already living on the river and so established the clan. Don Mose Jr., "Táchii'nii Group Stories," Part V, *Leading the Way* 2, no. 8 (August 2004): 2.

18. This practice, known in anthropological literature as "bride price" or "bride wealth," entails recognizing the loss of service in the bride's family to the family of the husband. Both groups join in a mutual agreement that shows acceptance of the change. This is not "buying" the bride but rather recognition of her value to both families involved.

19. LeGrand Richards (1886–1983) served as the presiding bishop of the LDS Church (1938–52) until he was called as a member of the Quorum of the Twelve Apostles, in which he served until his death. Famous for his knowledge and speaking ability, he wrote the widely read book *A Marvelous Work and a Wonder* (Salt Lake City: Deseret Book Company, 1976), about the coming forth of the Book of Mormon and the growing acceptance of the church.

Chapter 7

1. Jimmie Sinajini was a student, representing 200 others in a similar situation, who provided the test case for the Red Mesa and Oljato chapters. By 1975 these students were riding school buses anywhere from 80 to 166 miles a day (round trip) to get to school in Blanding. As responsibility for Indian education shifted from the BIA to counties and public school districts, so did the burden of constructing facilities in different Navajo Reservation communities. The lawsuit forced San Juan County to meet this need, which led to the building or improvement of elementary schools and high schools in Montezuma Creek, Mexican Hat, and Monument Valley.

2. This was also the time when Jim became involved in the investigation of the murder of two Navajo policemen (discussed later). No doubt tremendous personal pressure was placed on him to remove himself and family from a sometimes hostile environment.

3. Frogs are associated with water, have an iridescent sheen on their belly like a rainbow, and have the ability to bless people if treated kindly. See chapter 9 for additional information.

Chapter 8

1. "Yé'ii comes from the Navajo 'yiiyá' which means 'something scary.' It is something that has a boldness about it, like an eagle piercing through you with a look that brings a chill down your spine. A yé'ii does not necessarily look frightening, but it is scary because of its power and strength. . . . All Diyin Diné [Holy People] are capable of being yé'ii. They become yé'ii to us once they take on the features we see in the masks. Blessing Way songs describe how the yé'ii look, and the other ceremonies follow these descriptions in the masks and sandpaintings. The Nine Night ceremonies come after the Fall equinox and harvest, a time when people are happy. They include healing songs and Blessing Way songs. They have a sharpness to them because some holy beings are temperamental." John E. Salabye Jr. and Kathleen Manolescu, "A Blessingway Yé'ii Story," *Leading the Way* 5, no. 10 (October 2007): 12–13.

2. Talking God (Haashchééłti'í) is the only holy being who can be everywhere at once and serves as a spiritual guide for humans. He is in charge of things that have an easterly direction, such as early dawn and white corn, while Calling God (Hashch'é'ówąąn), his brother, is the guardian of the hogan and is responsible for evening twilight and yellow corn meal used in prayers. John E. Salabye Jr. and Kathleen Manolescu, "Haashchééłti'í dóó Hashch'é'ówąąn," *Leading the Way* 3, no. 11 (November 2005): 16–17, 21.

3. These twelve Holy People are made manifest during the ninth and last night of the Night Way ceremony known as the Yé'ii Bicheii dance. This is the culmination of the ceremony when Talking God and Hogan God preside over the dancers while the last man, Water Sprinkler God, provides humor and participates with the other dancers to make sure that they remain in line and perform well.

4. For nine nights and eight days activities are carried out by masked and unmasked men who assume the role and wear the mask of deity, performing various rites and services in preparation for the final night's performance. For a

concise accounting of these activities, see Berard M. Haile, *Head and Face Masks in Navaho Ceremonialism*.

5. The Yé'ii Bicheii ceremony heals people who are losing their eyesight or hearing or are paraplegic. A person acting as a Yé'ii cannot dance if the patient is a relative. The nine-day ceremony includes drumming each night on a basket turned upside down, a number of days when the Yé'iis visit schools and homes to receive goods that will later be redistributed at the ceremony, and the final night of dancing dressed in the Yé'ii mask and painted in white clay. Joe W. Yazzie, "Dancing as a Yé'ii," *Leading the Way* 5, no. 10 (October 2007): 1, 10–11.

6. "There are many Yé'iis. The Yé'iis are defined by the mask they wear. The most common ones are the Female Yé'ii, Haaschééłti'í (Talking God), Naayée Neizghaní (Monster Slayer), Tóbajishchiní (Born for Water), Clown (Water Sprinkler God--Tó Nah Nillie), Haasch'ééh (Man Who Dresses like a Woman), Ghą́ą'ask'idii (Hunchback), Zahat'oolzhaa'a (Monster Slayer and Born for Water together as one), Haashch'ééh Zhiní (Black God), and Haashch'ééh Tso (Big God). The spirit of the Yé'ii can affect anyone who sees them. This is why it's important to be respectful of all cultural teachings when the Yé'iis are present." Gibson Gonnie, "Yé'ii in Winter," *Leading the Way* 2, no. 1 (January 2004): 1–2.

7. This very important story has a number of versions that vary in detail but all end with the establishment of male-female gender roles that define appropriate behavior. For other versions, see Berard M. Haile, *Upward Moving and Emergence Way: The Gishin Biye' Version*; Jerrold E. Levy, *In the Beginning: The Navajo Genesis*; Aileen O'Bryan, *Navaho Indian Myths*; and Paul G. Zolbrod, *Diné bahane': The Navajo Creation Story*.

8. Blessing Way practitioner Anderson Hoskie explains the role of "two spirit people" (*nádleeh* ["changing"]: gays, lesbians, and transvestites) as follows: "Two spirit people are children of the rainbow. They are special because they live in both worlds. They are more knowledgeable about both parts, about both male and female. . . . The presence of two spirit people begins in the Navajo creation story about the separation of the sexes prior to the Emergence. The men were on the North side of a river, the women on the South side. . . . The men were doing a ceremony in a corral. There were kitchen utensils in there. On the left side were bows and arrows, on the right side were stirring sticks and female tools. No one stayed in the corral to watch over it. The corral got on fire. One man grabbed the bow and arrow while the second man grabbed the female tools. The men asked the second man, 'Why did you get the female tools?' He replied, 'We needed to save them. We need to pray for them.' Some men said, 'You should have gotten these first.' The group then came to understand that this man was a two spirit. The two spirits were able to do female chores. When the two sexes came back together, they learned the value of two spirits. They learned not to make jokes about them. . . . Two spirits receive the gift of having both sexes within them. They are multi-talented but cannot have children." Kathleen Manolescu, "Should Two Spirit People Marry?" *Leading the Way* 2, no. 3 (March 2004): 1, 12–13.

9. "Putting a saddle outside of the door" is a well-known metaphor for a husband being kicked out of his home and subsequently divorced.

10. Other teachings about the moon and its celestial journey are provided by John Salabye and Kathleen Manolescu. "The sun travels from the foot of the sky to

the top of its head plume. In the first quarter, the moon becomes full at the tip of the Earth's head plume. The crescent moon comes up in the West, and progressively becomes a full moon at the head plume of the Earth. When the moon is in its crescent position to the West, you were born. You were perfect at that time. When the moon becomes full, it means you are in balance with nature and healed. A Blessing Way ceremony is supposed to be done at the crescent of the moon. We say this time is háá hodidlééh, or fixing you back up. A full moon assures us that we will reach old age. A good mental attitude is an important part of healing." John E. Salabye Jr. and Kathleen Manolescu, "The Body's Seven Healing Points: The Application of Medicine and Pollen, Tádídíín dooldzéí á'ádaal'įįgo," *Leading the Way* 6, no. 9 (September 2008): 2.

11. Contact with lightning or lightning-struck objects can have long-lasting effects such as heartburn, dizziness, laziness, diabetes, cancer, and liver, kidney, or gallstone infections, which may not appear immediately. After the problem has been diagnosed, a ceremony is held to cure it. "There is the straight Lightning Way ceremony (Oo'oosnijí) plus the male and female Arrow Lightning Way ceremonies (Na'at'ooyee Biką'jí and Na'at'ooyee Bi'áádjí) to address problems from lightning. When these ceremonies fail, the Feather Way ceremony (Ats'oseejí) and Water Way ceremony (Tó yeejí) are a last resort." The Male Arrow Lightning Ceremony can last from one to nine days, depending on the complexity of the ceremony and the need of the patient. John F. Yazzie, "Male Arrow Lightning Way Ceremony," *Leading the Way* 5, no. 2 (February 2007): 2–5.

12. A person should not walk into a small whirlwind or dust devil because it will affect his breathing. These winds are believed to be the spirits of people who have died and have returned. Some of them may not be good. The same is true with tornadoes, but these winds will not harm the People because Navajos know the songs and prayers that can control them. Herbert Toledo, "Remembering My Dad: Hastiin Ts'ósí," *Leading the Way* 6, no. 3 (March 2008): 21.

13. A new husband is a servant to his in-laws, never sleeps in their home, and immediately responds to their requests. He is in charge of supplying enough chopped wood and water for their camp. For up to ten years he may be in this subservient status; but eventually they will start asking his advice and he will know that he has won their respect. If he receives a grazing permit from his wife's family, he knows that he is now accepted. Maggie Yellowhair gave John Salabye, a new in-law, this advice: "An in-law must be strong. He must know his priorities. A father's priority is to build a home. You find yourself a tree, a nice cozy place. Get some rags or canvas and make a shade. Go to your in-laws' trash dump and pick up some cans for a cup and coffee maker. Under the tree you can settle and cook your food. This is how you begin. It takes a man with courage to do this. Start in a really humble way. Initiate this kind of living. This condition won't last. Somewhere in the future you will have a nice home with nice things. A man's job is to build a hogan. You can't sleep long hours because you need to do this. The Sun won't wait for you. Don't be lazy. A 'real' man has a hoe, shovel, axe, and digging stick. These things are not only useful, but they help you become a man." John E. Salabye Jr. and Kathleen Manolescu, "Being a Husband," *Leading the Way* 4, no. 6 (June 2006): 3.

14. Snow and rain from the sky are male and provide the best growth for plants. After January bad things start to appear in the snow, colds and flu are pres-

ent, people freeze, and animals suffer. This is not true of the early storms. "Hot and cold are the same size. This means that these two extremes have the same dimensions and are part of the same whole. Both can be fatal. Once you learn to tolerate either one, it helps you withstand the other." Deana O'Daniel and Kathleen Manolescu, "Áłtsé yidzasgo," *Leading the Way* 1, no. 1 (November 2003): 9.

15. If creatures like snakes, spiders, and lizards are offended, they may tell the Holy People, who will exact a punishment.

16. Stories about Coyote, the trickster who can also be offended, are also told only in the winter, with two exceptions. If a story is explained during a ceremony in order to heal and teach the patient then it is appropriate. The other exception is when spring and summer rains have not come, causing the earth and its people to be parched and thirsty. The stories can then be told in midsummer in order to bring rain. John E. Salabye Jr. and Kathleen Manolescu, "Winter Stories Connect to the Stars," *Leading the Way* 2, no. 2 (February 2004): 2.

17. "The Ch'ąąshzhinii ceremony is done as part of the Enemy Way ceremony upon request. Not all Enemy Way ceremonies contain the Ch'ąąshzhinii ceremony and it is believed that relatively few people still know how to do it. The Ch'ąąshzhinii is done to treat problems related to falling or fainting. It is also done to communicate with Mother Earth, to pray for rain, and to help make someone immune to pain. . . . On the final day of the Enemy Way ceremony, muddy Ch'ąąshzhinii come into the hogan with an arrowhead. Two chants are done at the beginning of the ceremony and two chants are done at the end of it. An offering of white cornmeal is made to the East. The Ch'ąąshzhinii has his own set of songs and the group does a round dance inside the hogan. One of the Mud People goes out the chimney yelling four times to let the holy beings know that he is coming out. He then jumps into a mud puddle. . . . After the Mud People roll around in the mud with herbs, the patient rolls around in it too. Ch'ąąshzhinii capture people in the area to throw them into the mud to toughen them up. They will run after people on horseback if need be. Sometimes two Mud People will use a blanket to throw someone up in the air and then catch him in order to toughen him up." Clah Yazzie Sr., "Ch'ąąshzhinii: Mud People or Rainmakers," *Leading the Way* 5, no. 7 (July 2007): 6–8.

18. The power of frogs and turtles is explained in an Enemy Way story in which Monster Slayer and Born for Water sent word to Turtle and Frog, seeking advice about how to stay holy after taking scalps from their enemy. The two reptiles had learned how to protect themselves when they were captured by enemies who tried to kill them. The captors built a pit and threw them in, covered it with dirt, then built a fire on top. Frog urinated enough to allow the creatures to swim and thus saved them from the heat. Next their enemies put them in a pot of boiling water, but Frog got inside Turtle's shell as he swam back and forth and broke the pot. The enemies next tried to kill the two with clubs, but Turtle's shell protected both. Finally, their enemies became so frustrated that they tossed them in a river, hoping they would drown; both emerged from the water safe and victorious. Their sacred nature and cooperation allowed them to survive and escape with some of the enemies' scalps in their possession. As part of the Enemy Way ceremony, avoiding harm while handling enemy scalps was important. John E. Salabye Jr. and Kathleen Manolescu, "Turtle and Frog Overcome Their Enemies," *Leading the Way* 8, no. 6 (June 2006): 2.

19. Navajo Mountain served as a hiding place and shield of protection during the Fearing Time and Long Walk period (1860–68), when many other Navajos were brought to Fort Sumner. Extensive teachings concerning Protection Way ceremonies that include this mountain are found in Karl W. Luckert, *Navajo Mountain and Rainbow Bridge Religion.*

20. John Holiday, a Blessing Way singer from Monument Valley, explains the name of the La Sal Mountains. "Traditional beliefs say that all the mountains—Black Mountain Sloping Down or Sleeping Ute; Swirling Mountain [Navajo Blanket, a syncline east of Mexican Hat, Utah]; Black Mesa near Kayenta, Arizona; Head-of-Earth Woman [Navajo Mountain]; No Name Mountain [Henry Mountains, Utah]; and the Bears Ears—were gathered together to 'make' one mountain, then placed to the north. This is the La Sal Mountains. It has several peaks because it comprises these combined mountains." John Holiday and Robert S. McPherson, *A Navajo Legacy: The Life and Teachings of John Holiday,* 196.

21. Five different types of cedar grow in Utah, each of which has a use. Jim identified the one used for ceremonial purposes as red cedar (*Juniperus scopulorum*), which belongs to the cypress family and grows at an elevation of 5,000 to 9,000 feet. Anne Orth Epple, *A Field Guide to the Plants of Arizona,* 18.

22. Yucca (*hashk'aan: Yucca baccata:*) "was eaten raw or cut into pieces and sun dried. Hashk'aan cut in half would be dried and stored in black bags. The smaller sliced or diced yucca banana was used for making mush or pudding. . . . Ripe yucca fruit was boiled down like a jam, rolled out like a tortilla, and then formed into tight cylindrical rolls called neesdog. Neesdog was dried and saved for winter use. The desired amount would be peeled off like a potato, soaked in hot water until it reached the consistency of jam, and then added to cornmeal to make a mush." Mamie Becenti, Deana Dugi O'Daniel, and K. Manolescu, "Wild Edibles in Navajo Cooking," *Leading the Way* 2, no. 3 (March 2004): 1–4.

23. "As it was said, one day Mother Earth wanted to be the boss. She said, 'It's me. I'm it.' The people from above said, 'No, it's me. I'm the boss. You're down there, I'm up here. Everything grows from me.' Mother Earth and the Thunder People got mad at one another. Mother Earth said, 'Heck with you. Just because you're a man, you think you're all it. You're not.' The people upstairs then stopped everything. There was no rain, nothing. We know this to be true because of the dry period in history. The Anasazi and some Mexican tribes disappeared. A lot of people died. Mother Earth finally made peace. 'Let's work together.'" Francis T. Nez and K. Manolescu, "Fire: The Heart of Life," *Leading the Way* 2, no. 10 (October 2004): 16.

24. The Anasazi (*anna'* means war, alien, enemy and *sází* means ancestor), a Navajo term translated as "ancestral or alien enemies," inhabited the Four Corners region from 200 B.C.E. to A.D. 1300. The Navajos view them as a gifted people who eventually denied the blessings and powers given them by the Holy People and thus were cursed, punished, and destroyed for taking the sacred and making it profane. See Robert S. McPherson, *Sacred Land, Sacred View: Navajo Perceptions of the Four Corners Region.*

25. For a recent study that looks at linguistic relations between northern and southern Athabaskan speakers, see Edward J. Vajda, "Dene-Yeniseic in Past and Future Perspective."

26. Francis T. Nez shares a story that tells of language loss and the end of the world. "There was a certain spiritual being that appeared. He came around from out of the blue. At that time everyone had one language. Everyone understood one another well. This spiritual being spoke all different kinds of languages. Then the different tribes began to speak their own language: Japanese, Mongolian, Diné, English, and so on. When the people saw this spiritual being again, everyone spoke different languages. The spiritual being stood there and smiled, 'After the human was made, First Woman and First Man, they soon descended off into different colors, different languages. When all humans speak one language again, it's the end.' We know this time is coming near because everyone in the world is learning English today." Francis T. Nez and K. Manolescu, "Fire: The Heart of Life," *Leading the Way* 2, no. 10 (October 2004): 17.

27. See Karl W. Luckert, *A Navajo Bringing-Home Ceremony: The Claus Chee Sonny Version of Deerway Ajiłee.*

28. Both deer tobacco and mountain tobacco can have a calming effect on an individual. "When you face hardship in life, you can pick up tobacco to renew your thinking. This applies to such conditions as lost mental capacities, losing the will to live, mourning, and indecisiveness. When things are in this state, your heart and mind have no empty space. Tobacco creates space for good things to enter. It lets air permeate throughout your heart and mind. It helps make the transition to reality as it allows good things to enter your heart and mind." John E. Salabye Jr. and Kathleen Manolescu, "Rededicating Family Life—The Tobacco Songs," *Leading the Way* 5, no. 1 (January 2007): 21. Erwyn Curley adds: "The tobacco is a token or key to opening up my heart to the Great Spirit. This smoke helps me contact him. . . . The first smoke we blow to Mother Earth. The second smoke we blow to Father Sky, the Great Spirit. The third smoke we blow to the fire, our grandparents and their teachings. The fourth smoke we blow on ourselves." Erwyn Curley, "Pride and Strength with Humility," *Leading the Way* 4, no. 11 (November 2006): 4.

Chapter 9

1. "The ants were the first creatures to come into existence in the Black World. They were our first leaders. The black ants were leaders of the east, the red ants were leaders of the south, the yellow ants were leaders of the west, and reddish black ants were leaders of the north. The ants were also one of the first creatures to come out at the Emergence. . . . Ants are always busy. They never stop. They are also fierce fighters who will fight to the death. Don't eat ants. Don't urinate on them. Don't sleep near ants. Don't play near an anthill. Don't build a house where ants live. Don't have a ceremony where ants live. When people do not observe these taboos, they get urine problems, kidney problems. They have scaly, itchy skin. The Red Ant Way ceremony (Wóláchíí'jí) is done to correct problems related to disrespect for ants. It is a major ceremony with 1, 5, and 9 nights." John E. Salabye Jr. and Kathleen Manolescu, "Ants: The First Creatures," *Leading the Way* 4, no. 3 (March 2006): 21.

2. Many versions of the creation of the four worlds beneath this one, the events that happened there, and the emergence of the Holy People into the present world have been recorded. These are complex narratives that serve as the cen-

tral core of Navajo teachings from which many of the ceremonies are derived. See Washington Matthews, *Navaho Legend*; Aileen O'Bryan, *Navaho Indian Myths*; Berard M. Haile, *Upward Moving and Emergence Way: The Gishin Biye' Version*; and Paul G. Zolbrod, *Diné bahane': The Navajo Creation Story*.

3. "Turkey's tail was still in the rising water when he came through. The tips of Turkey's feathers were white from the foam created by the water. His tail feathers had a yellowish line, followed by a bluish line, with the rest of the feather black. These colors match the colors from the four times of day: the white of early dawn to the east; the yellow from evening to the west; the blue from midday to the south; and black from night to the north. Turkey brought these times of day and four sacred colors up to this world." John E. Salabye Jr. and Kathleen Manolescu, "Coyote's Name of Honor," *Leading the Way* 4, no. 10 (October 2006): 6–8.

4. For a detailed version of this emergence story and the role Locust played in winning the right to live in the Fourth World, see Franc Johnson Newcomb, *Navaho Folk Tales*, 43–56.

5. An example of the sacred power Coyote holds is found in the story about the time of Creation when the Holy People planned for birth and growth of plants. When they performed the first Blessing Way, the seeds germinated but did not grow very much. Coyote came upon the scene and asked to help, but the Holy People did not listen to him. After trying and failing, they turned to him and asked what he could do. Coyote howled "wu, wu, wuuuu" in each of the four directions, starting with the East, and the plants began to grow with fruits and pollen. Because of his assistance, the Holy People gave him the honor of establishing growth. John E. Salabye Jr. and Kathleen Manolescu, "Coyote's Name of Honor," *Leading the Way* 4, no. 10 (October 2006): 8–9.

6. In the Blessing Way songs Coyote is viewed as one of the wisest of the Holy People; however, in the healing ceremonies he is associated with evil. John E. Salabye Jr. and Kathleen Manolescu, "A Reader Asks," *Leading the Way* 6, no. 1 (January 2008): 4.

7. "Coyote said, 'When people with five fingers [humans] come into existence and I cross their path, they must give me an offering of minerals and pollen because I warn them of impending danger. I will be a messenger. This way, humans will learn to pray for themselves in order to avert danger.' . . . If you come across a coyote, it means that the holy beings are so concerned for you that they sent Coyote to warn you. It does not represent bad luck. When Coyote crosses your path, use pollen to make an offering to him. Speak his four sacred names [The One Who Yelps in the Early Dawn, . . . Mid-day, . . . Evening, and . . . at Night]. He is the only one who responds to these names." John E. Salabye Jr. and Kathleen Manolescu, "Coyote's Name of Honor," *Leading the Way* 4, no. 10 (October 2006): 9.

8. Ntł'iz is a male offering composed of small bits of white shell, turquoise, abalone, and jet that is sprinkled with prayer as a gift to the Holy People for assistance. Its female counterpart, corn pollen (tádidíín), is offered as a blessing for health, growth, and well-being. As in every aspect of the Navajo universe, they represent male and female complementary parts, with the male part being more aggressively potent.

9. A different perspective on coyotes and sheep is offered by Ryan Hosteen. "Coy-

ote keeps his sheep in every herd on Diné land. When he craves mutton, Coyote gets one or two sheep to eat. He doesn't ask, nor does he hesitate to take his sheep. . . . [As a Holy Person, he travels about acting as a messenger.] Coyote rewards himself for his holy work. He takes the choicest animals and leaves the old, young, unhealthy and skinny sheep that still need care. From the beginning, Coyote's sheep merged with the other Diné flocks. Some people didn't like this so they asked Coyote to take his sheep and keep them separate. To this Coyote replied, 'No, no, my dear silly Cousins. That is a frightening thought. You see, I'm a wanderer, always going to and fro. I'm hardly ever home and therefore I could not tend to my sheep.' Coyote continued, 'Besides, you would not tend your sheep if you thought I wasn't around to steal them. You would befriend laziness and neglect your property. This way poverty would come upon you. So just leave my sheep with yours so these things don't happen.'" Ryan Hosteen, "Coyote's Sheep: Mą'ii bidibé," *Leading the Way* 8, no. 1 (January 2010): 17.

10. Comb Ridge is a large sandstone rock formation that stretches for 100 miles from the Abajo (Blue) Mountains near Blanding in southeastern Utah to Kayenta, Arizona.

11. "This Coyote Star, Mą'ii bizǫ, was the source of confusion and disorder just as Coyote intended it to be. Accounts disagree on the identity of this 'Monthless Star,' so called because it is in the heavens for less than a full month, as well as on whether it is one star." Trudy Griffin-Pierce, *Earth Is My Mother, Sky Is My Father: Space, Time, and Astronomy in Navajo Sandpainting*, 87.

12. "Coyote added a month to the Navajo calendar to secure the continuation of life. His month was placed between September and November to accommodate the thirteen moons of the year. After October, Coyote sheds his hair." John E. Salabye Jr. and Kathleen Manolescu, "Coyote's Name of Honor," *Leading the Way* 4, no. 10 (October 2006): 9.

13. Big Snake was one of the four mythological protectors of Sun Bearer and Changing Woman. Its power may be used for both cursing and protecting and is often associated with lightning and other forces. See Robert S. McPherson, *Comb Ridge and Its People: The Ethnohistory of a Rock*, 60–81.

14. For a similar incident and an in-depth explanation of Navajo thought concerning what takes place in these encounters with snakes, see Maureen Trudelle Schwarz, *Navajo Lifeways: Contemporary Issues, Ancient Lifeways*, 111–33.

15. Lizards are said to be formed from the beads of a necklace worn by Big God. Once some of the Holy People sang four of his sacred songs without permission. When he learned that they had taken this liberty, he became enraged; as he stomped about and cursed the people, his beaded necklace fell apart. The turquoise beads became the collared lizard, the abalone became the leopard lizard, the white shell became the horned toad, and the jet became the eastern fence lizard. People should ensure that their necklaces do not break during a ceremony; otherwise they will have sores on their body. The collared lizard can be appealed to for wealth and growth by taking pollen that is sprinkled on its body and then placing it in a medicine bundle. John E. Salabye Jr. and Kathleen Manolescu, "Lizards and the Sweat Lodge," *Leading the Way* 8, no. 2 (February 2010): 6–7.

16. A common contemporary Navajo metaphor is associated with highways that have a yellow line on the left and a white line on the right side. This is com-

pared to the white cornmeal used to say prayers as a person faces east to pray in the morning and the yellow corn meal used for prayers in the evening as the person faces west. The lines on the highway remind people that as long as they remain between the prayers they will be protected.

17. The traditional name for a horned toad is "Wart of the Earth Boy/Girl," because it looks like a bump or a wart. John Salabye Jr. and Kathleen Manolescu explain: "The Horned Toad is a very powerful animal because he is dressed up with arrowheads. He is well-known for his hardiness, foreboding appearance, boldness, and spiritual strength. The other animals wanted to see how strong he was. They envied him. They decided that they wanted to get rid of him so they asked White Lightning to destroy him with his lightning. First the clouds came around. It got really dark. The winds came. It thundered. Rain and hail came around. Horned Toad was sitting out in the open. He was almost buried in hail. The hail was nearly level with his head. White Lightning struck Horned Toad with full force. He did this four times. It bounced off Horned Toad four times. Horned Toad saw hail and dirt blasting off his body. When everything cleared up, Horned Toad was still sitting there. He raked up the hail and put it in his mouth. He blew in all four directions and got rid of his enemies with his breath. . . . The Horned Toad is a very powerful animal because he is dressed up with arrowheads. You can wear arrowheads and be protected like the Horned Toad. When you find a Horned Toad, pick it up and put it to your heart. Say, 'Grandfather, my heart is going to be wet.' When your heart is wet, you are healthy." John E. Salabye Jr. and Kathleen Manolescu, "The Wart of the Earth," *Leading the Way* 6, no. 2 (February 2008): 15.

18. The deer is created in the image of the Holy People and has the powers from the mountains, Mother Earth, the Sky, and plants. Its antlers represent feathers and a life force. While hunting them in the old days, men did not use everyday language but imitated animal sounds. A hunter should perform a sweating ceremony both before and after the hunt and avoid intimacy with his wife. After the hunter kills the deer, he avoids going in front of the head until he is sure the animal is dead. The deer is then cut below the throat, and blood is put on the rifle from the end of the stock to the muzzle to show that the rifle will only be used to hunt game and that it is holy. "Once the animal is skinned, reverse the hide with the head going to the back end and the back end going to the head. This blesses the animal and yourself." Edison W. Emerson and Kathleen Manolescu, "Traditional Deer Hunting," *Leading the Way* 2, no. 12 (December 2004): 3, 19.

19. A Navajo story tells of a hunter getting ready to shoot a male deer when it suddenly turned into an oak tree. "The male deer reappeared and said, 'Before you hunt me, I will tell you how to butcher me, how to redeposit the bones and any wastes, and how to use the deer hide. Don't butcher me like a sheep. If I am going to be killed, I must be standing straight without wiggling my ears or tail. I must not be grazing. This is the only time to kill me. After you kill me, orient the carcass towards your home head first. Cut off my left whiskers and pray with them like you would pray with pollen. The only reason I turned into an oak tree is because I want my bones deposited with prayers at the base of the tree. If you observe these practices, deer will be plentiful. If you don't, we will become extinct.'" The hunter had a similar encounter with a doe that turned into a cliffrose bush, with instructions to cut off the right whiskers and pray with them. A

fawn later surprised the hunter from behind and warned that he should avoid it because it represented all of the bad things that could happen to him—lightning, cloudbursts, hail, and storms. The fawn then turned into a rock with spots of moss. John E. Salabye Jr. and Kathleen Manolescu, "Naazhééhjí Hane'—A Huntingway Story," *Leading the Way* 5, no. 10 (October 2007): 21.

20. "Tobacco is offered to the holy beings and tobacco songs are sung. Mind-altering plants are afraid of tobacco used in the sweat lodge. The deer does not distinguish between these two kinds of food. This is why it is associated with ajiłee. Ajiłee can also be defined as excessiveness due to too much eating, drinking, sleeping, working, or sex. These problems can occur if deer and elk rules are not observed." Ibid., 23.

21. Deer tobacco is made from the crushed leaves of the Utah service berry plant (*Amelanchier utahensis*), which belongs to the rose family and grows on rocky slopes, in piñon, juniper, and ponderosa pine forests at an elevation between 2,000 and 7,500 feet. Anne Orth Epple, *A Field Guide to the Plants of Arizona*, 91–92.

22. See Karl W. Luckert, *A Navajo Bringing-Home Ceremony: The Claus Chee Sonny Version of Deerway Ajiłee*, for a description of the smoking rite, origin, and use.

23. Women have their own power of fertility, life, and nurturing, which is in opposition to men's power associated with hunting, killing, and strong supernatural forces. The two may come together in certain circumstances, but generally they are kept separate to operate in their own spheres of influence and settings.

24. "[The bullroarer] is elliptical in shape and made of pine wood riven by lightning. Its front is mounted by eyes and a mouth of turquoise, the rear by a piece of abalone shell, to serve as its pillow. The whole is then covered with yucca pitch, lightning struck pitch, and charcoal gathered from a tree struck by lightning. A thong made of bighorn or sacred buckskin is attached through a hole in the butt end around which, too, it is wound when not in use. . . . [The medicine man] then encircles the hogan once or twice, violently whirling the roarer, during which time all remains in silence within. Upon returning to the hogan the thong is wrapped about it, in which shape the bullroarer is then used for pressing the limbs." Franciscan Fathers, *An Ethnologic Dictionary of the Navajo Language*, 414. The lightning-struck wood holds a powerful force that, along with the cries of the medicine man, the smell of pungent desert plants, and the sound of the bullroarer, will frighten away the evil afflicting the patient.

25. In traditional teachings Bear was one of the holy protectors, as was Big Snake. Noted for his ferocity and ability to fight, Bear is a highly respected deity whose physical representatives on earth hold strong powers and are not to be trifled with.

26. "In Navajo, [the constellation] Cassiopeia is a combination of the Bear and Thunderbird constellations. During the spring solstice the Bear and Thunderbird constellations touch. This results in a spark or sound, the beginning of thunder and white lightning. We say that Thunderbird makes its sound to wake up the plants and hibernating animals." John E. Salabye Jr. and Kathleen Manolescu, "The Bear and the Constellations," *Leading the Way* 6, no. 3 (March 2008): 3. Salabye provides additional information: "March 21st is the time of the spring solstice. The stars form the constellation Bear Lightning, which looks like a bird. When the bear and lightning noses touch each other, white lightning makes

known its presence. Animal hibernation ends with this signal. It is also a signal for everyone to stretch. Turn over and stretch all around so your body will feel vigorous. White lightning also signals the end of the Nine Night Ceremonies and the beginning of the Enemy Way Ceremony season." John E. Salabye Jr. and Kathleen Manolescu, "Wòòzhch'į́įd," *Leading the Way* 2, no. 3 (March 2004): 3.

27. "Once the first lightning and first thunder come in a new year, animals come out of hibernation and plants begin to grow again. When the Bear comes out, he holds his hand up. He opens up his den's doorway blanket to watch new life come alive at the peak of the mountain, along the rolling foothills, the streams and at the flatlands. When the Bear comes out of hibernation, medicine men make offerings to initiate their apprentices. When the Bear comes out, he expects to observe traditional apprenticeship offerings made at foothill streams. He purposefully leaves footprints out in the open as a sign for offerings to be made. Then he moves to a place higher up to watch and listen to the prayers. . . . The Bear was the leader of the mountains. He started to miss some of the animals. He wondered, 'Why is someone taking what belongs to the mountains without asking? He just goes out hunting without making offerings with prayers. He should make offerings to the young spruce tree, the gateway to the wilderness.'" Frank C. Young Sr., "Shash—The Bear," *Leading the Way* 6, no. 3 (March 2008): 4–5.

28. The Hoof or Claw Way is a three-day ceremony held for people who have concussions, fractured skulls, and broken bones. It is designed to restore strength for recovery, taking its name from the buffalo hoofs, deer hoofs, and bear claws placed on a rattle and used in the ceremony. The bear claws are particularly powerful because of this incident in which the bear went into shock then had its mind and strength restored during the ceremony.

29. "There are Blessing Way and Protection Way Bear prayers. The Blessing Way prayer is for obtaining things and establishing oneself with prestige, power, and privileges. The Protection Way Bear Prayer is done when someone senses danger and needs to be safe and protected. This prayer is also used when someone is in critical condition, lifeless, or near death. He may be slowly dying away from grief or traumatic experience; he may feel that he doesn't have much to live for. He may be spiritually or mentally unbalanced or even losing his mind. All due respect is given to the Bear by Navajo people, in part because it is associated with the treatment for someone who is battling the demons from bad decision-making and/or post-traumatic stress. When someone has become totally dependent on something hurtful, this prayer will draw him out so he can rehabilitate his mind, body, soul, and spirit." Young, "Shash—The Bear," 9.

30. "The Mountain Lion was present at the beginning of the clan system and in the creation of the earth. The Mountain Lion was one of the animals given to the first four clans for protection and it was to be respected that way. . . . Mountain lion pelts are seen as a kind of wealth, the same as unblemished buckskin or buffalo hide. A lazy person will not possess these items. He will be a beggar or a thief. . . . Mountain lion pelts are used to make the quivers that hold the bow and arrow, signifying protection in battle and on hunts. . . . In the Hunting Way stories, it is said that a Mountain Lion has a snake that lies across its back, from its head to the tip of its tail. If you looked at the movement of the Lion from above, it would look like a snake moving through brush. In the old hunting rituals, the Mountain Lion Way was a technique used whereby there was a 'surprise'

ambush." Anthony Lee, "Mountain Lion in Hunting Way Stories," *Leading the Way* 7, no. 5 (May 2009): 3.

31. "The chipmunk may appear to be a small and insignificant animal but he is part of the stories and practices in the Blessing Way, Enemy Way, Feather Way, and exorcist ceremonies. We think of Chipmunk as a neutral animal who was willing to work together with others. He is a role model for clan behavior as he reminds us that when someone is in need, our relatives should work together to help overcome sickness and poverty." John E. Salabye Jr., and Kathleen Manolescu, "Haazéísts'ósí—Chipmunk," *Leading the Way* 6, no. 12 (December 2008): 22.

32. Salabye and Manolescu add further detail: "Chipmunk approached Horned Monster [Déélgééd] every day. Because the Horned Monster was always hungry, everyone feared him. The Horned Monster thought Chipmunk was nothing so Chipmunk said [to Monster Slayer], 'He doesn't do anything to me. I even collect his chest hair to make a bed for my children to sleep on. I'll go ahead and see if he is dead. I'll run between his horns and call if he is dead.' When Chipmunk approached Horned Monster, he saw blood. Chipmunk put his paw in the blood and marked his body with it to create stripes. He also marked his face this same way. We can still see Chipmunk's stripes today. . . . The sound of Chipmunk is used during the Exorcist [Evil Way] Ceremony. The medicine man yells out the name of the patient and makes a war whoop sound, which represents the time when Chipmunk ran between the horns of the Horned Monster, making his sound. This is called chasing the evil away from you." Ibid., 21–22.

33. Navajo custom teaches that when a person asks for something four times, the request should be granted.

34. "The sheep is life. When you have sheep, you won't starve. They'll be your shoes, your clothing, and your well-being. It's all up to you. No one will do it for you. You'll be what you're going to be from that." Annie Dennison, "Herding Sheep," *Leading the Way* 7, no. 3 (March 2009): 13.

35. When the animals received their qualities and characteristics, the Holy People punished Snake because he had been mean. He used to be able to walk, but they took away his legs and made him crawl. They gave his lightning ability to move to the cat; when you look at a cat from above, the image of the snake can be traced from the cat's eyes along its back to the tip of its tail. Don Mose Sr. interview with author, January 25, 2011.

Chapter 10

1. "The holy beings studied the qualities of all of life in order to find a guide for people with five fingers [humans]. They found that plant life was exemplary: it did not lie, cheat, or use harsh words. It was always kind and gentle. Because of these qualities, the holy beings chose Corn Deities to be the guide for people with five fingers. . . . The spirit of corn gives us its defining characteristics: honesty, gentleness, love, steadfastness. These are the same qualities we expect to find in our mother." John E. Salabye Jr. and Kathleen Manolescu, "Corn, My Guide in Life," *Leading the Way* 4, no. 8 (August 2006): 4; and "Corn Teaches Me," *Leading the Way* 2, no. 7 (July 2004): 6.

2. Blue flower pollen (*tádidíín dootł'izh*: *Dalea parryi*) belongs to the pea family.

3. Navajo artist and author Shonto Begay believes that "one of the most important

teachings is to respect corn pollen. Pollen is in you. It is a life force. You become part of your pollen. When you respect pollen, you treat yourself as sacred." Kathleen Manolescu, "Pollen Is Life," *Leading the Way* 1, no. 1 (November 2003): 1, 14.

4. When a person is blessed in a ceremony, the pollen is applied to the body's seven healing points. Starting with the right side of the body, the person providing the blessing places the pollen or medicine with upward strokes on the feet, the lower legs, the open palms, the breast bone and upper back, the shoulder with movement toward the head, the forehead with movement toward the back of the head, and finally the tongue. When the holy wind entered the body at birth, it entered where the body bends or where there are whorls. The seven healing points are the connecting places important for administering the medicine. John E. Salabye Jr. and Kathleen Manolescu, "The Body's Seven Healing Points: The Application of Medicine and Pollen," *Leading the Way* 6, no. 9 (September 2008): 2. Father Berard Haile has identified slightly different locations for blessing: the sole of each foot, each bent knee joint, the side of each hip joint, the back of each shoulder, the palm of each hand, each cheek, each ear or temple, and the top of the head or away from the patient's mouth. Berard M. Haile, *The Padres Present the Navaho War Dance*, 37.

5. How ntł'iz received this sacred power is explained in the story about the time when Talking God took the four sacred minerals and planted them in the four directions. Although he watered them, they failed to grow. Coyote told him how to make them grow by starting with the East and putting white shell there, then turquoise in the South, and so forth. He blessed and prayed for them. As they grew they turned into four different types of yucca that represented the four directions. Now the stones and yucca were available for people to use in the future. Anderson Mariano, "Coyote, the Sacred Minerals, and Yucca," *Leading the Way* 8, no. 2 (February 2010): 24.

6. "Ntł'iz represents the intrinsic values of life, the things that come from your heart. Love, faith, hope, generosity, and patience are good examples of ntł'iz. . . . All offerings are taken to Changing Woman's home for inspection, a kind of quality control. . . . Yòdí represents our personal property. It is the property that we consider especially valuable . . . the fruits of the prayers done with ntł'iz become our yòdí. Ntł'iz plants a seed during prayer." John E. Salabye Jr. and Kathleen Manolescu, "Ntł'iz and Yòdí," *Leading the Way* 2, no. 3 (March 2004): 15–16.

7. A young cedar tree is also used in the Enemy Way ceremony when the stick described previously is cut from a sapling with no branches. The young woman carrying it, like the tree, must be young, strong, pure, and not yet have had her period.

8. Navajo interaction with the Ancestral Puebloans began in the worlds beneath this one and continued into the present. For a mythological explanation as to how the gods destroyed these people, see Robert S. McPherson, *Sacred Land, Sacred View: Navajo Perceptions of the Four Corners Region*, 77–131.

9. Staring is considered very impolite by traditional Navajo people and can be a form of directing power. This belief goes back to the time of the creatures called Bináá' yee agháni or Evil Eyes. Monster Slayer killed them after blinding them with smoke from salt tossed in a fire.

10. For a concise day-to-day description of the Enemy Way Ceremony, see Berard M. Haile, *The Navaho War Dance: A Brief Narrative of Its Meaning and Practice.*

11. Don Mose Sr. Navajo curriculum specialist for the San Juan School District, has been taught otherwise. While he confirms that the loss of the sacred name for a black person is a concern, a patient in a ceremony can still be healed by using the Navajo name for the place black people came from: their land of inheritance or the Black World. By using this ceremonial name, power can be gained over the offending spirit. Don Mose Sr. interview with author, December 14, 2010.

12. "Ants come from the Black World. They were the first creatures to come into existence here. Each ant species had its own leaders who were in charge of the different cardinal directions—black Ants the East, red Ants the South, yellow Ants the West, and red Ants with a black head and butt the North. . . . The Ants' homes [pueblo-type structures] were made out of the four sacred minerals. . . . The ants lived in total darkness in the Black World. After a time the ants started arguing with one another. They made enemies with one another and began fighting. Several ants got killed. This had never happened before. The ants got together to make peace. They brought the dead ants back to life. This is the beginning of the Upward Reaching Way Ceremony." John E. Salabye Jr. and Kathleen Manolescu, "Ants in the Black World," *Leading the Way* 8, no. 12 (December 2010): 2.

13. Many types of ants in the first world are mentioned, including Small Yellow Black Ants, Small Black Ants, Large Black Ants, Red Ants, Large Dark Red Ants, and Spider Ants. When comparing African Americans to the ant people, Jim believed that they were the Large Black Ants. In Sandoval's account of the Creation story recorded in 1928, he said: "Dark colored they were, with thick lips and dark, protruding eyes. They were the wolazhi'ni, the black ants. They also knew the secret of shooting evil and were powerful; but they killed each other steadily." In a note, Sandoval added: "Ants cause trouble, as also do wasps and other insects, if their homes are harmed. . . . Much evil, disease, and bodily injury is due also to secret agents of evil, in consequence of which the belief . . . shooting of evil [sting] is widely spread." Aileen O'Bryan, *Navaho Indian Myths*, 3.

14. Another time I asked Jim to explain further about the story associated with this teaching. After he told me that these were the big black ants, not the small ones, he said that he would have to wait until there was snow on the ground or on the tops of the mountains so that when he talked about it the ants would not be around to listen and become offended.

15. In another version of the shoe game story, the four questions were: (1) Should there be day all of the time or night all of the time? (2) Should there be eternal life or should there be death? (3) Should humans reach old age or stay young forever? (4) Should there be good all of the time or should there also be evil in the form of bad dreams or visions? Davidson James Brimhall, "Késhjéé' Shoegame," *Leading the Way* 2, no. 12 (December 2004): 1, 8.

16. For a concise explanation of a detailed game, see Davidson James Brimhall, "How to Play the Shoegame," *Leading the Way* 4, no. 1 (January 2006): 2–3.

17. Extensive literature on the Native American Church and its acceptance across the Navajo Reservation is available. Two standard works are Omer C. Stewart, *Peyote Religion: A History*; and David F. Aberle, *The Peyote Religion among the*

Navajo. Aberle suggests that the Native American Church had reached Red Lake by the early 1940s, which would make Jim too young to remember these early years. In some Navajo communities the practice spread slowly due to resistance from traditional medicine men and community members.

18. *Datura stramonium* is an annual herb with potent hallucinogenic chemical properties that can cause extreme sickness and death if received in an overdose.

19. Big Snake not only controls the snakes that populate the earth but also holds strong powers concerning dreams and hallucinations and can destroy the mind and consciousness.

Chapter 11

1. There are four types of Navajo divination or diagnosing, all of which are related and serve similar functions: wind listening, stargazing, crystal gazing, and hand trembling. They are used to examine the unknown, find lost people or objects, identify a thief or witch, locate water or other desirable resources, prevent danger or evil, and, most frequently, determine the cause of an illness in order to remedy it.

2. Jim is referring to the long and lengthy search for terrorist Osama Bin Laden (1957–2011). Bin Laden was later found living in a home in Pakistan, where he was killed in a strike by Navy Seals sponsored by the Central Intelligence Agency.

3. Evil avoids things that will harm it or that are unpleasant. Sharp yucca needles, bitter bile, the odor of pungent desert plants, and holy prayers are all ways to fend off harm.

4. This incident was very difficult for Jim to talk about. He gave few details other than his role, so the following information comes from articles published in the *Salt Lake Tribune* between July 28 and November 15, 1988. On December 4, 1987, after a basketball game at Monument Valley High School, a group of students and young adults held a bonfire in a nearby canyon. Navajo policeman Lee Roy Stanley visited the site where some of the participants had been drinking heavily. The officer exchanged words with some of the adults, and a fight ensued. Stanley was overpowered, shot, then put in his police van. Another officer, Andy Begay, who appeared was also overpowered and shot; the two policemen, still alive, were taken to Copper Canyon, where their vehicle was burned with them in it. All the people involved, on both sides, were from the Monument Valley area, so accusations, tension, and then silence engulfed the community. For months the investigation stalled. Once some of the students had broken silence, the police took three Navajo men into custody. The court found two of the men guilty and sentenced them to life in prison but acquitted the third. The family members of all involved suffered from the tragedy.

5. A stake president presides over a number of wards and branches in a certain geographical area of the LDS Church. He has the responsibility for the spiritual and temporal welfare of those who live within his ecclesiastical boundaries. Thus Jim appealed to the highest local authority who could direct him in spiritual matters.

6. The best study concerning Navajo beliefs about the afterlife is Berard M. Haile, "Soul Concepts of the Navajo." In this work Haile discusses the spirit world in the North, how the deceased interact, and their potential influence on the living.

7. The younger, more aggressive spirits are that way because they were not ready to die, had not lived a full life, and so linger with the living. Their desire to take the living or to interact with them creates fear of possession.

8. Called in Navajo *gad ni'eełii.*

9. Father Anselm Weber of Saint Michaels Mission reported the following explanation by a Navajo man (unnamed) concerning death and the afterlife: "After death, the Navajo spirit hovers near the body for about four days, during which time the relatives and neighbors must remain within the immediate vicinity of the home of the deceased. They are forbidden to work or to wash themselves. On the evening of the fourth day, a spirit comes and conducts the soul of the deceased to *tschindi tcha* [ch'įįdii tah—among the dead or spirit world], that is, into the communion of the spirits." Anselm Weber, "Suspicion Is Almost a Virtue Here," 32–33. An associated belief is that during this four-day period the spirit of the deceased is traveling to the land of the dead and may desire company.

10. Navajos had a wide variety of graves and accompanying burial practices in the old days. What Jim describes here is very much in keeping with traditional custom. See Albert E. Ward, *Navajo Graves: An Archaeological Reflection of Ethnographic Reality.*

11. Black ashes are repugnant to ghosts and make the wearer invisible.

12. Skinwalkers are one form of witchcraft practitioners who assume the shape of were-animals. The term is derived from the belief that the person actually puts on the skin of a wolf or coyote or some other such animal and by doing so assumes supernatural qualities used against an individual. Through evil prayers, ritual, and knowledge, the skinwalker performs antisocial acts shunned by a "normal" person. Good information on this topic can be found in Clyde Kluckhohn, *Navaho Witchcraft*; Margaret K. Brady, *Some Kind of Power: Navajo Children's Skinwalker Narratives*; and William Morgan, *Human Wolves among the Navaho.*

13. Corpse poison powder is made of decayed flesh or fluids from dead bodies and is used to cause fainting, lockjaw, swelling, unconsciousness, and general loss of health and vitality in a victim. The substance is said to be ground into a fine powder similar to corn pollen and administered by dropping it down a smoke hole in a hogan, putting it on someone who is asleep, or blowing it on a person in a crowd.

14. Although witchcraft can be practiced anyplace, Navajos often identify local spots where witches are said to gather. Here they work their powers against victims before going out at night to perform their misdeeds. These sanctuaries, *ant'įįh bighan* (literally "corpse poison house" so "home of witchcraft medicine"), are hidden sites that may take special powers to enter. For instance, an entryway may be a very thin crack that no human can fit through unless he has witchcraft powers. Then he can easily enter. The crevice opens into a large chamber where the witches congregate. What Jim describes here is typical of this setting associated with death and evil.

BIBLIOGRAPHY

Books, Articles, and Newspapers

Aberle, David F. *The Peyote Religion among the Navajo*. Chicago: University of Chicago Press, 1966, 1982.

Allen, James B. "The Rise and Decline of the LDS Indian Student Placement Program, 1947–1996." In Davis Bitton, ed., *Mormons, Scripture, and the Ancient World, Studies in Honor of John L. Sorenson*, 85–119. Provo, Utah: Foundation of Ancient Research and Mormon Studies, 1998.

American Heritage Dictionary. 2nd college ed. Boston: Houghton Mifflin Company, 1985.

Bahr, Howard M., ed. *The Navajo as Seen by the Franciscans, 1898–1921: A Sourcebook*. Native American Resources Series, 4. Lanham, Md.: Scarecrow Press, 2004.

Benedek, Emily. *Beyond the Four Corners of the World: A Navajo Woman's Journey*. Norman: University of Oklahoma Press, 1995.

Birtcher, Anna Begay, and Normand Birtcher. "Blending Cultures—Medicine Man/ Temple President." In *The Blossoming: Dramatic Accounts of the Lives of Native Americans in the Foster Care Program of the Church of Jesus Christ of Latter-day Saints*, ed. Dale L. Shumway and Margene Shumway, 239–48. Orem, Utah: Granite Publishing, 2002.

Blanchard, Kendall A. *The Economics of Sainthood: Religious Change among the Rimrock Navajos*. Cranbury, N.J.: Associated University Press, 1977.

Brady, Margaret K. *Some Kind of Power: Navajo Children's Skinwalker Narratives*. Salt Lake City: University of Utah Press, 1984.

Brooks, Juanita. *Jacob Hamblin: Mormon Apostle to the Indians*. Salt Lake City: Westwater Press, 1980.

Brugge, David M. *Navajos in the Catholic Church Records of New Mexico, 1694–1875*. Research Report 1. Window Rock, Ariz.: Navajo Tribe, 1968.

279

Cannon, Anthon S., ed. *Popular Beliefs and Superstitions from Utah*. Salt Lake City: University of Utah Press, 1984.

Chadwick, Bruce A., Stan L. Albrecht, and Howard M. Bahr, "Evaluation of an Indian Student Placement Program." *Social Casework: The Journal of Contemporary Social Work* (1986): 515–24.

Corbett, Pearson H. *Jacob Hamblin: The Peacemaker*. Salt Lake City: Deseret Book, 1952, 1973.

De Hoyos, Genevieve. "Indian Student Placement Services." In *Encyclopedia of Mormonism*, 2:280. 5 vols. New York: Macmillan, 1992.

Epple, Anne Orth. *A Field Guide to the Plants of Arizona*. Helena, Mont.: Falcon Press Publishing Company, 1995.

Evans, Will. *Along Navajo Trails: Recollections of a Trader*. Ed. Susan E. Woods and Robert S. McPherson. Logan: Utah State University Press, 2005.

Farella, John R. *The Main Stalk: A Synthesis of Navajo Philosophy*. Tucson: University of Arizona Press, 1984.

Faunce, Hilda. *Desert Wife*. Lincoln: University of Nebraska Press, 1928, 1981.

Franciscan Fathers. *An Ethnologic Dictionary of the Navajo Language*. Saint Michaels, Ariz.: St. Michaels Press, 1910, 1968.

Frisbie, Charlotte J. *Kinaaldá: A Study of the Navaho Girl's Puberty Ceremony*. Salt Lake City: University of Utah Press, 1967, 1993.

———. *Tall Woman: The Life Story of Rose Mitchell, a Navajo Woman, c. 1874–1977*. Albuquerque: University of New Mexico Press, 2001.

———. "Temporal Change in Navajo Religion 1868–1990." *Journal of the Southwest* 34, no. 4 (Winter 1992): 457–514.

Garr, Arnold K., Donald Q. Cannon, Richard O. Cowan, and Richard N. Holzapfel. *Encyclopedia of Latter-day Saint History*. Salt Lake City: Deseret Book Company, 2000.

Gottlieb, Robert, and Peter Wiley. *America's Saints: The Rise of Mormon Power*. New York: Harcourt Brace and Jovanovich, 1984.

Griffin-Pierce, Trudy. *Earth Is My Mother, Sky Is My Father: Space, Time, and Astronomy in Navajo Sandpainting*. Albuquerque: University of New Mexico Press, 1992.

Haile, Berard M. *Head and Face Masks in Navaho Ceremonialism*. Salt Lake City: University of Utah, 1947, 1996.

———. *The Navaho War Dance: A Brief Narrative of Its Meaning and Practice*. Saint Michaels, Ariz.: Saint Michaels Press, 1946.

———. *The Padres Present the Navaho War Dance*. Saint Michaels, Ariz.: Saint Michaels Press, 1946.

———. "Soul Concepts of the Navaho." *Annali Lateranensi* 7 (Winter 1943): 59–94.

———. *Upward Moving and Emergence Way: The Gishin Biye' Version*. Lincoln: University of Nebraska Press, 1981.

Harris, Lacee A. "To Be Native American—and Mormon." *Dialogue* 18, no. 4 (1985): 143–52.

Henderson, Eric. "Kaibito Plateau Ceremonialists: 1860–1980." In *Navajo Religion and Culture: Selected Views, Papers in Honor of Leland C. Wyman*, edited by David M. Brugge and Charlotte J. Frisbie, 164–71. Museum of New Mexico Papers in Anthropology Number 17. Santa Fe: Museum of New Mexico Press, 1982.

Holiday, John, and Robert S. McPherson. *A Navajo Legacy: The Life and Teachings of John Holiday*. Norman: University of Oklahoma Press, 2005.

"Introduction." In *The Book of Mormon: Another Testament of Jesus Christ*, i. Salt Lake City: Corporation of the President of the Church of Jesus Christ of Latter-day Saints, 1981.

Iverson, Peter. *Diné: A History of the Navajos*. Albuquerque: University of New Mexico Press, 2002.

Kluckhohn, Clyde. *Navaho Witchcraft*. Boston: Beacon Press, 1944, 1970.

Kluckhohn, Clyde, and Dorothea Leighton. *The Navaho*. Cambridge, Mass.: Harvard University Press, 1946, 1974.

Lamphere, Louise, Eva Price, Carole Cadman, and Valencia Darwin. *Weaving Women's Lives: Three Generations in a Navajo Family*. Albuquerque: University of New Mexico Press, 2007.

"The LDS Placement Service: 'It's Not a Form of Kidnapping.'" *Navajo Times*, July 27, 1978, A-4.

Leading the Way, vols. 1–9 (monthly), 2003–11. Publisher/Editor Kathleen Manolescu. Gamerco, N.Mex.

Lee, George P. *Silent Courage: An Indian Story—The Autobiography of George P. Lee, a Navajo*. Salt Lake City: Deseret Book, 1987.

Levy, Jerrold E. *In the Beginning: The Navajo Genesis*. Berkeley: University of California Press, 1998.

Liebler, H. Baxter. *Boil My Heart for Me*. Salt Lake City: University of Utah Press, 1969, 1994.

Linford, Laurance D. *Navajo Places: History, Legend, Landscape*. Salt Lake City: University of Utah Press, 2000.

Luckert, Karl W. *A Navajo Bringing-Home Ceremony: The Claus Chee Sonny Version of Deerway Ajiłee*. Flagstaff: Museum of Northern Arizona, 1978.

———. *Navajo Mountain and Rainbow Bridge Religion*. Flagstaff: Museum of Northern Arizona, 1977.

Matthews, Washington. *Navaho Legends*. Salt Lake: University of Utah Press, 1897, 1994.

McClintock, James H. *Mormon Settlement in Arizona*. Tucson: University of Arizona Press, 1921, 1985.

McCloskey, Joanne. *Living through the Generations: Continuity and Change in Navajo Women's Lives*. Tucson: University of Arizona Press, 2007.

McConkie, Bruce R. *Mormon Doctrine*. Salt Lake City: Bookcraft, 1966.

McNeley, James Kale. *Holy Wind in Navajo Philosophy*. Tucson: University of Arizona Press, 1981.

McPherson, Robert S. *Comb Ridge and Its People: The Ethnohistory of a Rock*. Logan: Utah State University Press, 2009.

———. "He Stood for Us Strongly: Father H. Baxter Liebler's Mission to the Navajo." *American Indian Culture and Research Journal* 23, no. 2 (August 1999): 109–26.

———. *A History of San Juan County: In the Palm of Time*. Salt Lake City: Utah State Historical Society, 1995.

———. "Naalyéhé Bá Hooghan, 'House of Merchandise': Navajo Trading Posts as an Institution of Cultural Change, 1900–1930." *American Indian Culture and Research Journal* 16, no. 1 (Winter 1992): 23–43.

———. *Navajo Land, Navajo Culture: The Utah Experience in the Twentieth Century*. Norman: University of Oklahoma Press, 2001.

———. "Navajo Livestock Reduction in Southeastern Utah, 1933–1946: History

Repeats Itself." *American Indian Quarterly* 22, nos. 1 & 2 (Winter/Spring 1998): 1–18.

———. *The Northern Navajo Frontier, 1860–1900: Expansion through Adversity*. Logan: Utah State University Press, 2001.

———. *Sacred Land, Sacred View: Navajo Perceptions of the Four Corners Region*. Provo, Utah: Brigham Young University Press, 1992.

Moore, Carrie A. "Debate Renewed with Change in Book of Mormon Introduction." *Deseret News*, November 8, 2007. http://www.deseretnews.com/article/695226008/Debate-renewed-with-change-in-Book-of-Mormon (accessed January 5, 2011).

Morgan, Brandon. "Educating the Lamanites: A Brief History of the LDS Indian Student Placement Program." *Journal of Mormon History* 35, no. 5 (Fall 2009): 191–217.

Morgan, William. *Human Wolves among the Navaho*. Yale University Publications in Anthropology 11. New Haven, Conn.: Yale University Press, 1936.

"Mormon Church in Navajoland." *Navajo Times*, July 27, 1978, A-2.

Newcomb, Franc Johnson. *Navaho Folk Tales*. Albuquerque: University of New Mexico Press, 1967.

———. *Navajo Neighbors*. Norman: University of Oklahoma Press, 1966.

O'Bryan, Aileen. *Navaho Indian Myths*. New York: Dover Publications, 1956, 1993.

Pavlik, Steve. "Of Saints and Lamanites: An Analysis of Navajo Mormonism." *Wicazo Sa Review*, 8, no. 1 (Spring 1992): 21–30.

Peterson, Charles S. *Take Up Your Mission: Mormon Colonizing along the Little Colorado River, 1870–1900*. Tucson: University of Arizona Press, 1973.

Quinn, D. Michael. *Early Mormonism and the Magic World View*. Salt Lake City: Signature Books, 1987.

Reichard, Gladys A. *Navaho Religion: A Study of Symbolism*. Princeton: University of Princeton Press, 1974.

———. *Prayer: The Compulsive Word*. New York: J. J. Augustin, 1944.

Richardson, Gladwell. *Navajo Trader*. Tucson: University of Arizona Press, 1986.

Salt Lake Tribune. July 28 to November 15, 1988.

Schwarz, Maureen Trudelle. *Molded in the Image of Changing Woman: Navajo Views on the Human Body and Personhood*. Tucson: University of Arizona Press, 1997.

———. *Navajo Lifeways: Contemporary Issues, Ancient Lifeways*. Norman: University of Oklahoma Press, 2001.

Shumway, Dale L., and Margene Shumway. *The Blossoming: Dramatic Accounts of the Lives of Native Americans in the Foster Care Program of the Church of Jesus Christ of Latter-day Saints*. Orem, Utah: Granite Publishing, 2002.

Smith, Brian L. "Indian Placement Program." In *Encyclopedia of Latter-day Saint History*, 539. Salt Lake City: Deseret Book Company, 2000.

Stewart, Omer C. *Peyote Religion: A History*. Norman: University of Oklahoma Press, 1987.

Stolzman, William. *The Pipe and Christ: A Christian-Sioux Dialogue*. Chamberlain, S.Dak.: Tipi Press, 1986, 1998.

Tate, LaVerne Powell. "A Family of Traders." *Blue Mountain Shadows* 29 (Winter 2003): 67–80.

Topper, Martin D. "'Mormon Placement': The Effects of Missionary Foster Families on Navajo Adolescents." *Ethos* 7, no. 1 (Winter 1979): 142–60.

Vajda, Edward J. "Dene-Yeniseic in Past and Future Perspective." http://www.adn. com/2010/07/05/1354714/new-language-research-supports.html (November 10, 2010).

Vogel, Dan. *Indian Origins and the Book of Mormon: Religious Solutions from Columbus to Joseph Smith*. Salt Lake City: Signature Books, 1986.

Vogt, Evon Z., and Ethel M. Albert, eds. *People of Rimrock: A Study in Values in Five Cultures*. New York: Atheneum, 1966, 1970.

Walking Thunder. *Walking Thunder: Diné Medicine Woman*. Ed. Bradford Keeney. Philadelphia: Ringing Rocks Press, 2001.

Ward, Albert E. *Navajo Graves: An Archaeological Reflection of Ethnographic Reality*. Ethnohistorical Report Series 2. Albuquerque: Center for Anthropological Studies, 1980.

Waters, Frank. *Pumpkin Seed Point: Being within the Hopi*. Chicago: Sage Books, 1969.

Weber, Anselm. "Suspicion Is Almost a Virtue Here." In *The Navajo as Seen by the Franciscans, 1898–1921: A Sourcebook*, ed. Howard M. Bahr, 24–37. Lanham, Md.: Scarecrow Press, 2004.

White, Richard. *The Roots of Dependency: Subsistence, Environment, and Social Change among the Choctaws, Pawnees, and Navajos*. Lincoln: University of Nebraska Press, 1983.

Wilkins, David E. *The Navajo Political Experience*. Tsaile, Ariz.: Diné College Press, 1999.

Witherspoon, Gary. *Language and Art in the Navajo Universe*. Ann Arbor: University of Michigan Press, 1977.

———. *Navajo Kinship and Marriage*. Chicago: University of Chicago Press, 1975.

Wood, Beth. "LDS Indian Placement Program: To Whose Advantage." *Akwesasne Notes* 10, no. 5 (1978): 16–18.

Wyman, Leland C. "Navajo Ceremonial System." In *Handbook of North American Indians: Southwest* 10, 536–57. Washington, D.C.: Smithsonian Institution, 1983.

———. *The Red Antway of the Navaho*. Santa Fe: Museum of Navaho Ceremonial Art, 1973.

Wyman, Leland C., and Stuart K. Harris. *The Ethnobotany of the Kayenta Navaho*. University of New Mexico Publications in Biology 5. Albuquerque: University of New Mexico Press, 1951.

Zolbrod, Paul G. *Diné bahane': The Navajo Creation Story*. Albuquerque: University of New Mexico Press, 1984.

Manuscripts

"Agreement of Parties." *Sinajini* v. *Board of Education* case materials on file at the Dinébeiina Nahiilna Be Agaditahe (DNA) Office, Mexican Hat, Utah.

Boxer, Elise. "'To Become White and Delightsome': American Indians and Mormon Identity." Doctoral dissertation, Arizona State University, 2009.

Branch President materials for Indian Student Placement Program of the Church of Jesus Christ of Latter-day Saints "Leadership Program." Special Collections, Harold B. Lee Library, Brigham Young University, Provo, Utah.

Flake, David Kay. "A History of Mormon Missionary Work with the Hopi, Navajo, and Zuni Indians." Master's thesis, Brigham Young University, 1965.

Foster Parent Guide. Unified Social Services of the Church of Jesus Christ of Latter-day Saints. Salt Lake City: Indian Student Placement Service, March 1970.

Garrett, Matthew. "Mormons, Indians, and Lamanites: The Indian Student Placement Program, 1947–2000." Doctoral dissertation, Arizona State University, 2010.

"Indian Student Placement Services Fact Sheet." Special Collections, Harold B. Lee Library, Brigham Young University.

Lindquist, Geraldine Taylor. "The Indian Student Placement Program as a Means of Increasing the Education of Children of Selected Indian Families." Master's thesis, Utah State University, 1974.

Palmer, John Franklin. "Mormon Settlements in the San Juan Basin of Colorado and New Mexico." Master's thesis, Brigham Young University, 1967.

Riggs, Lynette A. "The Church of Jesus Christ of Latter-day Saints' Indian Student Placement Service: A History." Doctoral dissertation, Utah State University, 2008.

Interviews

Billy, Florence. Interview with Ernesteen Lynch, August 12, 1990. LDS Native American Oral History Project (no number), Charles Redd Center for Western Studies, Brigham Young University, Provo.

Dandy, Betty. Interview with authors, April 26, 2008.

Dandy, Charlie, and family (wife Virginia and daughter Corilyn). Interview with authors, May 29, 2008.

Dandy, Jim. Discussion with author, September 24, 2007.

Goatson, Elouise T. Interview with Farina King, November 10, 2007. LDS Native American Oral History Project (no number), Charles Redd Center for Western Studies, Brigham Young University, Provo, Utah.

Halona, Tonia. Interview with Jim M. Dandy, April 10, 1991. LDS Native American Oral History Project (no number), Charles Redd Center for Western Studies, Brigham Young University, Provo, Utah.

Hogue, Jerrald. Interview with Ernesteen Lynch, August 21, 1990, LDS Native American Oral History Project (no number), Charles Redd Center for Western Studies, Brigham Young University, Provo, Utah.

Holiday, Marilyn. Discussion with author, September 23, 2007.

Hunt, Lucille. Interview with authors, June 11, 2009.

Jett, Stephen. "Wildcat Peak," personal communication with author, 1987.

Long, Clayton. Interview with authors, June 22, 2009.

Mose, Don, Sr. Interview with authors, June 22, 2009; December 14, 2010; January 25 and June 7, 2011.

Mose, Don, Sr., and Clayton Long. Interview with authors, June 22, 2009.

Richards, Zonnie. Interview with authors, May 29, 2008.

Sakizzie, Ella. Interview with author, May 14, 1991.

INDEX